Intimate Partner Violence

Intimate Partner Violence

Angela J. Hattery

ROWMAN & LITTLEFIELD PUBLISHERS, INC.
Lanham • Boulder • New York • Toronto • Plymouth, UK

ROWMAN & LITTLEFIELD PUBLISHERS, INC.

Published in the United States of America
by Rowman & Littlefield Publishers, Inc.
A wholly owned subsidiary of The Rowman & Littlefield Publishing Group, Inc.
4501 Forbes Boulevard, Suite 200, Lanham, Maryland 20706
www.rowmanlittlefield.com

Estover Road, Plymouth PL6 7PY, United Kingdom

British Library Cataloguing in Publication Information Available

Library of Congress Cataloging-in-Publication Data

Hattery, Angela.
  Intimate partner violence / Angela J. Hattery.
    p. cm.
  Includes bibliographical references and index.
  ISBN-13: 978-0-7425-6072-7 (cloth : alk. paper)
  ISBN-10: 0-7425-6072-4 (cloth : alk. paper)
  ISBN-13: 978-0-7425-6073-4 (pbk. : alk. paper)
  ISBN-10: 0-7425-6073-2 (pbk. : alk. paper)
  eISBN-13: 978-0-7425-6573-9
  eISBN-10: 0-7425-6573-4
  1. Family violence—United States. 2. Family violence—United States—Prevention.
I. Title.
  HV6626.2.H38 2009
  362.82'920973—dc22
                                        2008021880

Printed in the United States of America

⊗™ The paper used in this publication meets the minimum requirements of American National Standard for Information Sciences—Permanence of Paper for Printed Library Materials, ANSI/NISO Z39.48-1992.

To Travis and Emma

May you find someone you respect and who respects you the same, someone you love who loves you back.

Love, Mom

To Earl Smith

I could not have done this without you.

Angela

Contents

Foreword

Philosopher Celia Green once said, "The way to do research is to attack the facts at the point of greatest astonishment." Truly excellent research attacks that point and then follows it to its roots, attempting to deeply and broadly understand its subject. This book is an example of such research.

Dr. Angela Hattery has been studying violence against women since her days as a master's student, and since 1999 she has intensively researched intimate partner violence in multiple locations and contexts in the United States. Throughout, she has resisted the trap of believing she has found the one true way to understand the phenomenon. Instead, she has followed each promising thread, intent on seeing how the entire system operates. She has unfailingly recognized good ideas and new insights wherever they might be found.

This openness actually comes as no surprise to me. Dr. Hattery and I began an unusual interdisciplinary study in 1999 that in its unassuming way paved the road for this remarkable book. I am a theater scholar and director, but we had—and continue to have—more in common than not, both as women and as students of American culture. Together we decided to explore the family dynamics of intimate partner violence through the dual lenses of theater and sociology in a study based on Sam Shepard's 1986 play *A Lie of the Mind*. The play has been criticized by some for its somewhat sympathetic treatment of a male batterer, Jake. But in the end it was Jake who made us ask the hardest, most interesting questions. Along with the violent men we interviewed here in Winston-Salem, Jake provided our "point of astonishment." As we began our interviews, we wondered if, through this violent, desperate man, Shepard had somehow let us in on a dirty little secret of our violent world. Had he told us what violent men really think and feel? Had he given us a theatrical version of Donna Ferrato's remarkable photographs of violent families?

As we got deeper into the project, we found ourselves asking each other why so few people (if any) had systematically looked at IPV from the batterer's perspective. Were we all brainwashed by the "boys will be boys" mentality we kept encountering? Every interview with an abusive man inspired a torrent of questions and insights, and we came to believe that studying IPV only by focusing on the victims was tantamount to studying murder without looking at murderers or burglaries without looking at thieves. We simply could not have done the research for *A Lie of the Mind* without looking at IPV from the man's point of view, but in turn we saw that the sociological phenomenon itself could not be adequately understood without an analogous focus. We simply had to understand constructions of masculinity in order to understand IPV or, for that matter, *A Lie of the Mind*.

In all of this, what was remarkable to me was that, unlike other interdisciplinary colleagues I had worked with, Dr. Hattery was willing to see our interaction as a circuit. Not only was I benefiting from her expertise, but she was willing to allow my strengths to inform her work. Further, she could see *A Lie of the Mind* for what it is: an authentic cultural document that asks some extremely interesting questions. She saw that, despite its limitations as a *scientific* document, it did express one very clear and troubling version of American family life, and—as such—it held within it insights that a good sociologist could use as a springboard. She has done just that.

Since those early days and our relatively small interview sample of men and women, Dr. Hattery has gone on to broaden the sociological study's scope and to deepen her understanding of the many competing factors that contribute to IPV. Her work is more complete and more nuanced now, and it includes a much-needed examination of how race intersects with gender and class in the IPV puzzle. She has also moved beyond the Southeast to include a more diverse sample of men and women. In Clifford Geertz's terms, this study might be looked at as a "thick description," which helps us understand the isolated elements and players in the IPV picture, the internal relationships of those elements, and—finally—how IPV works within a larger cultural system.

Certainly no one interested in why and how IPV occurs will be able to read this book without knowing that class inequities, gender construction, and racism must all be examined in order to even understand—let alone stop—this violent epidemic. Dr. Hattery has shown us Candy's bruises, Ella's $40,000 hotel bill, and Hank's assertion that he loves the "motherfucking lazy bitch" he lives with. Now it is time to recognize how these astonishing "artifacts" express the bigger picture of IPV in the United States.

Cynthia Gendrich, Ph.D.
Wake Forest University

Acknowledgments

This book has been a long time coming. My interest in this issue began when I was a graduate student at the University of Wisconsin, Madison, taking a class in women's studies. We read Angela Browne's book *When Battered Women Kill*. Having grown up in a safe, nonviolent home, I was mesmerized by the level of terror and torture so many people live with on a daily basis. I set out to conduct research on intimate partner violence for my dissertation. As I was putting my dissertation proposal together in the summer of 1993 I was also staring into the eyes of my newborn baby daughter, Emma. I knew then that I could not conduct this type of research and come home each day and cradle a baby girl who was no doubt starting as hopeful a life as the women whose lives would ultimately become filled with severe violence. I decided on a different project for my dissertation (*Women, Work and Family: Balancing and Weaving*, 2001) but always knew I would return to this important work. Now, nearly fifteen years later, I am thrilled to finally be making a contribution to the study of violence that in many ways has always been part of my intellectual journey.

As authors always note, the writing of a book, though an extremely solitary endeavor, could not be done without the help and advice of many people. I would like to publicly acknowledge those who have helped with this book. Any errors that remain are mine alone.

I am grateful to my editors at Rowman & Littlefield, Alan McClare and Michael McGandy. The stories contained in this book are gut-wrenching, so while completing another project (*Globalization and America*) with Alan and Michael I approached them with this manuscript. They were immediately enthusiastic about this project and encouraged me to complete it. Working with

Rowman & Littlefield has been seamless, and I am grateful to the many people there who allowed me to write the book I wanted to write.

I am grateful to Professor Rebecca Bach (Duke University) and Professor Janel Leone (Syracuse University) who provided thoughtful and insightful reviews. Their comments forced me to write more clearly and tighten the arguments I present in this book.

Many people helped me to arrange the interviews with the men and women whose stories are the basis for this book: Joetta Shepherd and Kevin Sidden and their staff at Family Services of Winston-Salem, North Carolina; Pat Dean-McRay and her staff at the battered women's shelter in Winston-Salem, North Carolina; and Michele Valletta and her staff at Child Protective Services in Olmsted County, Minnesota. She carefully coordinated my schedule, thus allowing me to collect interviews with men and women with whom they work. I will always remember the cooperation and warm welcome they gave me, especially my last meeting with the staff wherein I introduced them to a gift of "North Carolina BBQ."

I am also grateful to the highway patrolman in Zumbrota, Minnesota, who rescued me at 3 a.m. on Highway 52 after my rental car hit a raccoon. The ninety minutes I waited for a tow truck in the backseat of his cruiser proved more interesting than I could have imagined. Once I warmed up as he blasted the heat, he, too, told story after story of battering in the all-white suburbs wherein judges, lawyers, and "city fathers" were engaging in some of the most brutal, but hidden, interpersonal violence that will never be told in a social behavioral scientist way. It will simply move from one generation to the next.

I am grateful to Melissa Williams, Wake Forest University class of 2005, who took an interest in my project and conducted evaluation research for Family Services, Winston-Salem, North Carolina. That project became, at a later date, the subject for her honors thesis in sociology. Her work greatly informed my understanding of the efficacy of the batterer intervention program, *TimeOut*, in Winston-Salem.

I am grateful to Sarah Hazlegrove who efficiently and tirelessly transcribed the majority of the interviews. Despite less-than-ideal equipment and recording situations (babies were often crying, television sets were on), the work Sarah did for me was impeccable. I gratefully acknowledge the transcription work of Peggy Beckman, Joan Habib, and Donté McGuire who each transcribed the remaining interviews.

I am grateful for the funding we received at various stages of this project, including that from the Social and Behavioral Sciences Research Fund at Wake Forest University. I thank Provost Mark Welker for this award and for all of his support for this project. I am also grateful to the American Sociological Association's Fund for the Advancement of the Discipline which provided the funding for a good portion of this project. A special thank you to Paul Ribisl, Dean of Wake Forest College, for providing the indexing software necessary for me to complete the index. I am very grateful.

I am grateful to my colleagues at Colgate University, especially Chairperson Mary Moran, Professor Rhonda Levine and Dean Doug Johnson for offering me the chance to spend the 2008–2009 academic year at Colgate as the A. Lindsay O'Connor Professor of American Institutions. They have welcomed me into their intellectual community, and I look forward to sharing the release of this book with my colleagues and students at Colgate.

I am grateful to Professor Cynthia Gendrich (Wake Forest University) who conducted the early interviews with me. She also contributed the foreword to the book. Her insights into the project and her support and friendship were so important to its success.

Thanks to Emily Kane, you taught me to do sociology. Thanks to Paul Wellstone, you believed in me when I was your student at Carleton, you helped me through some very dark days, and you and your wife, Sheila, worked tirelessly to keep intimate partner violence on the agenda of lawmakers. To Bob and Diane Hattery, who taught me I could be anything I wanted to be and to tackle any problem I wanted to, your vision allowed me to find my own way.

I owe a very special thanks to my research partner, Professor Earl Smith (Wake Forest University). He not only believed in this work but dedicated many years of his own life to a collaborative partnership that resulted in expanding the interviews beyond North Carolina to Minnesota. Our coauthored book, *African American Families* (2007), explores the webs of dysfunction — IPV, incarceration, HIV/AIDS — that plague African American families in the contemporary United States. He painstakingly read every page of this manuscript, and he challenged me to make this the best book on intimate partner violence on the market today. Thank you.

Finally, to the men and women who so graciously opened up their lives to us, I am grateful. They shared the deepest, most intimate — and oftentimes painful — parts of their stories with us, in offices, in their homes, in the hospital, and even from jail cells. Without you there would be no book.

Angela J. Hattery
Winston-Salem, North Carolina

Introduction

When things were good, they were so good. Like I said, I was always secure with him. He might try to hit me and he might try to kill me, but nobody else was going to do it. Nobody else was going to talk bad to me or hurt me or talk bad about me. That just wasn't going to happen. I was secure in that sense with him. *He was going to protect me from everybody else.*—Candy, twenty-something white woman, North Carolina

On April 16, 2007, the worst school shooting in the history of the United States—to date—took place when a gunman shot thirty-two members of the Virginia Tech University campus community before turning the gun on himself and becoming the thirty-third "victim." Early speculation about the motive focused on a possible domestic dispute.

Perhaps the most troubling aspect of this situation is the fact that many accounts of the morning of April 16, 2007, indicate that the campus police did not immediately recognize the risk that the shooter presented to the entire Virginia Tech campus *because the first homicide committed that morning was believed to be a domestic violence homicide.*[1] "Virginia Tech President Charles Steger said authorities believed that the shooting at the dorm was a domestic dispute and mistakenly thought the gunman had fled the campus. 'We had no reason to suspect any other incident was going to occur,' he said" (Lindsey 2007).

The events surrounding the Virginia Tech shooting are troubling for many reasons, first and foremost because the decision by the Virginia Tech president implies that domestic violence homicide is nothing to take too seriously, and certainly it does not constitute a threat to public safety in the larger community. And yet in many cases of domestic violence homicide, other victims are maimed and/or murdered. Even more troubling is the fact that in examining other school shootings, a clear and disturbing pattern emerges (Newman et al. 2005). Beginning with the Texas Tower shootings at the University of Texas, Austin, in 1966, many school shootings either began with or involved domestic violence homicide. In the Texas Tower shootings, the shooter, Charles Whitman, murdered his wife and his mother the night before the terrible rampage in Austin. Luke Woodham, the school shooter in Pearl, Mississippi, also began his rampage by shooting his girlfriend and mother. And, of course, the most recent tragedy at Virginia Tech was believed to begin with a domestic violence homicide. In all of these cases, had law enforcement and emergency responders taken the initial domestic violence homicide as a matter of public safety, perhaps the greater tragedies would have been avoided.

April 2007 was indeed a deadly month. Earlier that month a 19-year-old Texas A&M student was murdered by her ex-boyfriend. After killing her, he barbequed her body on his backyard grill in an attempt to dispose of it. A few days before that a University of Washington college student was murdered by her ex-boyfriend who shot and killed her *on campus*. Those who are not moved by the tragedy of domestic violence, conceptualizing it as something that women often bring on themselves, should care because it is a threat to public safety in this society. And, though high school and college students are far less vulnerable to domestic violence homicide than adult women, the community living situation that characterizes college campuses and the high concentration of people on high school campuses creates a situation ripe for the "spillover" of domestic violence into what have become some of the worst school shootings in U.S. history.

The violence continued into May 2007 when in Moscow, Idaho, a man shot and killed two police officers and wounded bystanders in a standoff with police. This man's rampage began with the murder of his wife, whose body was found after the man committed suicide inside the courthouse where he had barricaded himself during the standoff.

Taken together, these events, both on and off campuses, are part of a larger culture of violence in the United States. Tragically, forty times more women are killed by their intimate or ex-intimate partners *each year* in the United States than the total killed at Virginia Tech that fateful day in April 2007. On average, four domestic homicides occur *each day*. Millions of women live in fear of their intimate and former intimate partners. The tragic events at Virginia Tech became second-page news, having received more coverage but no more analysis than did the tragic stories of battered women introduced in this book. These women's stories bring to light a dirty secret that most Americans are even less willing to discuss than school shootings.

Lost in all of the media attention and hype around the shootings at Virginia Tech is the fact that to date all of the school shooters, from Columbine to

Jonesboro, Arkansas, to Virginia Tech, have been men. Violence is *gendered*. And intimate partner violence (IPV) is *doubly* gendered in that the victims are almost always—95 percent of the time—women.[2]

Little attention is paid in the public sphere, the media, or the academic literature to the epidemic of intimate partner violence. Sociologist Lisa D. Brush argues that sociologists, even those who identify themselves with the study of social problems, no longer study individuals' lives:

> It has become unfashionable to speak of first-order social problems—the events or beliefs or dilemmas that threaten peoples' livelihood or safety or health and well-being—rather than the second-order construction or third-order reception and interpretation of the discourse about such problems, the people who suffer them, and how to organize relief. It is hard to find a *Social Problems*[3] article that presents research and theory-testing as a means of remedying suffering by laboring to understand the world in order to change it (or at the very least to change social policy!). (Brush 2006, 1)

This book not only provides another exposé of the tragedies of intimate partner violence, but it does so using the voices of actual battered women and the men who batter them. Second, rather than painting batterers as crazy men and battered women as helpless victims, the analyses presented here identify the structural and cultural factors that create an environment where gendered violence is normalized and unfortunately all too common. By constructing acts of battering as "rule" enforcement and "role" enforcement, I argue that individual men and communities use intimate partner violence to discipline women for "misbehaving." Equally important, IPV is a "tool" used to keep all women in their "proper place" in the gender hierarchy (Epstein 2007), thus maintaining the status quo dictated by gender inequality regimes (Acker 2006).

THE PROBLEM

As noted, intimate partner violence is an epidemic societal problem.[4] We should care about IPV because it affects our mothers and sisters and partners and friends, and because it is our fathers and brothers and male partners and friends who are responsible for this violence. IPV kills fifteen hundred women per year and sends millions to local emergency rooms for medical treatment (Bureau of Justice Statistics 2003).

So, Will's at work one day and I'm, I'm home. Bri's at school. And I was sleeping up in my bedroom, and all of a sudden, my bedroom door came flying in.

GW [Stella's ex-boyfriend] had broken through a window downstairs, come in and kicked open my door, and I was in T-shirt and panties and it was winter out, so I was barefooted. And he jumped on top of me and started choking me. Then he yanked me up, and started banging my head against a cement wall. And I managed to get my feet up against his chest and push him backwards, and I ran down the stairs, and got to the front door, but its one of those, you have to turn the door knob and the thing at the same time. One of those old fashioned locks. And he got me before I could get it out and he grabbed me around the waist and threw me backwards and I hit the banister to the stairs, which was solid wood, and I slid down. He ripped the phone out of the wall and then he was standing over me with a baseball bat. And I thought, this is it. I'm going to die.—Stella, twenty-something white woman, Minnesota

Until very recently, domestic violence, as it has been referred to, was a problem to be dealt with inside the family. Furthermore, domestic violence was essentially legal; men were legally allowed to beat their wives as long as they did not kill them or the violence did not become extreme (Browne 1987).[5] As evidence of this, many feminist scholars cite "the rule of thumb," noting that men were legally sanctioned to beat their wives as long as they did so with an instrument that did not exceed the diameter of their own thumb (Browne 1987).[6] In the late 1970s and early 1980s second wave feminists began to draw attention to the situation of domestic violence and its victims. The writings of these scholars (e.g., Browne 1987; Kirkwood 1993) were critical in that they brought this common experience of IPV to the attention of the larger American population. However, as awareness of IPV has grown, our discussions of it have remained narrowly focused on conceptualizing and defining IPV as a "women's problem." Certainly IPV is a women's problem. Millions of women are injured and thousands are killed each year as a result of IPV. And certainly, women face many problems as they experience IPV, such as the difficulty of finding a safe place to live (Tiefenthaler et al. 2005). However, it is their male partners who beat them.

A significant barrier to effectively dealing with IPV is our continued conceptualization of it as a "women's problem," thus focusing on or examining only the women who are victims. I argue that we need to redefine and reconceptualize IPV as a "men's problem" and as a problem faced by couples in our society. I also argue that it is a social problem, one that has significant costs to our society. The most notable costs are those associated with law enforcement, the criminal justice system, welfare payments and shelter costs for women who leave, health care costs as a result of injury, labor costs as a result of sick leave, and of course the innumerable and inestimable costs to our children who grow up with this violence and so often go on to perpetuate its cycle.

I argue further that it is precisely this tendency to categorize and segregate by gender that creates the environment in which IPV is not only common but more or less accepted and expected. And, though I explore in this book both the race and class underpinnings of IPV, it is fundamentally a product of *gender inequality regimes* (Acker 2006). Extrapolating from the work of Cynthia Fuchs Epstein, I suggest that the existence of IPV fundamentally reminds us as individuals and as a society that men and women live in different social worlds. IPV is a powerful tool in enforcing and reinforcing gender hierarchies and gender inequalities. And, as we shall see in subsequent chapters, "triggers" to IPV can be understood as reactions to the perception (by men) that women are trying to act "equal," that they have lost sight of their "proper place." I term this type of IPV "role enforcement."

Epstein, in her 2007 Presidential Address to the American Sociological Association (ASA), argued that one of the core concepts in understanding gender is recognizing that, historically, patriarchy has constructed men and women as "different" and that the closer women get to men at work in earning potential, in holding public office, in running corporations, and in gaining educational credentials, the more important it is for patriarchy to identify and reinforce gender differences. She writes:

> The enforcement of the distinction is achieved through cultural and ideological means that justify the differentiation. This is despite the fact that, unlike every other dichotomous category of people, females and males are necessarily bound together, sharing the same domiciles and most often the same racial and social class statuses. Analyses of these relationships are difficult given the ways in which they are integrated with each other and the extent to which they are basic in all institutions. (Epstein 2007, 4)

In other words, just as Ku Klux Klan violence arose during the Reconstruction period in the South to enforce racial boundaries threatened by the emancipation of millions of slaves—in short, to remind African Americans of "their place"—so, too, gendered violence can be understood as a tactic for reminding women of *their* place. Furthermore, Epstein notes that the need to enforce between-group boundaries is greatest when there is a high degree of intimacy between the group members. This framework suggests it is not surprising that Klan violence was far more prevalent in the South, a geographic landscape in which African Americans and whites shared the intimate spaces created by wet-nursing, domestic service, and so on, than in the North (see Hattery and Smith 2008). So, too, is the rate of gender violence high. In fact, it is significantly higher than racial violence, because men and women share intimate space not just as spouses and partners but as siblings, parents, and children. In the context of this intimacy, and in a time when women are gaining access to freedoms and opportunities that have been denied them for so long, it is not surprising that we see the high rates of IPV that characterize the contemporary United States.

ASSUMPTIONS

People always ask why I focus my attention on men who batter, with particular attention to those who also grew up in violent homes, instead of focusing on the more common experience: men who do not batter *despite* the fact that they were raised with violence.

This is an interesting question and one that I have thought about long and hard. I've come to realize that people who ask me this question are in fact applying a different set of assumptions to understanding intimate partner violence than they apply to most other aspects of life. The question arises from their assumption that the common experience should be studied rather than the exception to the rule.

Asking why I do not study men who are not batterers rises from the assumption that all men are bad, and therefore we had better study the process by which men, indeed most men, can and do become "good" (Zimbardo 2007).

This runs counter to the assumptions that permeate all aspects of sociology. Nearly all of sociology is based on the exception. And, the discipline rests firmly on the assumption that people are generally good, and we need to understand what happens when things go wrong.

Allow me to illustrate. I do not ask my colleagues who study poverty, "Why don't you study the more common experience of being middle class or moderately affluent in order to understand what those folks did right?" This query would rest on the assumption that most people are poor but that a few figure out how to make money and not become or remain poor.[7]

Similarly, I do not ask my colleagues who study incarceration, "Why don't you study the more common experience of those who never go to jail?" That, too, would imply that most people are destined for jail but for some lucky event in their lives that keeps out of jail. And, fortunately, most Americans are lucky.

I study men who batter because I believe they are the exception to the rule. I believe that men (and women) are born fundamentally good, not bad. But, being raised in a patriarchal, violent society, many boys, far too many, grow up learning to beat women. Though statistically they may be the exception to the rule, I am also interested in the ways in which patriarchal culture normalizes violence against women. Though men who engage in IPV may still be the exception to the rule, I will argue in chapter 5 that in fact IPV and other forms of violence against women are an expected outcome of patriarchy. This can be seen in the recent remarks by Isaiah Thomas, former Indiana University and NBA standout and former manager of the New York Knicks. Thomas, in a deposition taken as part of a sexual harassment lawsuit filed against him, indicated that it was offensive for a white man to call an African American woman a "bitch," but he was not equally troubled by the same word being used by an African American man.

> Jurors heard the Knicks coach say he wouldn't stand for a white man calling a black woman a "bitch"—but wouldn't be as angry if the same words came from the mouth of a black man. In a videotaped deposition played for the jury at fired Knicks exec Anucha Browne Sanders' sexual harassment trial, Thomas said he drew a distinction between whites and blacks when it came to the B-word. Asked if he was bothered by a black man calling a black female "bitch," Thomas said: "Not as much. I'm sorry to say, I do make a distinction." (Zambito 2007)

And, of course, I must point out here that Thomas is considered one of the "good guys" in basketball. People note that he is sophisticated, articulate, and not a thug like some of his peers. What is notable about his statement is that it points out the pervasiveness of misogynistic beliefs among everyday kinds of men.[8]

Now, a caveat: in fact I am especially interested in men who were raised with violence but not socialized to be violent themselves. They do not learn to beat women, even though most of us would not be surprised if they did. As a feminist I am interested in these men who throw off the trappings of patriarchy. Men who do not batter, especially those who were raised in violent homes, are interesting because they fail to conform to hegemonic constructions of masculinity, which I will explore in this book. Yet, this project is based on an examination of the reasons that men do beat the women they love and the ways that this shapes their relationships and the individual lives of both the men and women who live with this violence.

Finally, as a researcher, I will continue to base my research on two major assumptions: (1) that people are born "good," and it is society that teaches them to be "bad"; and (2) that the interesting part of science lies in these exceptions to the rule, even if they, too, are far too "common," as I will argue is the case with men who batter.

My thoughts here are in many ways similar to those of the late African American historian and sociologist William Edward Burghardt DuBois, who argued for most of his academic/activist career for a more accurate account of U.S. and world history. He said, "We have the record of kings and gentlemen *ad nauseam* and in stupid detail; but of the common run of human beings, and particularly of the half or wholly submerged working group, the world has saved all too little of authentic record and tried to forget or ignore even the little saved" (1951).

THIS BOOK

The approach of this book is unique in that it is not limited to a discussion of IPV per se. Though the stories of men and women living with IPV will be presented and analyzed, several chapters of the book will examine the ways in which IPV is a structural, perhaps inevitable, outcome of the ideology and false consciousness that is a part of the patriarchal socialization process. Patriarchy proscribes a certain set of gender relations as well as imposes limits and constraints upon educational attainment, labor force participation, and economic freedom for women. Patriarchy results in restricted constructions of motherhood and fatherhood and constrains women's reproductive lives. For example, women continue to be socialized to believe that it is better to have a man who beats you than no man at all (Rich 1980). Women continue to earn seventy-five cents on the male dollar, leaving them economically disadvantaged (England 2005; Levine, n.d.; Padavic and Reskin 2002).

Until we address these fundamental, root causes for staying in a relationship with a batterer, such as economic dependency, battered women will continue to make unsuccessful attempts to leave, returning because they cannot "make ends meet" (Edin and Lein 1997). Therefore, IPV, a gendered phenomenon, and all of its causes and outcomes, must be examined within the larger system of patriarchy. Only when we understand the ways in which patriarchy creates unequal gender outcomes can we begin to consider social reconfigurations that will eliminate (or at least reduce) the violence plaguing so many of our families.

But, IPV is not structured only by a system of patriarchy. It is also structured by a system of racial superiority and capitalism and of the intersections of these systems with patriarchy. I will argue later in the book that one of the battering "triggers" for men is feeling that their masculinity is threatened. One of the patterns that emerged from these interviews is that when men feel emasculated they will often try to reassert their masculinity through violence. One of the fundamental tenets of patriarchy is the requirement that men be the breadwinner in their families. But, one of the outcomes of capitalism is that this is a difficult if not impossible task for a large number of American men. And the situation is far worse for minority men, especially African American men. Thus, this book will not only present data on the experiences of whites and African Americans, but it will utilize the lens of integration provided by the race, class, and gender theory to analyze the differences that exist across race, class, and gender demarcations. Until we understand better the nuances of IPV as it is structured by systems of domination (racism, sexism, classism, and so forth) we will be unable to work toward building a society free of violence and oppression. This book is also framed by the notion that IPV consists of individual, structural, and cultural components. Thus, I devote a chapter to each of these components, and each includes an analysis framed by the race, class, and gender paradigm.

The Stories

What makes a book like this compelling are the stories of the men and women — regular, everyday people like those we work with, those we meet in the aisle of the grocery store, and those we live near. The stories here are of regular, everyday people who live with a secret, and that secret is IPV.

The stories that constitute the data utilized in these analyses vary. Some of the men and women we met had experienced only one violent episode before the violence was interrupted. Others have lived for fifteen or twenty years with severe violence. Many of the women we met have an injury report that would fill a medical chart — broken bones, miscarriages, blackened eyes, broken teeth, pulled hair, and even scars from being bitten in the face. The stories presented here chill the spine. But, until we can be honest about IPV and examine it systematically, we will be powerless in reducing and eliminating it as a major cause of injury and death to women in this country.

Chapter 1, "Setting the Stage," presents the most recent statistics and empirical data to paint a broad picture of IPV in contemporary U.S. society and provide an overview of race, class, and gender theory, which I use to contextualize and advance our understanding of IPV.

NOTES

1. At the time of this writing it has not been determined if in fact the first homicide was a domestic violence shooting. My claim here is only that at the time of the events, the decision to not alert the campus about the first homicide was based on the belief that it was a domestic violence homicide and thus was considered an isolated event. In fact, according to the official report commissioned by the governor on the tragic shootings, "Had university officials not waited more than two hours to tell the campus about the initial shootings, lives could have been saved when Seung-Hui Cho later began his massacre inside a classroom building." See *Report of the Virginia Tech Review Panel*, www.governor.virginia.gov/TempContent/techPanelReport.cfm.

2. Among scholars of domestic violence are two schools of thought. Feminist scholars tend to focus on severe battering when they describe its gendered quality. In contrast, Michael Johnson and others prefer to distinguish what they term intimate terrorism from situational couple violence. They note that while 95 percent of the victims of intimate terrorism are women, situational couple violence involves similar numbers of men being violent toward women as women being violent toward men. I will examine this distinction in chapter 1.

3. *Social Problems* is the journal of the Society for the Study of Social Problems (SSSP).

4. IPV in the gay, lesbian, bisexual, and transgender communities is an important issue. For the purposes of this book, however, I am restricting my discussion of IPV to the heterosexual community. For an excellent report on IPV in the lesbian community see Renzetti 1989.

5. In an examination of Palestinian women from the West Bank and Gaza Strip, Haj-Yahia (2000) found that even among fundamentalists this seemingly universal truth holds for these women subjected by their mates to annual incidences of psychological, sexual, and economic abuse as well as physical violence. Battering, then, especially in legally constructed unions like civil and religious marriage, has been researched and argued by scholars to be legal in many countries, including the United States, well into the twentieth century (Browne 1987; Weitzman 1998; Leone et al. 2004). This finding correlates well with the early text by Engels in which he argues that women all over the world who enter into marriage become the property of their husbands. While originally contested, family scholars using the then unique database of the Human Relations Area Files, located at Yale University, confirmed this "husband's right" (Murdock 1954, 1983).

6. Note that legal scholars who trace the origins of the "Rule of Thumb" conclude that it is probably half true and half not true. In other words, men were legally sanctioned in beating their wives, but only in accordance with an actual rule comparing an instrument to the thumb of the husband (Kelly 1994; U.S. Commission on Civil Rights 1982).

7. Recent IRS reports on wealth suggest that in fact more and more Americans may soon be considered "poor" as more and more wealth concentrates among an ever-decreasing proportion of the U.S. population. www.commondreams.org/archive/2007/10/12/4509/.

8. "He has no right to put her down, and then think it's ok for me to put her down but it's not alright for a white man to put her down. What are you talking about? She is a human being and as a female, and in particular as a black female, I took tremendous offense to that." C. Vivian Stringer, Rutger's head basketball coach, October 26, 2007. ESPN, http://sports.espn.go.com/ncw/news/story?id=3081048.

Chapter One

Setting the Stage

In the Arab-Muslim world, argues David Landes, certain cultural attitudes have in many ways become a barrier to development, particularly the tendency to still treat women as a source of danger or pollution to be cut off from the public space and denied entry into economic activities. When a culture believes that, it loses a large portion of potential productivity of the society. A system that privileges the men from birth on, Landes argues, simply because they are male, and gives them power over their sisters and other female members of society, is bad for the men. It builds in them a sense of entitlement that discourages what it takes to improve, to advance, and to achieve. This sort of discrimination, he notes, is not something limited to the Arab Middle East, of course. Indeed strains of it are found in different degrees all around the world, even in so-called advanced industrial societies. (Friedman 2006, 412–13)

Every scholar of any topic must begin by examining the work on which his or hers is built. A thorough understanding of previous research is critical to advancing knowledge in any field. Similarly, it is not enough to simply describe a social phenomenon; if we truly seek understanding then we must ground these descriptions in a theoretical framework. This chapter provides the reader with some statistics that create a context for understanding intimate partner violence, a review of previous research on IPV, and a review of the race, class, and gender paradigm which provides the theoretical underpinning for this book. Because intimate partner violence can mean many things to different people, I begin with some definitions that will be employed in this book.

DEFINITIONS

Intimate partner violence (IPV) refers to the physical, emotional, psychological, and sexual abuse that takes place between intimate partners. The focus

11

of this book is limited to a discussion of violence between heterosexual partners. I do not use the term "domestic," as I am not referring to violence that
occurs between other members of the domestic household, such as the abuse
of children by parents. In addition, "domestic" implies a shared residence.
Many of the casualties of IPV do not live together, or the violence began before they moved in together and often continues long after they physically
separate. Finally, I choose the term "intimate partner" rather than "domestic
partner" in order to underscore the nature of the relationship—these are intimate partners who claim to love each other—yet they may or may not be
legally married. IPV is present in both marital and cohabiting relationships. I
do not differentiate between these legal statuses but rather focus on the intimate nature of the relationship.

Intimate Terrorism versus Situational Couple Violence

As noted above, I prefer the term "IPV" to others that are also common in the
field, such as "domestic violence" and "battering." However, as noted in the
definition above, IPV involves many forms of violence, including physical
violence. Because this is the case, I sometimes use the term "battering" or
"men who batter." This is in recognition of both the physical violence that
takes place and the need to utilize clear language.

Among scholars of IPV a critical debate centers on "mutual combat," a
term coined by Gelles and Straus (1988). Michael Johnson and his colleagues
have extended this debate and attempted to distinguish between two different
forms of IPV: (1) situational couple violence and (2) intimate terrorism.
These corresponding forms of violence against women differentiate themselves in terms of the *lethality* of the violence and the *level of control* in the
relationship.

> The importance of categorizing types of violence, rather than viewing partner
> violence as a continuum of severity or frequency of physical violence, rests on
> the assumption that intimate terrorism and situational couple violence involve
> qualitatively different patterns of control rather than high or low levels of phys-
> ical violence. (Leone et al. 2004, 473)

Intimate Terrorism: Johnson and his colleagues (Johnson and Ferraro 2000;
Leone et al. 2004) describe intimate terrorism as "a partner's attempt to exert
control over his partner using a broad range of power and control tactics,
which include physical violence" (2004, 473).

Situational Couple Violence: In contrast, situational couple violence "does
not exist within a general pattern of controlling behavior. This form of

violence is not motivated by a desire to control and overpower a partner or a relationship, but rather occurs when specific conflict situations escalate to violence" (Leone et al. 2004, 473).

Though these distinctions may be important, especially to practitioners and intervention specialists, I find them to be problematic for two reasons: (1) this distinction often blurs or hides the ways in which IPV is about gender and power, and (2) the fact that in many violent relationships both types of violence exist.

The data collected, analyzed, and presented in this book come primarily from men and women whom Johnson and his colleagues would define as engaging primarily in "intimate terrorism." This is a function of the data collection strategies employed for my study. It is not problematic, however, because the analyses in this book are not based on the schematic developed by Johnson and others but rather on the race, class, and gender paradigm. Furthermore, unlike most of the studies conducted by Johnson and colleagues that rely on large-scale, mostly superficial data collection techniques, this book is based on thick descriptions generated by in-depth, life history interviews and weaves the stories both of women who are battered (and sometimes batter back)[1] and men who batter, shedding light on the often hidden details of intimate partner violence as it is experienced by men and women in America.

A BRIEF HISTORY OF THE DOMESTIC VIOLENCE MOVEMENT

The earliest research on "domestic" violence dates to the 1970s. The second wave of feminism with all of its consciousness raising, support groups, public marches, and rhetoric brought battering to the mainstream discourse. Women like Susan Brownmiller and Lenore Walker helped to bring battering to the attention of lawmakers and law enforcement agencies.

During the late 1970s and early 1980s shelters for battered women began to spring up all over the country, though they are still outnumbered three to one by shelters for abandoned animals (Browne 1987; Koss et al. 1994). More recently, researchers and advocates for victims of domestic violence have put together protocols for dealing with domestic violence that have been codified into laws such as mandatory arrest. Yet we still know very little about the inner workings of IPV, and we are still relatively unsuccessful in reducing its prevalence.

Domestic violence remains a misdemeanor in most states, punishable by probation rather than jail time. In fact, in many communities batterers can opt for a treatment program (as many of those interviewed for this book did) and forgo jail time altogether. In these treatment programs batterers learn the rhetoric, but they seldom cease battering. Most of the men whose stories are told in this book admitted openly and freely that they were still in abusive relationships with their partners, and some admitted, or their partners confessed, that battering episodes had occurred just a day or two prior to my interview.

SOME FACTS

From Durkheim (1982, 50–59) we learn that "social facts" are things. That is, they prove the existence of a social reality in addition to an individual reality. In order to understand the power of the stories of the women and men that are told in this book, we must first have a context for these experiences. Statistics on IPV provide an appropriate context that allows us to better interpret these experiences. The statistics on women who are battered are followed by statistics on men who batter.

Women Who Are Battered

Many women in the United States experience violence within their own homes, exacting from them severe physical, emotional, and economic costs (Browne 1987; Koss et al. 1994). The Centers for Disease Control (2006) estimates that women are nine times more likely to be injured in their homes than in the streets; domestic violence accounts for more injuries to women than car accidents, muggings, and rapes combined (Browne 1987). In 2006 women *reported* 4.8 million acts of violence.

Domestic violence can also be lethal; 1,544 women were murdered in 2004 by their intimate or former intimate partners (Centers for Disease Control 2006). Domestic violence homicide accounts for 33 percent of all female homicides each year (Rennison 2003; *USA Today* 2003) with beatings being the most common method of murder (Browne 1987; Fields 1977–1978).

In addition to the injury tolls associated with intimate partner violence, it has many other negative consequences for women. Intimate partner violence forces many women into poverty and homelessness both during and after marriage and partnership; in fact an estimated 25–50 percent of homeless women left violent homes (Mason 1993). Also, the majority of women who are welfare (TANF) recipients have experienced IPV (Brush 2000, 2001; Brush, Raphael, and Tolman 2003; Renzetti 2001; Taylor Institute 1997).

Intimate partner violence also affects women psychologically. Browne (1987) noted that an inordinate number of women (50 percent) whom she interviewed considered or attempted suicide; rates were higher among those who killed their abusive partners than those who did not. Many others exhibited symptoms of depression, post-traumatic stress disorder, and/or anxiety disorder (Browne 1987, Walker 1979, 1984). Psychological injury can also render women unable to hold steady jobs, thus leaving them in poverty, homeless, or simply unable to leave their abusers because they are economically unable to do so (Browne 1987; Brush 2000, 2001; Brush, Raphael, and Tolman 2003).[2] See box 1.1 for statistics on intimate partner violence in the United States.

Box 1.1.   Statistics on the Impact of IPV

4.8 million acts of intimate partner violence are reported by U.S. women each year.
 CDC Fact Sheet, 2006

1,544 women were murdered in 2004 by their intimate or former intimate partners.
 CDC Fact Sheet, 2006

Females accounted for **39 percent** of hospital emergency department visits for violence-related injuries.
 National Center for Injury Prevention and Control. 2003. *Costs of Intimate Partner Violence against Women in the United States*. Atlanta, GA: Centers for Disease Control and Prevention.

31,260 women were **murdered** by an intimate from 1976 to1996.
 U.S. Department of Justice. 1998. *Violence by Intimates: Analysis of Data on Crimes by Current or Former Spouses, Boyfriends, and Girlfriends.*

25 percent of women report being raped.
 Warshaw, R. 1988. *I Never Called It Rape: The MS. Report on Recognizing, Fighting, and Surviving Date and Acquaintance Rape.* New York: Harper & Row.

8 in 10 rape victims are raped by someone they know.
 Centers for Disease Control, http://www.cdc.gov/nchs/fastats.htm.

1 in 4 women report having sex with their male partners when they did not want to.
 Russell, D. E. H. 1990. *Rape in Marriage.* Bloomington, IN: University of Indiana Press.

Men Who Batter

Large-scale surveys (Tjaden and Thoennes 2000) reveal that approximately one in four men (25 percent) indicate that they engaged in an act of violence against their intimate partner during the previous year. The most common types of violence include slapping, pulling hair, throwing things at their partner, and "beating her up" (Tjaden and Thoennes 2000).

Given these statistics it is not surprising that the research on men who batter is focused primarily in two areas: differentiating men who batter from the rest of the male population (Hanson et al. 1997; Holtzworth-Munroe and Stuart 1994)—what makes batterers different from "regular" men—and evaluating the efficacy of interventions with men who batter (Hirschel, Hutchison, and Dean 1992; Pate and Hamilton 1992; Sherman et al. 1992).

One of the shortcomings of the existing research on men who batter is that very little has focused on the *batterers' perceptions* of the violence they engage in (Goodrum, Umberson, and Anderson 2001). Rather, what we know about the dynamics of battering in couples we have learned almost exclusively from the accounts of the female victims (Browne 1987; Goodrum, Umberson, and Anderson 2001).

In that context, the vast majority of research that relies on the voices of batterers is focused on evaluating various intervention programs. A variety of programs have been implemented with limited success in treating battering primarily because, according to Adams (1988), they seldom incorporate the victim's perspective into treatment. Rather, Adams suggests that many interventions attribute the battering to external forces, such as alcoholism or depression. By designing treatment protocols around these "social problems," which are clearly linked to battering (Hanson et al. 1997), instead of the core issue, which Adams defines as the batterer's need to retain and enforce power over his partner, many interventions are only moderately effective (Adams 1988; Hattery, Williams, and Smith 2004).

Other scholars have noted that batterers use denial to protect their self-concepts, often failing to acknowledge the inappropriate nature of their actions; batterers have very little understanding of the violence from the perspective of their wives or partners. These researchers speculate that batterers have a limited ability to take the role of the other in the context of this power relationship (Goodrum, Umberson, and Anderson 2001). Thus, Adams (1988) suggests that a successful intervention requires the identification and understanding of the ways in which both partners perceive the violence in the relationship. This is similar to Scully's (1990) research with convicted rapists.

Finally, scant literature exists about nonwhite men who batter. Smith (2008) addresses this void and argues that while an examination of rates of battering shows no difference between African American and white men, other issues need to be taken into account when trying to understand cross-cultural issues related to men who batter. Indeed, recent large-scale, nationally representative surveys have established stable estimates of the prevalence of IPV in our society—one in four women report at least one violent episode in their lifetimes, and one in four men report perpetrating IPV—and its relative blindness to social demarcations of race/ethnicity, social class, or region of the country (Tjaden and Thonnes 2000). However, recent research does identify the ways in which race (and class) shape the experiences of both battered women and men who batter (Hattery and Smith 2007a; Hill 2005; Hill-Collins 2004; hooks 2004). Though these processes and outcomes will be examined in depth in chapter 5, this finding that race and class influence the shape that IPV takes calls out for using the tenets of the race, class, and gender paradigm to contextualize and analyze the data presented in this book. Thus I turn now to a brief discussion of race, class, and gender theory as it has developed to guide the research that attempts to understand and explain the phenomenon of violence between intimate partners.

RACE, CLASS, AND GENDER THEORY

This book takes a different approach to examining IPV than most others have. Rather than fitting squarely into a family violence or feminist framework—the two most common theories used to analyze IPV—the framework for the analyses discussed throughout the many chapters of this book will be the race, class, and gender paradigm. My analyses consider the ways in which IPV is experienced and dealt with differently by men and women, African Americans and European Americans, the working class and poor, and to a lesser extent, the affluent.

I argue that the most effective way to analyze and explain the phenomenon of IPV is through the lens that focuses our attention on the context of a web of intersecting systems of oppression: primarily the systems of racial domination, class oppression, and patriarchy. This assumption guides the analyses which will examine the various ways that these systems (racism, sexism, and classism) work independently and intersect, become mutually reinforcing, and thus shape the contours of IPV.

Every system of domination has a countersystem of privilege. In other words, oppression is a system of both costs and benefits. For example, we know that African American men die prematurely: seven or eight years earlier than their white counterparts (Hattery and Smith 2007a). Generally a discussion of this gap in life expectancy focuses on the reasons that

African American men die early, including jobs that involve physical labor, poverty, lack of access to health care, discrimination, and the stresses associated with being an African American man. Yet, a race, class, gender framework forces us to ask the opposing question: why is it that white men live so much longer? Posing the question this way reveals that the gap is also created by the fact that white men tend to have more access to white collar employment, the best quality health care, and their affluence affords them the ability to have the "dirty" work in their lives taken care of by others, mostly African American men and women. Thus the intersection of race and social class creates *simultaneously* a disadvantage for African American men and an advantage for white men. Furthermore, when we dig deeper into this question of life expectancy, we see that significant gender differences exist as well. Specifically, not only do women live longer than men, but the racial gap is significantly smaller for women than for men. In short, our understanding of racial disparities in health and illness are improved when we layer these explanations: focusing not only on gender or race, but on the ways they interact to produce outcomes that vary by both statuses.[3]

At the structural level, the race, class, and gender framework illuminates the ways in which different systems of domination are mutually reinforcing: patriarchy is woven with racism (or race supremacy), both of which are woven with capitalism. For my work then, the race, class, and gender perspective provides a framework for understanding, for example, the ways in which white, affluent men feel threats to their masculinity, or beat their wives, or are dealt with at the police station—ways that are very different from the experiences of African American men.who may experience different threats to their masculinity, and who are certainly exposed to a criminal justice system that can only be characterized as racially unjust (Hattery and Smith 2007a, b).

This attention to race, class, *and* gender is rather unique in the literature on IPV. For example, researchers who attempt to include the stories of a racially and ethnically diverse sample often fail to include variance by social class.[4] Furthermore, it is critical to point out that the race, class, and gender paradigm requires more than the simple inclusion of individuals of different race/ethnic groups, social classes, and genders into the sample. The paradigm also *requires* that the data be analyzed with attention to the inequality regimes based in the systems of patriarchy, capitalism, and racial domination (Acker 2006). Analyzing the data with attention to these systems of power also separates this book from much of the research on IPV, even that which includes a racially diverse or class-diverse sample.

Race and Class: Images of Batterers and Battered Women

As a society we have an image of IPV. The truth is that no description of a batterer exists. Men who batter are of all races/ethnicities, all ages, all levels of education, all different occupations, they practice all religions, and they live in all different regions of the country.

Similarly, we have an image of what constitutes a battered woman. We imagine that most battered women are poor and nonwhite. They are hit, beaten to a pulp, and often must seek serious medical help for their injuries. In so doing they show up at (1) emergency rooms, and (2) when they have little children, they become occupants of battered women's shelters. Yet, just as is the case with batterers, women who are battered come from all social locations; they are of all race/ethnic groups, all ages, all religions, all levels of education, and they live in all regions of the country. Some victims of IPV experience just physical violence whereas others experience serious emotional and sexual abuse alongside physical abuse. This book tells the stories of women and men who come from different walks of life and who have different experiences with IPV. This diversity is one of the strengths of this book.

The Question of Race: IPV in the African American Community

Because the data for this book come from a racially and ethnically diverse sample, it is important at the outset to consider some of the ways in which IPV may be shaped by race/ethnicity. I argued at the beginning of the book that IPV is the "dirty little secret" that Americans do not want to talk about. Among African Americans the subject is taboo as well (Hattery and Smith 2003, 2005). Furthermore, the underlying reasons for the taboo nature of IPV in the African American community are significantly shaped by race. Though researchers are often focused on the fluctuations and seeming contradictions among different forms of oppression within communities, often members of these communities either are not aware of or choose to remain silent on forms of internal oppression. Black feminists (King 1988; Hill-Collins 2004; hooks 2000, 2004) have pointed out, for example, the ways in which sexism and gender oppression are rendered invisible in the African American community. The concerns of African American women *as women* are dwarfed by discussions of race as well as by a fear of contributing to existing negative images and myths of African American men. The consequences of this invisibility have been deadly for African American women.

> Currently, one of the most pressing issues for contemporary Black sexual politics concerns violence against black women at the hands of Black men. . . . Much of this violence occurs within the context of Black heterosexual love

relationships, Black family life, and within African American social institutions. Such violence takes many forms, including verbally berating Black women, hitting them, ridiculing their appearance, grabbing their body parts, pressuring them to have sex, beating them, and murdering them. (Hill-Collins 2004, 225–26)

That is, the "internal silence" within African American civil society turns out to be as dangerous as the outwardly conflicted racial violence heaped on African Americans from without. Hill sums it up nicely when she says, "Black Communities must begin facing up to the lethal consequences of our own sexism. The time is over for expecting black women to be silent about the sexual violence and personal suppression they experience in ostensible fidelity to our common cause" (2005, 171).

Intimate partner violence in the African American community is both serious and controversial. Yet, as both Hill and Hill-Collins note, it is time to begin honest discussions of the violence that African American women experience at the hands of African American men who proclaim to love them. And, though patriarchy in the African American community is tied up in ideologies of racial superiority, we need to examine both the intersections of race and gender, and we also need to deconstruct them and examine gender oppression as it exists singularly in the African American community.

The Question of Social Class

What we do not have in the accumulated data on IPV are good, accurate portraits of those women who are white and of upper-class status. What we rely on instead when we attempt to paint a picture of the upper-class victims are the cases in which a woman's story has been told, often through either a biography or a court record, or most frequently through the analytical writings of therapists. These stories are difficult to unearth. From Anna Quindlen, former op-ed writer for the *New York Times*[5] to Farrah Fawcett, the actress and sex symbol, women in the upper classes have been the victims of IPV, but their stories are rarely heard outside a tight-knit "community" of close friends and therapists. Why? They, like all battered women, are mostly afraid and ashamed to go public with their pain (Weitzman 2001).

Susan Weitzman's study of upper-class women who are battered is possible because of a particular niche that she occupies: that of therapist. As part of her practice, upper-class women who are having "trouble" in their marriages come to her for therapy, and during the course of this therapy stories of violence tumble out.

This is not the case for poor women who must seek shelter away from their batterers in ways that upper-class battered women often do not. With financial resources and a full range of social capital to draw on, these women can make choices. Poor women almost always have no choices to make. In fact, when presenting on the topic of IPV I am often asked if the women I interview seem to experience the telling of their stories as cathartic. My answer is always "yes." On one occasion a colleague in the audience said, "Do you suppose that's because affluent women can afford therapy, but the women you interview can only find therapy in a research study?" I think the answer to this is also yes. As a result, researchers have access to certain parts of the population (in this case middle-income women and poor women), and they do not have access to other parts of the population—in this case affluent women. I am grateful for studies like Susan Weitzman's, but they are less possible for sociologists to conduct.

Hence, the literature is skewed with a variety of types of accounts of poor women who find themselves in predicaments they do not control. I have found that both types of studies are limited in that they do not capture the full range of experiences and the ways they are shaped by social class. Also, race and ethnicity are almost always absent.

But perhaps the biggest flaw in previous research is that seldom do studies of IPV incorporate the experiences of *both* men and women, batterers and battered, in the same study.[6] Interviewing both battered women and the men who batter them provided me an opportunity to see both sides of the same relationships—"his" and "hers"—and also allowed me to understand more fully the ways that men, who are much less frequently included in studies of IPV, understand their own attitudes and behavior. Taken together, data from both men and women allow for richer analyses and a more complete understanding of IPV in contemporary America.[7] (A lengthy description of the methods and sampling as well as a list of the subjects, identified by pseudonym, can be found in the appendix.)

PROFILES OF THE MEN AND WOMEN WHOSE STORIES ARE TOLD HERE

The men and women whose stories are told in this book come from a variety of backgrounds. Just over half of the men and women live in the South, and the vast majority of these men and women have never lived outside the South. Most were born and raised and continue to live in the community in which the interviews were conducted. The other half of the people we spoke with live in the upper Midwest. The majority of these folks had lived their whole lives in this region of the country, though most had moved as adults to the actual community in which we interviewed. Just about half of the men and women identify as white and the other half identify as African American. The majority of these men and women come from the lower end of the socioeconomic spectrum, most are working class, though some of them are college educated and hold professional jobs.

THE ORGANIZATION OF THIS BOOK

The book is organized so that each chapter focuses on a different issue within the discussion of IPV. Chapters 2 through 4 are devoted to the three different "causes" of IPV. One of the main risk factors for IPV among both men and women is exposure to violence in childhood and adolescence. Therefore, I begin with an examination of individuals' experiences with violence, both sexual and physical, in childhood, adolescence, and adulthood. This allows me to examine childhood exposure to violence as a potential pathway into adult intimate relationships that included violence (chapter 2). In chapter 3 I examine structural causes of IPV, specifically the ways in which three systems of domination, patriarchy, capitalism, and racial domination, shape both the risk for IPV and its contours. In chapter 4 I turn to an examination of the role that cultural factors play in the development and preponderance of IPV. Specifically, I examine social constructions of masculinity and femininity and the ways in which these constructions, as they exist in the contemporary United States, create a situation that is ripe for high levels of IPV.

The second part of the book is devoted to different outcomes of IPV. In chapter 5 I look at the ways in which race shapes the probability for and contours of IPV. Specifically, this chapter compares interracial and intraracial experiences with IPV. Chapter 6 is devoted to a discussion of the early warning signs of IPV[8] as well as the fatalistic interpretations that many victims and offenders hold about their relationships. Many battered women and their batterers believe they are destined for each other, and thus, though they desire a decrease in the violence, they do not desire to separate their lives. Chapter 7 offers a look forward. In this final chapter I propose both individual and structural transformations that would reduce the epidemic rates of IPV that so many men and women in the United States live with and are perpetuated from generation to generation.

NOTES

1. At the time of writing this book men who have been battered by their spouses and significant others had begun a movement. See http://menshealth.about.com/od/relationships/a/Battered_Men.htm.

2. In chapter 3 I return to a longer discussion of the experiences of battered women.

3. Deborah King (1988) refers to this as "double jeopardy," and Maxine Baca Zinn and Bonnie Thorton Dill (2005) refer to this as the "matrix of domination."

4. A common problem that plagues much research on IPV is that most investigations have ignored its occurrence among the affluent. IPV is far more hidden in affluent families who have more access to resources that result in their underrepresentation in social service agencies that are used to recruit subjects. For example, affluent women rarely use the battered women's shelter, and affluent men can afford legal representation that limits their required participation in court-ordered intervention programs. Similarly, the small financial incentive that is offered to subjects for an interview is less attractive to affluent potential subjects. While this study will not be able to adequately deal with IPV in affluent families, a few affluent subjects are in the sample, and their experiences will be analyzed with special attention to social class.

5. When Quindlen came to Wake Forest several years ago to speak at convocation, absent was any mention of her book *Black and Blue* that details the experience of a battered woman.

6. This sample, though small, is racially/ethnically diverse, but this is less the case when it comes to socioeconomic diversity. However, the inclusion of both men and women will perhaps be the greatest contribution of this book.

7. This book is based on in-depth, one-on-one interviews with twenty-five men who batter and thirty-five battered women. These interviews were conducted between July 2001 and August 2004. The interviews were conducted by me and several colleagues who worked on different portions of the project. Dr. Cynthia Gendrich worked on the early portion of the project (2001) and Dr. Earl Smith worked on the latter (2003–2004), during which time the bulk of the interviews were collected in both North Carolina and Minnesota.

8. Angela Browne (1987) coined this term.

Chapter Two

Individual Factors That Contribute to Intimate Partner Violence

She would go downtown and take out warrants out on him and restraining orders and he'll go back and one night she took and killed him, you know they got into a fight, and one night she took and got it, they got into a fight, and she grabbed a pistol and shot him in the head, and he got killed the day before I had to go to court and go to training school, and uh, I went to training school at the age of 14 years old. I didn't know where my mother was at, she was going with guys that would sell her drugs, you know, she was doping you know.—Eddie, forty-something African American man, North Carolina

The previous chapter provided an overview of intimate partner violence in the United States. This chapter is the first of three that explore different causes of intimate partner violence: individual (chapter 2), structural (chapter 3), and cultural (chapter 4).

In this chapter I focus on individual factors that contribute to intimate partner violence. First I examine the role that sexual abuse in childhood plays in the likelihood that women will be beaten in their adult relationships. Second, I examine the role that child abuse and exposure to IPV in childhood plays in the probability that men will grow up to become batterers. In both cases, exposure and victimization to violence in childhood lead to an increased probability for IPV—both perpetration and victimization—in adulthood. We begin by examining the relationship among women.

INDIVIDUAL PREDICTORS OF IPV FOR WOMEN

In the interviews I conducted with women, I focused on their experiences growing up, dating, and in their adult intimate relationships. During these discussions, the number of experiences with sexual abuse that tumbled out of them was surprising and troubling. The analyses in this chapter highlight the ways that experiences with sexual abuse in childhood and the teen years affect women's ability to cope with battering in their adulthood.

Sexual Abuse in Childhood and Adolescence and Battering in Adulthood

A key issue facing scholars, policy makers, and practitioners is the ability to predict who will batter and who will be battered. And, though many feminists agree (Brownmiller 1975; MacKinnon 1989; Rich 1980; Sanday 1981, 1990) that the single best predictor of battering or becoming a victim of IPV is *gender* (85 percent of battering is done by men to women) (Tjaden and Thoennes 2000), this chapter will examine the role that childhood sexual abuse (CSA) plays in the pathway to becoming a victim of IPV. Specifically, I will (1) describe the relationship between CSA and IPV and (2) identify the *process* by which CSA shapes women's experiences with IPV.

Abuse in Childhood and Abuse in Adulthood

At least half of all women report at least one incident of *physical abuse* by a parent or caretaker before age 18 (Tjaden and Thoennes 2000). Though women who were victims of child abuse are not significantly more likely to grow up to be battered in adulthood (46 percent are but 53.3 percent are not), women who *were* victims of child abuse are *twice as likely* to experience IPV as women who were not physically assaulted in childhood (46.7 percent compared to 19.8 percent) (Tjaden and Thoennes 2000). In other words, more than half of women who were physically abused in childhood *do not* grow up to be battered in adulthood, but the *risk* for IPV is *twice as high* for female victims of child abuse as for those women who were not abused as children.

The relationship between being sexually abused in childhood and being raped in adulthood follows a similar pattern. Women raped as minors are *twice as likely* to be raped in adulthood (18.3 percent compared to 8.7 percent). However, as was the case with child abuse, most women who are raped in childhood are *not* raped in adulthood—18.3 percent of those raped in childhood are raped as adults, but 81.2 percent of those raped in childhood are *not* raped as adults.

In summary, we have good estimates of both sexual and physical abuse in both childhood and adulthood, and we understand something about the increased risk victims of both physical and sexual abuse in childhood have *for the same type of violence* in adulthood. In short, though most children who

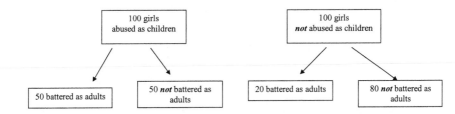

Figure 2.1.   Relationship between Abuse in Childhood and Being Battered in Adulthood

experience sexual abuse or physical violence *are not* victimized in adulthood, victims of childhood sexual or physical abuse *are twice as likely* to experience the *same type of abuse in adulthood as their non–childhood victim counterparts*.

The question becomes how abuse in childhood creates a pathway to abuse in adulthood. In her study of stripping and prostitution, Raphael explicates the ways in which sexual abuse and exploitation diminish self-esteem and can create a pathway to intimate partner violence. She notes that prostitution and violence destroy the body's boundaries. "If your body does not present limits to other people, you begin to feel that you do not have a right to exist, to take up space" (2004, 164). Beyond her work, however, little empirical research exists on the relationship between *sexual abuse* in childhood or adolescence and *physical abuse* in adulthood. Also, because my sample is limited to women who have been battered, I am unable to use experiences with sexual abuse in childhood to *predict* the likelihood of being battered in adulthood. This chapter focuses on experiences of a group of battered women who were also victims of severe CSA and illuminates the ways in which this early childhood sexual abuse led to poor partnering decisions and limited agency in ending IPV when it did occur.

An Important Research Note: Developing Rapport

Each interview began by asking the women to describe the families in which they grew up.[1] In some cases the women talked at length about abusive fathers or stepfathers. In other cases they made a brief reference to their fathers, stepfathers, or their mothers' boyfriends that led me to believe that some abuse had occurred. In most cases, as the women became more comfortable and we established more rapport, the stories literally tumbled out. When one conducts research on such a painful topic, it is critically important to establish trust and rapport with the subject. I have found that victims of gender oppression (rape, IPV) are often ashamed of their experiences, and they have encountered people who are literally shocked by their stories. Therefore, they tend to start out mildly and slowly drop more and more outrageous experiences on the table. It

is critical that the researcher express sympathy but not shock at these revela-
tions. By accepting the extraordinary experiences of these women, the researcher develops the trust necessary for the revelation of increasingly intimate and increasingly shocking events.[2]

Though not all girls who are sexually abused in childhood and adolescence
grow up to be battered women, a significant relationship does seem to exist
between being a battered woman and early experiences with rape and incest
(Lawless 2001, Wesley 2006).[3]

Among the women in this study, CSA fell into three distinct categories:
premature sex engagement, incest, and childhood prostitution. I begin with
some descriptive data on the forms of childhood and adolescent sexual abuse
(CSA) and then examine the two "survival" strategies that put victims of CSA
at risk for IPV: (1) marrying as teenagers to escape incest and prostitution,
and (2) choosing intimate partners who could protect them from outside violence but who ended up abusing them.

Childhood Sexual Abuse: Premature Sex Engagement

Premature sex engagement refers to experiencing one's first sexual intercourse at a very young age (13 or 14) with an older man. The most typical
pattern involved 13- and 14-year-old girls having their first sexual experiences with men ten years older, men in their mid-twenties. However, in some
cases the first sexual experiences of these young teenage girls involved much
older men—in their thirties or forties.[4] Though this fits the definition of statutory rape, these women primarily defined these experiences as "consensual."
The issue of consent in these cases is a tricky and complex one, as Odem
(1995) points out in her historical study of sexuality; the "age of consent"
laws effectively remove the possibility that girls under the age of 18 can
legally consent to *any* sexual activity. Recently some states have modified
their statutory rape laws to require age differences of at least a year; for example, sex between two 17-year-olds no longer meets the legal requirements
of statutory rape.[5]

This issue is further complicated by the blurring of the term "consent." Diana Scully (1990) points out that convicted rapists' definitions of rape hinge
on *their* perceptions of a woman's consent rather than the women's own perceptions. And research on incest and CSA notes that in many cases victims do
report "consenting." I argue that the women whom I classify as experiencing
premature sex engagement fall into the same category as victims of CSA and
not into the category of those cases now excluded from statutory rape. In all
cases, the age difference between the girls and the men they had sex with was
at least ten years. Furthermore, this age gap results in both a power differen-

tial and an experience differential that often left these girls feeling exploited, even when they consented.

Veta, for example, told of her first sexual experience when she was 16. Her "partner" was a 42-year-old married man by whom she would become pregnant. In discussing the awkwardness of the age difference Veta recalled telling her parents she was pregnant. When they insisted that she bring the father of her child to their home to meet him, she realized she was bringing home a man who was not only married to someone else but *older than her parents*.

Of the twenty African American women I interviewed, eighteen (90 percent), experienced premature sex engagement (several via incest and/or prostitution). Though common among white women as well, somewhat fewer (ten of fifteen or 67 percent) experienced premature sex engagement. Furthermore, only one experienced incest, and none experienced prostitution. These patterns reinforce those that are reported by national studies which reveal that African American teenage girls are one and a half times more likely to have had sexual intercourse than their white peers (Dye 2005).

Not only was early teenage sexual activity common, but it almost *always* involved older, and presumably more experienced, first sex partners. And, for African American women, these sexual experiences at 14 or 15 almost invariably led to pregnancy and a birth before the mother turned sixteen.[6] With rare exceptions, girls who had their first child by age 16 dropped out of high school and failed to earn a general education diploma (GED). Race differences exacerbate the problems associated with teen childbearing. For example, because African Americans have higher levels of *unintended unemployment* (Hattery and Smith 2007a; Padavic and Reskin 2002) and because African Americans and women require more education to make the same wages as white men (Padavic and Reskin 2002), the long-term consequences of these experiences significantly shape the life chances of African American girls (Hattery and Smith 2007a; Maynard 1997) and their children. The failure to complete high school left these women even more vulnerable to IPV because they had little earning power in a changing economy where low-skilled employment continues to disappear. This form of economic dependency is highly correlated with IPV (Browne 1987; Brush 2000, 2001).

Clearly race shaped both the likelihood of experiencing premature sex engagement as well as its consequences. The fact that *nearly all* of the African American women I interviewed experienced premature sex engagement suggests that, as scholars and practitioners (teachers, social workers, and health care providers), we need to adjust our understanding of the "typical" experiences of African American teenage girls to include this type of experience. Second, because we know that premature sex engagement has many consequences for young women, especially African Americans, these race differences demand our attention. The consequences range from those associated with early sexual intercourse (Alan Guttmacher Institute 2006), to those associated with the exploitation inherent in these experiences (Wesley 2006; Sweet and Tewksbury 2000), to those associated with teen childbearing (Hattery and Smith 2007a; Maynard 1997).

Incest and Child Molestation at Home

Incest and child molestation are reported by 15 to 25 percent of adult women (Tjaden and Thoennes 2000). Several white and African American women whom I interviewed admitted to childhood sexual abuse by fathers, stepfathers, and mothers' boyfriends. Among the thirty-five women I interviewed, five (15 percent) reported at least one experience with incest.

Candy is a white woman from North Carolina who was molested at age 15 by her mother's boyfriend. As a result of this abuse she became pregnant and was thrown out of the house. Shortly thereafter she married a young man her own age but because of his drug addiction they divorced a year later.

Debbie is an African American woman from North Carolina who was not only molested by her father but tortured physically as well. Among other things, her father slapped her, banged her head against the wall, forcibly cut her hair—while he made her lie on the cement floor of the garage—and burned her with a welding iron. Debbie's father also kept the family—she has eight brothers—isolated, and made the children quit school when they reached the age of 16 so that they could go to work. He demanded that they bring their wages home for his use. By age 17 Debbie had moved out of the house. Shortly after, she met John, and they married within weeks.

Consistent with national level data (Tjaden and Thoennes 2000) very few race differences exist with regard to the women's experiences with incest. The race differences that did emerge in this study revolved primarily around women's willingness to talk about the incest.[7] Regardless of their willingness to disclose the details, scholars and practitioners need to assume a high probability for CSA when working with young women, especially young women who are in trouble or "at risk" (Gaarder and Belknap 2002; Sweet and Tewksbury 2000; Wesley 2006).

PREADOLESCENT PROSTITUTION: THE LIQUOR OR DRINK HOUSE

Among the women I interviewed, none of the white women but 15 percent (three of twenty) of the African American women had experiences as child prostitutes. One case involved "situational prostitution," the other two cases involved *continuous* child prostitution in drink houses run by the fathers/stepfathers of the women.

I begin the discussion of liquor houses with a caveat: I do not imply here that childhood prostitution is a normative or even a common experience for young African American women. I do suspect, however, that Winston-Salem, North Carolina, is similar in many regards to other southern communities with a single major employer; in Winston-Salem this employer is RJ Reynolds Tobacco. In these communities relationships often form between the company, its executives, and the illegitimate economy that exists in all communities. As in many southern communities until very recently, work was segregated (Hattery and Smith 2007a; Hill-Collins 1994; Shapiro 2003), and RJ Reynolds was no exception. Though a few African Americans were hired to sweep floors and do the most menial labor associated with cigarette production, for the most part they were excluded from working at the town's primary company. As is typical in many southern towns, African Americans were, however, called on to "service" the white community as housekeepers, nannies, gardeners, and as liquor suppliers (Korstad 2003; Tursi 1994). This was an especially important function during Prohibition, and the habit local white men developed then of going into liquor houses to imbibe persists today. When conditions like these exist, the environment is primed for many exploitative and oppressive behaviors, among them prostitution. Therefore, I believe there is much to learn from the case of Winston-Salem, North Carolina.

A liquor house is a type of unregulated social club. Usually it is located in an apartment in a public housing project. In a typical liquor house, a man allows a woman (and often her children) to live rent free upstairs in exchange for her (and her children) running the liquor house on the main level of the home. And, this arrangement usually involves an exchange for sex with the woman whenever he desires it.[8]

When I inquired about the men who frequented the drink houses, Evie told me that of course there were the locals, men who lived in the projects, but that the primary customers were white male executives from RJ Reynolds Tobacco Company. These men would come during their lunch hour and at happy hour (usually after 4 p.m.) to consume alcohol, smokes, and have sex before returning to their quiet, white, middle-class neighborhoods.

> Some of the Reynolds men got paid on Wednesday. They'll come in, maybe, and buy . . . give me a five, and maybe they done bought four drinks and I would have the change. Sometimes they would sell fish in there. And a lot of times, some of the guys would get the cigarettes and change cigarettes for drinks. And it was just like, I wonder that the people that lived out by a car [meaning out in the suburbs]. There was nice section. But they would come in

our neighborhood, and drink, and buy women and stuff like that.—Evie, fifty-
something African American woman, North Carolina

Both women who worked in (and in fact grew up in) liquor houses were
initially lured into this work by their fathers/stepfathers who told them they
could earn a little money making sandwiches and pouring drinks. Evie recalls
that by age 12 she was frying fish and totally managing the food side of the
operation. In addition, Evie admitted that her father prostituted her as well;
she was required to "perform favors" for the men in the drink house.

You can't imagine what it's like to have to sit on the laps of men when you are
a 10-year-old. I hadn't even learned to ride a bike yet.—Evie, fifty-something
African American woman, North Carolina

Perhaps most striking about these stories of preadolescent prostitution is
the way that they are shaped by both race and social class. Not only were the
women subjected to this type of sexual abuse African American and poor, but
the situation itself was in part created out of race and class inequalities that
exist in the community. In a segregated community like Winston-Salem, few
legitimate ways exist for African Americans to earn a living, and those that
do exist are primarily restricted to educated, middle-class, and professional
African Americans and to women who were employed as domestics (Hill-
Collins 1994). Poor whites were able to find work in the RJ Reynolds cigarette factories, but African Americans were excluded from this employment
option. Thus, African Americans living in the housing projects created a "service" economy that filled a niche, one that would never have been allowed in
most white neighborhoods regardless of its social class composition (Korstad
2003; Tursi 1994). Thus race, class, and gender were powerful forces in shaping both the individual experiences these women had with preadolescent
prostitution as well as the phenomenon itself.[9]

In response to the CSA these women experienced, they employed two related survival strategies: (1) marrying to escape the abuse and (2) choosing
dangerous partners. Both strategies put these women at risk for IPV. I turn
now to a discussion of the survival strategies and incredible violence that
these women endured at the hands of their abusive partners.

SEXUAL ABUSE AND A DRIVE TO ESCAPE

By age 17, seeking answers and help, Debbie became a disciple of James and
Tammy Bakker's PTL ministry. Homeless for a time, she slept in a trailer on
the grounds of the PTL Club in Charlotte. There she met a young man. After

a few weeks they had sex, and feeling guilty, they married. Within months her husband became abusive both physically and sexually. In addition to moving out of the house during the period of incest and molestation, it was also common for these women to marry early, a practice that was encouraged by the victims' own mothers. Debbie describes her decision to marry John.

> It was after three days we met that we kissed. And we never really discussed that kiss or nothing. We just liked each other right away. So he took me to a jewelry store and bought me an engagement ring and a wedding band. Then he had this necklace around his neck that said "I love you" that somebody gave to him. So he took it off and put it around my neck. Then I put the engagement ring on and he asked me to go with him. And I said, "Sure." *I wanted to be free from my family. I thought if I get married, my name changes and I'm free from my family.*— Debbie, thirty-something African American woman, North Carolina

For many women like Debbie, getting pregnant and/or married was perhaps the only route for escape (Lawless 2001). *All* of the women who acknowledged that they had been sexually abused or prostituted in childhood entered their first intimate, romantic sexual *relationship* before they were 18. Frequently these relationships involved living together (married or not) within weeks or months of getting together. Moving in with another man seemed the most obvious escape route, one that almost always led to physical, emotional, and sometimes sexual abuse at the hands of their lovers (Brandt 2006; Griffing et al. 2005). In their attempts to escape the sexual abuse they were experiencing at home these girls often left with the first man who would take them away (usually by marrying them), and within months it was clear to these girls that they had traded one sort of violence and abuse for another. Debbie paints a graphic picture:

> I wanted to please him [sexually], because my mom never talked to me or nothing. I had to figure out what I'm supposed to do. I knew you screwed, but I wanted more than that. So I looked at the videos. And when I did something on him that I learned from the video, he was like, "Oh, where did you learn to do that? You had to do it before somewhere else." But then he got sexually abusive. He wanted to like use objects on me and all kinds of stuff. When he did that, that's when I started hating him. And I wouldn't let him do it and he would get mad. And then he would tear my pictures up of my family and burned them. He tore up some of my clothes he bought me. One time he got so mad, we was going down the road and he ran his car into an overpass bridge. We were both in it, and he was going 80 miles per hour. He totaled the car, but we both walked out of it. [AH: *Was he trying to kill you?*] Yeah. He wanted to kill both of us.—Debbie, thirty-something African American women, North Carolina.

Many, many women I interviewed reported having sex when they did not want to, though they seldom called it rape. And, many reported that sex seemed to be a tool of the violence or an attempt to make up after a battering episode. They described not only the hurt of being raped by their intimate partners, the men who claimed to love them, but also the consequences, such as unintended pregnancy. We can also assume that many women were at risk for contracting HIV/AIDS as well, though it is difficult to pinpoint the incident that leads to transmission when acts of consensual intercourse are mixed in with acts of rape or nonconsensual intercourse. Cheri describes her experience:

So, you know, the park. We smoke a little blunt. And then we have sex in the car, which was ironic, 'cause we'd never done this before. Ok, my pants still on my ankles and then he just starts beating me on my face. Yeah. I mean, his was too [pants were down]. That's how, soon as he done it, it happened. He didn't even get up off of me. He just started beating me, talking about, that's what I was doing, that's what I gave to somebody else and just rambling on and on and on. And I crawled out of the car and crawled under my car. Then my stubborn butt wouldn't leave 'til he gave me my two hundred dollars back. Then, he was like, he was like, well, go clean your face up. . . . I had about six bones broken over here. This was broken and this was broken. And to this day, I can't see out this eye. I have a dislocated retina. And, like, this bone was broken and stuff. And, so, I went a whole day without going to the emergency room 'cause I was scared. So, when I finally went to the emergency room, 'cause the eye wouldn't open up is what made me go, and I was in so much pain, I found out I was pregnant. So, I told . . . so I told the abortion clinic, if ya'll don't get this baby out of me, I am. So they got me a volunteer to help pay for it, but by the time they came through, I was five months pregnant. So then that almost killed me.— Cheri, thirty-something African American woman, North Carolina

The strategies employed by Debbie, like those of so many other women I interviewed, extend a well-established finding by scholars who study CSA: that CSA is a major pathway to careers in stripping and prostitution (Monto and Hotaling 2001; Sweet and Tewksbury 2000; Wesley 2006) and juvenile delinquency (Gaarder and Belknap 2002; Goodkind, Ng, and Sarri 2006). I argue that seeking out sexual partners as a means of escape is similar to stripping and prostitution in that they all involve trading sexual access for economic support. In contrast, the battered women I interviewed who had *not* experienced CSA left intimate partner relationships the *first time* they were hit. As a result, they were seldom forced into the cycle of trading sexual access for the economic support of a man who would also abuse them.

With regard to social class, the strategy of trading sexual access for economic support, though used by many women for centuries and in all cultures, is by and large a strategy that affluent women do *not* need to rely on. The middle-class women in the sample *did not* establish a pattern of trading sexual access for economic support to flee abusive relationships. Instead, they relied on their own economic assets.

Andi is an African American woman I interviewed in Minnesota. Andi's is yet another case of premature sex engagement. At 13 Andi had her first sexual relationship with a man ten years her senior. He was 23. She ultimately bore two children by this man though they never married. Because he was also a drug dealer and violent with her and the children, she decided that she needed to escape.

> Yeah—I got my older son, I got all my stuff and we went to Chicago. Um, with me working for the moving company, I knew this guy who drove a truck, and so he was up there and he had to go back to Chicago, so he took us to Chicago. I stayed in a hotel for about a week and then went to a shelter. I stayed in the shelter, but, mind you, I'm a hot girl, so, I don't know, but I stayed in the shelter for, like, three days—and then met this guy. One day when I was outside of the shelter. And I do not know what was going through my mind, but I liked him; he was like, "Why don't you come to Minnesota with me." So I came to Minnesota. I'd been in Chicago for a-week-and-a-half. [*AH: And how quickly did you move to Minnesota?*] The next day after I met him. It was like—no, I didn't—it was like one of those stupid you're risking your life moves—but I was like, "*Hey—What do I have to lose right now? I have absolutely nothing.*" So—he was—He had already came up here to Minnesota 'cause his brother got murdered and they couldn't stay in Chicago because the people who killed his brother were actually trying to kill him. So he were up here and he was supposed to be in Chicago picking up this girl who says she was pregnant by him but she said she didn't want to go, so he brought me back up here instead and told his family that I was her. I was living with him and his family—with him and his mom, and his grandma and younger brothers and sisters. I thought it was—I thought it was weird. Really, really weird. But, I mean, we talked to each other every day and we started getting involved with each other and everything. [*AH: Were you sleeping with him?*] Eventually—yeah. Yeah. The reason it's weird to me that we started getting closer, he started getting real close to my kids and my kids started getting close to him. So I kept working and he finally got a job. And—he was working at [Simoniz] at first, 'cause he had never had a real job and he had always been hustling down in Chicago—that was the life out there. So he got his job at Simoniz in Apollo Air—and so we decided we wanted to get an apartment of our own. So we got an apartment of our own.

Everything seemed pretty good for a minute. It was all right—I mean but it
was a two bedroom apartment and everything. He got a job at Target, so that
was a better job so we were living on our own, we got furniture and stuff—
'cause we work hard to get furniture and everything, make sure the kids are
okay, had daycare set up; all that was good—but then one night he flipped
out because he found out I had smoked a blunt which I shouldn't have but it
was a temptation. He found out I had smoked a blunt and that I had been
around some guys. So he flipped out and we got into this fight and everything. . . . Well, first he had just grabbed me, and like, slammed me into the
wall; and me, I'm not gonna just stand there—so, like, I try to shove him off
me. And I grabbed his shirt up, like, roped it up—like that—and then I kept
telling him "get off me," and stuff and, no, he steady slinging me around
and stuff and he ended up hitting my face against the wall.—Andi, twenty-
something African American woman, Minnesota

Andi's story, though perhaps extreme in that it involves moving several
hundred miles, is typical of the stories I heard from the women I interviewed.
What Andi's story illustrates is the cycle that many of the battered women I
interviewed fell into, specifically their drive to replace the financial security
they traded when they left abusive circumstances. These women often reported that they felt that their options were limited to either living alone and
in poverty or taking a chance to improve their economic conditions by moving in with a man.

Though this may seem obvious, something that all women face, for many
of the battered women I interviewed, leaving a violent or sexually abusive
relationship—often leaving fathers, stepfathers, or older men—had plunged
them into such severe poverty that they were homeless. In addition, moving
out often meant that they lost their jobs because they either failed to come to
work during the transition or they could not continue to go to work *and* care
for their children. It is common in low-income families for parents to "split
shifts" so that one parent watches the children while the other works, thus
eliminating or significantly reducing child care costs (Hattery 2001b). Leaving the abusive relationship often meant leaving behind the only child care
that was available and "affordable." Therefore, the pressures these women
felt to find a new relationship were significant and pressing. Most of the
women I interviewed reported that after leaving an abusive relationship
they often established a new relationship within weeks, often with someone
they barely knew or with someone they knew had a reputation for violence,
and more often than not, this relationship turned violent as well.

This confirms the findings of other scholars who found similar patterns in
studies of homeless women who reported high rates of violence in their relationships. "It is evident that the women entered into initial adult relationships

for multiple reasons (often related to childhood issues)—to escape the home environment, to prove to themselves and others that they could 'do it right,' to achieve what they discerned as safety, security, comfort, or love" (Wesley and Wright 2005, 1089). In short, as Wesley and Wright note, women who have experienced abuse typically find that their options "shrink." And, this is compounded by race and social class. Women with fewer of their own economic resources were more likely to jump directly into new relationships in order to avoid what they saw as a real chance they would otherwise be homeless. And, because of the strong correlation between race and social class (Hattery and Smith 2007a; Shapiro 2003) this pattern was more pronounced among African American women than their white counterparts. Thus, the data presented here further our understanding of the links among CSA, IPV, race, class, and homelessness.

TRADING SEXUAL ACCESS FOR PROTECTION

Women who have been raped or sexually assaulted often view men as dangerous (Brownmiller 1975; Griffin 1979; Koss 1985; Koss et al. 1994). If they are sexually assaulted by someone they know, they often report feeling as if they can no longer trust anyone. Women who are raped by a stranger may develop a generalized distrust of the world (Griffin 1979; Koss 1985; Koss et al. 1994). Living with the awareness that they can be victimized again, some women may put up with sexual and physical abuse by their intimate partners in exchange for the protection these men provide from the outside world (MacKinnon 1989; Rich 1980, 1995). As a result of the CSA the women in this sample experienced, they entered their adult lives in a nearly obsessive search of exactly that kind of male protection.

Ironically, wanting a protector is, by definition, wanting someone capable of violence. To defend a woman from another man's physical violence, he must himself be capable of inflicting physical harm or of providing the threat of physical harm. Clearly not all protectors *use* physical violence, either against women or men, but the paradox lingers—and it played itself out especially clearly in Candy's relationship.

Candy, whose story was presented earlier, was molested at age 15 by her mother's boyfriend. Like many of the other women's stories told here, she sought adult intimate partners who would protect her even while abusing her. Candy lives/lived[10] with Mark, a physically dominant man who is horribly abusive. Among many incidents, he choked her until she was unconscious, beat her against the stick shift of their car until her pelvis broke—causing her a few days later to miscarry their child—slapped her, pulled her hair, jumped on her and broke several ribs—almost causing an additional miscarriage and landing Candy in the hospital for two days—and bit her in the face at least ten times. At 5'9" and 120 pounds, Candy is extremely thin. At 300 pounds, even Mark's slaps are extremely dangerous. Candy also indicated that Mark had raped her "once or twice." At the time of the interview, this level of battering had been going on for four to five years. However, Candy rationalizes that although Mark may beat her, abuse her emotionally, and rape her, *he does not allow anyone else to treat her this way.*

Candy stays with Mark because he provides protection from the violence she fears she might otherwise experience at the hands of a stranger. The abuse she experiences with Mark is predictable, making it preferable to the unpredictable nature of sexual harassment and sexual and physical assault that women face in the workplace and outside world (MacKinnon 1989; Rich 1980, 1995). Recall Candy's quote that opens the introductory chapter, which I repeat here in brief:

"He might try to hit me and he might try to kill me but. . . . *He was going to protect me from everybody else.*—Candy, twenty-something white woman, North Carolina

Candy's quote illustrates not only an extreme example of the types of violence these women live with, but it also demonstrates her cognizance of her situation. Many people believe that battered women have no agency or that they do not know how to make good choices. Candy's statement is clear: she understands very clearly the trade-off that she is making. And, though extreme, Candy's case illustrates the trade-off that many battered women make: choosing life-threatening violence that is predictable over the kind of random violence they perceive awaits them in the streets. In Candy's case this choice also puts her at risk of becoming one of the 1,300 women who are murdered by their partners and ex-partners each year. And, it illustrates, profoundly, the mistake U.S. society makes in teaching women to fear strangers when in fact their greatest risk for violence is in their own homes.

A LIFE OF ILLEGAL AND ILLEGITIMATE BEHAVIOR

Sexual assault and sexual abuse are significant events in any woman's (or man's) life. As noted by Pipher (1994) and Wolf (1992), many girls and women who are raped or sexually abused rely on dangerous coping strategies: they medicate the pain with alcohol or drugs, they attempt to become "sexually invisible" by developing anorexia, bulimia, and overeating. Some will go so far to end the pain as committing suicide or going "crazy." There is little one can do to protect girls and women from being the victims of rape and sexual abuse, but those who deal with its victims note the importance of support and a healthy environment in which to heal. The women I interviewed had neither a healthy environment nor the financial resources to get the support they needed. For Evie in particular, the effects of being forced to work as a child prostitute in her father's drink house, living in a violent household, and living in poverty had lifelong effects.

Evie was exposed to many different avenues for making money in the illegitimate economy while she was working at the drink house. As one can imagine, she ruled out prostitution and escaped it as soon as she could. Though, as was the case with many of the other victims of childhood sexual abuse, she did sometimes trade sex for the financial support of a male partner: a place to live, some food on the table, or some drugs. However, for the majority of Evie's life, she supported herself in all sorts of ways. Her father was a numbers writer,[11] and she learned the numbers trade in the liquor house. As a teenager, she began running numbers for her father. She also learned to deal drugs. Sometimes she would hold a part-time job; for example, she worked for a while in a laundry, but she was always engaged in running numbers and dealing, even when she was employed. Evie told of how dry cleaning customers would drop off or pick up laundry and ask to see her. They would place bets or buy drugs from Evie; she weaved legitimate work in with illegitimate work. Evie also learned about the opportunities to make money by selling products on the aftermarket. She would steal clothes and accessories from stores at the mall and sell them in aftermarket outlets.

As we talked more and more about her adult life, Evie talked about the only legitimate job she had ever had. She worked as a cook at the county hospital for the last four years, a job she got when she was 46 years old. It was Evie's first "real" job, not because, like many white, middle-class women, she had been out of the labor market raising children and taking care of a home, nor because she was on welfare, but because she had always supported herself in the illegitimate economy. When I met Evie in the shelter, she had lost her job at the hospital due to a single absence that resulted from battering. (I will return to this issue in chapter 4.)

Living her whole life in the illegitimate world and being abused physically, sexually, and emotionally left Evie with very little hope and trust that things would work out. Evie had never experienced any measure of stability—except for constant instability—and this adversely affected her decision making. As Evie was describing her foray into legitimate employment, she smiled for a moment. She loved to cook and was happy that she could earn a living doing something she loved. The other staff in the hospital kitchen were impressed by her skills, and when I asked what her signature dish was, she gleamed and replied: "My turkey and stuffing! Everything made from scratch."

In the midst of this conversation Evie stopped, opened up her pocketbook, and pulled out a receipt. She had been living in and paying rent to a local flop hotel for the last four years to the tune of almost $40,000.[12] I was shocked, and when I remarked that for that sum, with her good job at the hospital, she could have bought a small house or at least paid on a mortgage, her face sunk. Yes, she knew that. When I asked her why she had not invested in something more permanent, even an apartment, which would have cost less per month and allowed her to save some money, she replied that it was her fear of instability. She assumed that she would lose her job. She was actually shocked herself that she had managed to keep a legitimate job for four years. To put it simply, the long-term effects of sexual abuse in childhood, when coupled with a life of poverty and an unhealthy home life, had far-reaching, lifelong effects that extended into nearly all aspects of "normal" adult life.

RACE, CLASS, AND GENDER: ANALYZING THE DATA

This discussion has focused on the relationship between women's experiences with sexual violence in childhood and adolescence (CSA) and intimate partner violence (IPV) in adult relationships. Here I employ the race, class, and gender paradigm to analyze the individual variations in experiences with both CSA and IPV. I also use the paradigm as a framework for understanding the ways that race and class structure the lives of individual actors so that opportunities are either created or denied. Because CSA and IPV are both types of violence against women and fundamentally about gender, I begin with a discussion of sexual abuse as *gendered*.

The sexual abuse experienced by these women illustrates a culture of misogyny (Brownmiller 1975; MacKinnon 1989; Rich 1980; Sanday 1981, 1990/2007). The abuse serves to teach and reinforce the lesson that women are of lower or perhaps no value relative to men, other than as sex objects, reinforcing Raphael's finding (2004). The abuse also serves to reinforce the masculine identities of the perpetrators, reminding women and men of the power of patriarchy in shaping relationships and households. If we assume that girls learn many of their lessons about men from the men with whom they live growing up, then the lessons in these households were (are) the lessons of patriarchy; women have no value, women are to be controlled and punished by men, and sexual abuse is defined as normal and often appropriate (Geffner 1997).

The lessons learned in the liquor houses are further shaped by race. One of the lessons learned by the girls who worked as prostitutes in the liquor houses is that the bodies of African American girls and women are of even less value than the bodies of white women. The white men who abused these girls and paid to rape them (how can a 12-year-old consent to sex, even as a prostitute?) engaged in this activity in the African American community, *not* in the white community. These white men used their race and gender privilege to abuse these young African American girls. Though rates of sexual abuse by stepfathers and mothers' boyfriends is also high in the white community, the *systematic* abuse of young white women by men from outside the community, specifically *nonwhite men*, is not only less common, *it simply does not exist*.

This structured exploitation can be linked to another form of exploitation in southern communities: the sexual abuse of African American women by white men during slavery and the era of Jim Crow (see especially Davis 1983). During the 250 years of chattel slavery in this country white men routinely had nonconsensual sex with African American women slaves (Johnston 1970, 217).[13] This circumstance occurred at all levels of the social class strata all the way up to the third president of the United States, Thomas Jefferson (Lanier 2000). After the official end of slavery, many southern white households employed an African American woman as a housekeeper or domestic. The systematic sexual abuse of these women is well documented (Halsell 1969) and again, extends all the way up the social class ladder to long-time U.S. Senator Strom Thurmond who "sowed his wild oats" with the young African American woman working in his parents' house. She became pregnant and gave birth to their child, Essie Mae Washington (Staples 2004). We can see then the way that a system of racial domination, and to a lesser degree social class inequality, can create an environment ripe for the systematic sexual abuse of African American girls by white men. It was and always has been part of the structure of the American South.

The experiences of the liquor houses are also shaped significantly by social class. Middle-class and affluent communities typically do not have these outward manifestations of the illegitimate economy. African Americans who live in middle-class and affluent neighborhoods and communities are not likely to experience the type of abuse I heard about and detail here. However, this does not mean that middle-class African Americans are immune to this type of situation. Many middle-class African Americans who can afford houses in white neighborhoods and communities are redlined; they can purchase homes only in predominantly African American neighborhoods which are, as a result of these practices, typically fairly heterogeneous by social class (Massey 2005; Massey and Denton 1993; Shapiro 2003), in contrast to white neighborhoods and communities which are very homogeneous by race *and* social class. Therefore, though middle-class African Americans are not likely to be victims of the types of exploitation associated with the liquor houses, they may be aware of these establishments within their residential communities. Thus, the lens provided by the race, class, and gender paradigm provides the framework for examining the ways that three distinct systems of oppression—race, gender, and social class—are interwoven and shape the lives of those living underneath and within these systems.

National level data indicate that African American women are more likely to experience rape and sexual abuse (Tjaden and Thoennes 2000), and though the stories of CSA in this book come from African American women as well as white women, these interviews also confirm the national level data. Though many of the white women I interviewed had experienced molestation or incest, virtually *all* of the African American women I interviewed experienced CSA in the form of (1) incest, (2) childhood prostitution, and/or (3) premature sex engagement. Analysis of National Violence Against Women (NVAW) data also indicates that African American women are more likely to experience severe IPV than are their white counterparts (Hattery and Smith 2003, 2005). Though many reasons for this can be cited, I would argue that *one key issue is the increased exposure of African American women to CSA that ultimately increases their risk for IPV in adulthood.*

Furthermore, though rates of IPV are relatively stable across time and across racial/ethnic boundaries, my analyses of the NVAW data (Hattery and Smith 2003, 2005) demonstrate that race/ethnicity shapes the *forms* of violence that women experience. Overall, African American women are disproportionately likely to experience lethal and near lethal violence. For example, they are more likely to have a weapon (knife or gun) used against them, and they are more likely to be "beat up" (Hattery and Smith 2003, 2005). And, my interviews confirmed this quantitative finding as well. White women were less likely to report injuries that required a visit to the emergency room and/or other forms of medical attention than were their African American counterparts. African American women reported incidents such as being hit in the head with a ball-peen hammer, being hit in the mouth so hard that one woman's teeth punctured both her top and bottom lips, being threatened with a shotgun, and being beaten beyond recognition—reported by the male batterer who was also a boxer and had recently killed another boxer in the ring.

Similarly, research on the effects of child physical and sexual abuse demonstrate that African American children who are abused and/or neglected are more likely to be involved in criminal activity as juveniles and adults than are white children who experienced abuse and/or neglect in childhood (Widom and Maxfield 2001). For girls, arrests were most often reported for alcohol and drug violations (Widom and Maxfield 2001), which is consistent with the research on "self-medicating" by female victims of CSA (Browne and Finkelhor 1986; Hanson 1990; Kendall-Tackett, Williams, and Finkelhor

1993; Rind, Tromovitch, and Bauserman 1998; Sturza and Campbell 2005). These data provide empirical evidence to corroborate the qualitative findings presented here: African American women who are victims of CSA are at increased risk for IPV as a result of the damaging effects of CSA that remain untreated and uninterrupted (Raphael 2004). Because minority and low-income girls are more likely to experience CSA, and because minority and low-income women are more vulnerable to and at higher risk for IPV (regardless of their experiences with CSA), additional attention and resources must be dedicated to our most marginalized and vulnerable citizens. I turn now to a discussion of the impact of childhood violence on men.

THE IMPACT OF VIOLENCE IN CHILDHOOD ON MEN

Growing up in a violent household, particularly one that involves IPV, is a significant predictor of violence in adulthood. Family scholars like Straus and Gelles talk about this as the intergenerational transmission of violence theory. Violence is transmitted from parent to child, from father to son. In their study of men, Ehrensaft, Cohen, and colleagues (2003) report that experiencing child abuse *doubles* a man's risk for beating his intimate partner. But witnessing violence in childhood *triples* a man's risk for becoming a batterer.[14] Few researchers dispute the fact that child abuse and/or growing up witnessing parental intimate partner[15] violence is detrimental to the healthy development of children.

Yet discussions of the intergenerational transmission of violence theory are wrought with controversy. Critics of the theory point to the fact that the majority of boys who grow up in violent homes do not grow up to abuse either their children or their female partners (Kaufman and Zigler 1987). This is an important critique. Other researchers are critical of the term because it implies a genetic transmission. I will discuss this critique in the concluding chapter, arguing that the intergenerational transmission of violence theory can be of value in examining the ways that men, especially violent men, *teach* their sons to be men. This is completely different from the genetic implications implied by the intergenerational transmission of violence theory.

Yet, as I stated in the first pages of this book, to ignore the fact that boys who grow up experiencing violence and/or witnessing it often grow into men who perpetrate it would be to ignore one of the processes by which IPV becomes part of intimate relationships. Indeed Murray Straus makes an interesting analogy: "It happens that research on smoking and lung cancer is very similar to that on having been abused and abusing. Two-thirds of those who smoke a pack of cigarettes a day or more do *not* die of lung cancer or other smoking related diseases. Yet we do not take that as invalidating the theory that smoking causes lung cancer" (1991, 184).

Finally, it would also be dismissive to ignore the powerful impact of childhood violence on the men I interviewed. Many of these men grew up in households that were violent. Men like Darren grew up in households where their fathers physically abused their mothers.

> I saw the violence growing up. I can remember him standing over my mother with an iron in his hand and me drawing a .22 rifle on him to make him back up. Stuff like that. I can remember him choking my mother when I was seven, eight, nine years old. And all my friends are going to the kitchen window. There he is; he's got her over the sink. It was violent. Nobody was ever hospitalized or anything like that, but it was usually associated with his drinking.—Darren, forty-something white man, North Carolina

In addition to the physical violence that occurred between Darren's parents, he described his father as emotionally absent; in fact, he indicated that his father was incapable of expressing emotion. After his parents divorced he saw his father only five or six times in the next twenty years, at which point his father died. On one of the rare occasions that Darren did see his father, they argued about his father's absence and lack of guidance, and Darren's father became physically violent with him.

> He got up and he backed me up against a wall, and he was just quivering from head to toe. . . . He said, son, I love you, but I'll kill you. . . . He was just unable to handle the emotional side about losing his family.—Darren, forty-something white man, North Carolina

Other men grew up in homes in which their fathers were physically abusive to them.

> Yeah, yeah, but I don't want him [my son], you know what I mean, to grow up and go through what we been through, you know what I'm sayin', I believe in discipline, I give out spankin's, but I just don't want him to go through what me, my brother, and my sister went through with this dude [his stepfather], you know what I'm sayin', 'cause I still got scars from when he beat us. He beat me with an extension cord, hit me in the face, yeah, he left a scar down my face, you know what I'm sayin', so I had to stay out of school for a while on that, you know. He used to taunt my brother all the time. You're a punk, you're a pussy, you're a pussy, you know what I'm sayin', you ain't never gonna be nothing, you're stupid, dumb, you see what I'm sayin', so me and him, he had grabbed me by my neck and broke my glasses because this one particular day

he kept calling my brother a punk, you're a punk, you're a pussy, you're a punk, so he had went outside and got into some altercation with some dude, [laugh]) he came home, the dude kicked his ass [laugh] so when he came home I was like I guess you the punk and the pussy now, you know, so I guess that comment made him mad, and he grabbed me by my neck, so me and him start fightin', you know, but just by me making that comment I didn't care about gettin' beat up or getting a whippin', I just feel good that he got hit (laugh) you know what I mean, that was a great feeling, you know what I mean.—Manny, thirty-something African American man, North Carolina

Finally, though much less common, several of the men I interviewed grew up in households in which one parent killed the other, as noted in Eddie's quote that serves as an epigram to this chapter.

THE IMPACT OF PROSTITUTION ON SONS

The previous discussion detailed the impact of prostitution on girls and young women. Many of the men I interviewed also grew up with mothers who worked as prostitutes, usually as part of a drug addiction. Again, the impact on these young men was severe. Boys growing up in these households were often introduced to the drug culture and began using themselves. I would also argue that these boys and young men were learning important lessons about women: that women were not to be respected or trusted. Unfortunately they carried these views into their own adult relationships, as noted by Eddie, whose mother killed his father.

At the course of time I even would see my mother stick needles in her arms, shooting heroin, you know, and it just became a life for me that I had developed some bad habits from the people that I was hanging around and from I seen in my past, all that I knew what I knew and during the course of years, during the course of these years, in school, I would go to school, you know, lay my head on the desk, wouldn't focus on the work, or cuss the teacher out, skip school, goin' to school, having marijuana, school just wasn't important to me. It had no benefits to me whatsoever, because I had already had made up mind that I was going to be a drug dealer because, you know that's all I had seen, that's all I had developed. I thought that getting high and drinking was the way to go because that's all I developed throughout my years of coming to be a early teenager and uh, because all the abusive and damage I seen from my parents, all the damage of the people that I seen and hung around them. It became a habit to me and by the time I was 16 years old I was selling drugs and uh toting guns, and snorting cocaine, smoking crack at the age of 16 years

old, um, stealing cars, you know, the situation had gotten worse. I was snorting heroin, you know. The situation had just gotten bad at the age of 16 and
therefore due to the fact that I had been in so much trouble, the judge sentenced me to go to Morganton High Rise for young men, a young prison camp
in Morganton, North Carolina, and I was there and I went there; I caught 10
years when I was 16 years old. The judge gave me 10 years.—Eddie, forty-
something African American man, North Carolina

RACE, CLASS, AND GENDER APPROACH

Much research documents the fact that rates of physical abuse of boys crosses
all race and class lines (Tjaden and Thoennes 2000). Thus, the role that race and
class play in the intergenerational transmission of violence is in some ways min-
imal. However, the interviews that I conducted with batterers of different
racial/ethnic and class backgrounds illuminate the ways in which race and class
do shape the relationship between male child abuse and battering in adulthood.
The situation for men is similar to that for women: because minorities and the
poor are significantly less likely to report abuse or have it interrupted when it occurs, the cycle of interpersonal violence is more likely to continue.

African American men also face distinct differences that shape their likelihood
for seeing interpersonal violence propagated from one generation to the next.
Most of these forces, such as unemployment and incarceration, will be discussed
in the next chapter. However, it is important to point out here that young African
American men are disproportionately likely to be exposed to other individual risk
factors that shape their decisions and behaviors in adulthood, such as drug abuse,
prostitution, and homicide. African American men (and women, as noted above)
are far more likely than their white counterparts to grow up in families that sub-
sist in the illegitimate economy, a risk factor for exposure to drug abuse and prostitution (for a lengthy discussion see Hattery and Smith 2007a). And homicide
rates are substantially higher in the African American community; for example,
homicide constitutes the fifth leading cause of death for African American men.
As is the case with Eddie, one can only speculate about the impact that witnessing a domestic violence homicide had on his experiences with violence in adulthood. This increased exposure to severe violence certainly impacts the likelihood
that African American men will grow up to batter their intimate partners.

CONCLUSION

Clearly the relationships among CSA, IPV, race/ethnicity, and social class are
complex. I have argued here that African American women's disproportion-

ate exposure to CSA puts them at increased risk for IPV in adulthood. As noted by sociologist Deborah King (1988), the impact of race, class, gender, and other social statuses is not "additive" but rather intersectional or "multiplicative." In order to understand the differences in the experiences of IPV for African American and white women we need to understand the complexities of being a white woman and/or being an African American woman and how this status intersects with other systems—access to shelters, to health care, to stable employment, and to the criminal justice system—that shape both the risk for IPV as well as the services available for women who find themselves faced with IPV. The same is true of social class. The fact that social class and race are so conflated exacerbates the situation for African American women. In terms of CSA and IPV (the focus of this chapter) we need to pay attention to the fact that African American women who are sexually abused as girls will, on average, have less access to treatment (mental health services, counseling) that if successful in producing healing, may reduce their risk for IPV in adulthood.[16]

Most boys who grow up in violent homes do not grow up to become abusive themselves. But the impact of the abuse they witness or experience is severe nonetheless. Many of the men I interviewed, white and African American, grew up in homes that were extremely violent. In some cases they experienced violence themselves, but far more commonly they watched their fathers (or stepfathers) beat their mothers. This confirms the finding that Straus and Gelles and others have reported—that boys who grow up watching their fathers (or stepfathers) beat their mothers are at the greatest risk for growing up to beat their own female partners (Ehrensaft et al. 2003). I will return to this discussion of intergenerational transmission in the concluding chapter.

Furthermore, it is clear that we cannot understand African American women's experiences with IPV until we understand their relation to African American men (Hattery and Smith 2007a). Because of a long history of segregation and antimiscegenation laws coupled with the continued abhorrence by whites of black-white marriage, most African American women who are in relationships are in relationships with African American men—intermarriage rates for African American women are less than 5 percent. Thus, an additional "risk" that African American women face is linked to their partnerships with African American men, who, like them, are situated in a particular space in the opportunity structure that heightens the probability that they will engage in violence against their female partners (Hattery and Smith 2007a).[17]

Finally, I note that one question that is always asked with regard to these "stories" is why these women sought out relationships with men as a route to escape sexual abuse. Part of the answer is quite simple: in most cases these women were poor and unable to make a living on their own. In short, they

were economically vulnerable. Of all the themes that run through the literature used in developing this book, that of "economic vulnerability" was the
most frequently cited by interviewees.

Furthermore, the majority of African American women and some (about 25
percent) of the white women I interviewed were pregnant as teenagers. Most
dropped out of school. Thus, they were extremely limited in their ability to provide for themselves economically, and they sought out relationships with men
whom they thought could put a roof over their heads, some food in their children's bellies, and provide them with some level of support. This is one of the
most powerful ways in which class inequality shapes exposure to IPV. Why? Because women who are marginalized and denied access to the opportunity structure are vulnerable to and at increased risk for violence both in the streets and at
home.

Though I will make many policy recommendations in the final chapter, I
note here that because of the strong relationship between adult IPV and childhood sexual abuse (for women) and child abuse and witnessing IPV (for
men), interventions with the child victims of abuse, including those who witness it, are critical and are likely to produce a sharp reduction in the incidence
of IPV in adulthood. In the next chapter I will examine the structural causes
of IPV, such as unemployment, poor health, and incarceration.

NOTES

1. Incidentally, the interviews with the men began this way as well.

2. This is what made my interview with Debbie so noteworthy. She began the interview by saying that her father tortured her. Because women were so much more
likely to start off slowly, using less charged language, I have to admit that at first I
wondered if Debbie was being facetious. Within minutes, as her story unfolded, I realized that her term, torture, was indeed apt.

3. Furthermore, because African American women are significantly more likely
than their white counterparts to report being raped or sexually abused in childhood or
adolescence (Tjaden and Thoennes 2000), the impact on young African American
women and girls is even greater.

4. In some cases the age differences were smaller, only ten years. Yet, I argue that
for a teenager this age difference still represents a huge gap in knowledge about sex
and power in the "relationship."

5. The case of Genarlow Wilson in Georgia, who spent several years in prison for
having consensual sex with a 15-year-old—he was 17—led to the revision of the state
statutes there and elsewhere.

6. Half of the white women who experienced premature sex engagement also became teen mothers, and they too struggled to complete high school and acquire any
human capital.

7. Whereas both Valerie and Candy were willing to disclose the most intimate details of the abuse, African American women were more reluctant and preferred to simply indicate that it had occurred. This finding may be related to the overall pattern: African American women in general are less willing to disclose violence by relatives or intimates (CSA and IPV) because they are more distrustful of the police and follow a strong norm against airing "dirty laundry" in public (see Hattery and Smith 2003, 2005). Either way, the fact remains that girls who are sexually abused are most likely to experience that abuse at the hands of relatives and acquaintances.

8. Typically drink houses are open nearly twenty-four hours a day. The women I interviewed told me that they were horrible places to grow up in because customers, mostly men, come in all times of the day and night to get a drink, a plate of food, play cards, and buy cigars or cigarettes. A typical liquor house stocks not only liquor, wine, and beer but will often serve cold sandwiches during the afternoon and fish, pork chops, and french fries in the evening. Evie talked, almost with pride, about how she could make the sandwiches and even pour a shot of whiskey by the time she was 10. Her face turned dark and tears filled her eyes as she talked about the men she encountered there and what they made her do—employing the euphemism that she had to "sit on their laps."

9. Note that the burgeoning international child sex trade is similar. The vast majority of children sold into childhood prostitution are not only poor themselves but come from some of the poorest countries in the world.

10. Candy's order of protection (a 50-B) prohibits them from living together. However, according to Candy, they are living with each other on and off, and they are continuing to have a sexual relationship, another violation of both the 50-B and the terms of Mark's treatment program.

11. Individuals will place "numbers" on the day's horse races with a bookie. Depending on the outcome, they can win considerable amounts of money for a small investment, sometimes as little as a quarter. When they "hit," the bookie collects a percentage of the take. (See Drake and Cayton 1945, 380–81, for a further explanation and discussion of what they refer to as the "policy station.")

12. I saw the receipt that she pulled from her handbag.

13. From the work of Johnston we find the following. "The Negro slave woman was an absolute dependent; dependent upon white men who dominated the little isolated world of the plantation" (1970, 217).

14. Ehrensaft, Cohen, and colleagues (2003) also report that child abuse and witnessing parental violence puts individuals (both men and women) at risk for drug abuse, mental health "diseases," and other negative behavior.

15. I use the term parental here to stand for violence perpetrated between the intimate partners who are raising children. I fully recognize that in many cases the batterer or the victim may not be a parent to the child. The adults may be stepparents, foster parents, even grandparents who are raising the child. The use of the term "parental" is merely a tool to reduce the cumbersome nature of the discussion for the reader.

16. This is just one example. African American girls who are sexually abused are also less likely to have access to the criminal justice system, whose intervention may

provide the validation that sexual abuse victims need to avoid issues of low self-esteem and self-hatred. Lack of access to the criminal justice system for African American girls who are sexually abused will result in higher rates of vulnerability for IPV as these young women transition into adulthood. It is also important to note here that one reason these girls do not have sufficient access to the criminal justice system has to do with the long-standing belief that they should not tell police authorities about their abusive male partners. As sung by the late Billie Holiday:

> Well I'd rather my man would hit me
> Than for him to just up and quit me,
> Ain't nobody's business if I do.
> I swear I won't call no coppa,
> If I'm beat up by my Poppa
> Ain't nobody's business if I do
> —Billie Holiday, 1930s

17. See especially Smith 2008.

Chapter Three

Structural Supports for Intimate Partner Violence

Capitalism, Racism, and Patriarchy

> The truth that [Michael] Jackson's spectacular crossing confirms is the immutability of the boundary between "black" and "white" and, just as important, the value of not being "black." For here we have the spectacle of a fine-looking, talented young Afro-American man spending a good part of his fortune on plastic surgeons and submitting himself to considerable physical pain, not to mention public ridicule and contempt, and all for what? *To achieve something the meanest, filthiest Euro-American bum on the streets has: being "white."* (Orlando Patterson 1999, 257)

In chapter 2 I explored individual factors—namely sexual abuse and exposure to violence in childhood—that increase risk for experiencing or perpetrating IPV in adulthood. In this chapter I turn to an examination of structural factors that contribute to intimate partner violence. Specifically I will focus on the systems of capitalism, patriarchy, racism, and the institution of incarceration.

Karl Marx, writing in the *Eighteenth Brumaire of Louis Bonaparte* (1869, 15), makes the following analysis which still today forces us to clearly disentangle individual actions from structural constraints. He put it thus:

> Hegel remarks somewhere that all facts and personages of great importance in world history occur, as it were, twice. He forgot to add: the first time as tragedy, the second as farce. And the same caricature occurs in the circumstances attending the second edition of the Eighteenth Brumaire! *Men make their own history, but they do not make it just as they please; they do not make it under circumstances chosen by themselves, but under circumstances directly encountered, given and transmitted from the past.*

Thus, my argument pertaining to the behavior of batterers is in line with analyses that distinguish between what any one individual might do or say and how their actions are shaped by their circumstances. It is, of course, the classic problem that sociologists pose when trying to make sense of unclear or irrational human actions: distinguishing the roles of individual agency and structural constraints.

SYSTEMS OF OPPRESSION IN LATE CAPITALISM: PATRIARCHY AND INTIMATE PARTNER VIOLENCE

The economy and intimate partner violence (IPV) are interconnected in many different ways at both the macro and micro levels. At the macro level, tangible financial costs are associated with IPV in various sectors of our economy, from lost wages, to the cost of housing women and children in shelters, to the costs directly associated with law enforcement, the courts, and incarceration. These costs are often difficult to estimate, but the Centers for Disease Control (CDC) has estimated the costs of IPV to the health care system alone at *$4 billion* annually.

At the micro or individual level,[1] finances and money are strongly linked to IPV. A common belief about couples is that they fight about two things: money and children. Money is no doubt an important part of family life. Couples argue about how to obtain it, how to spend it, how to manage it, and who should be earning it and by what means. As I will discuss at length in chapter 4, hegemonic masculinity proscribes that "real" men be successful breadwinners, and all the men I interviewed indicated that money was something

Table 3.1. Estimated Total Costs of Intimate Partner Violence against U.S. Adult Women, 2003

Type of Cost	Estimated Total Cost
Health Care	$ 4,050,211,000 ($4 billion)
Lost productivity	
Paid work	$ 858,618,000
Household chores	$ 727,831,000
Present value of lifetime earnings	$ 892,733,000
Total Costs (Direct + Indirect)	$ 5,801,561,000 ($5.8 billion)

Source: Department of Health and Human Services, Centers for Disease Control and Prevention, National Center for Injury Prevention and Control. 2003. Costs of Intimate Partner Violence against Women in the United States. Atlanta, Georgia, March 2003, http://0-www.cdc.gov.mill1.sjlibrary.org/ncipc/pub-res/ipv_cost/ipv.htm.

they argued about. Specifically for white men, their female partners' critiques of them as breadwinners were significant triggers for IPV.

Control of the family economic resources is important for many different reasons. But in families that involve abuse and violence, the degree to which women have access to these resources is critical to their ability to exit or escape these relationships (Tiefenthaler, Farmer, and Sambira 2005).[2] In addition, access to financial resources is directly linked to the mode of leaving. However, access to financial resources is by no means a guarantee of exit. Many affluent battered women do not leave their abusive partners for the same reasons middle-class or poor women do not: because they love their partners, and because they believe they will change.

Affluence is a complex part of the IPV puzzle. Battered women in affluent households often have the resources to leave but frequently also have a great deal to lose if they do leave. Many examples of this exist in the worlds of sport, business, entertainment, and politics. For example, Felicia Moon, wife of football superstar quarterback Warren Moon, was so badly beaten up by her husband one night that she called the police, who arrested Mr. Moon for misdemeanor battering.[3] At the trial, the prosecutor produced photographs that demonstrated that Mr. Moon had beaten his wife into an unrecognizable state, yet Mrs. Moon stood by her man and in her testimony blamed his violent outburst on herself. As a result, Mr. Moon was not convicted and the couple remained together. Why? I would argue because in the balance, Mrs. Moon, like many wives of powerful, influential, affluent men, had a lot to lose, mainly money. Though Mrs. Moon could most likely have accessed the assets to exit, she chose not to.[4]

Though social class may have only a limited effect on *whether* battered women leave, it most certainly affects the *ways* in which they do (Tiefenthaler, Farmer, and Sambira 2005). Affluent women rarely wind up in shelters, for example, because they frequently have access to resources that will facilitate temporary housing arrangements. That is, they can afford to stay in a hotel, rent an apartment, or even live with family or friends who are also more likely to have the resources necessary to accommodate a long-term guest.[5]

On a personal note, during the first week of interviews in Minnesota, I had lunch with a childhood friend. We have known each our whole lives. As soon as we sat down to our salads and diet drinks, she told me she was getting a divorce. As I expressed the usual "I'm sorry," she told me a tale of emotional and physical abuse. She noted that her soon-to-be ex-husband had come to call her "cunt" more than anything else and that he repeatedly told her and her son that they were the biggest mistakes of his life. On the Fourth of July (in

2004) he hit her. Three weeks later, when she and I met for lunch, she had already filed for divorce, they had sold their home, and she had bought and moved into her own home. The rapid exit and the buying of her own home are clearly examples of class privilege that the majority of women I interviewed were not afforded.

Though class privilege can provide alternatives to staying in an abusive relationship or fleeing to a shelter, affluence does not protect women from experiencing IPV. When I analyzed data from the NVAW survey (Tjaden and Thoennes 2000) specifically to examine the relationship between types of violence experienced and social class, I found that rates of violence remained high among middle-income, upper-middle-income, and affluent women. The data in table 3.2 are limited to middle- and upper-income households, those who are affluent or class privileged. In the analysis, the rates of violence reported by middle- and upper-class women were compared to the rates reported by working-class and poor women. On only a few types of violence (as denoted by the asterisks) were rates of violence *less common* among affluent than working-class and poor women. Thus, it is safe to say that affluence is not a buffer from IPV.

I turn now to an exploration of the complex relationship between IPV and economics. It can be best described as a "chicken and egg" relationship. In

Table 3.2. Physical Violence Experienced by Affluent Women: Percent of Women Reporting Each Type of Physical Violence

	HOUSEHOLD INCOME	
Types of Physical Violence	*Upper-middle* *50–80 K*	*Upper* *>80K*
Partner throws something at woman that could hurt her*	9.4%	7.2%
Partner pulls woman's hair*	9.1%	8.3%
Partner slaps woman	20.2%	18.8%
Partner kicks or bites woman	6.0%	4.3%
Partner chokes or drowns woman*	5.4%	4.9%
Partner hits woman with an object	6.8%	5.4%
Partner beats woman*	8.7%	8.6%
Partner threatens woman with a gun*	5.1%	2.9%
Partner threatens woman with a knife	3.4%	4.3%
Partner uses a gun on woman	2.0%	1.8%
Partner uses a knife on woman	1.7%	2.4%

Note: Analyses were performed using the data collected as part of the Violence and Threats of Violence Against Women survey, a national probability sample of men and women. Descriptions and data can be found at http://www.icpsr.umich.edu/cgi-bin/SDA.

*Indicates physical violence that is significantly lower among affluent women than middle-class and poor women. All other forms of physical violence are not significantly different by household income (social class).

Significance based on chi-square analyses with P-values <.10.

some cases the batterer prevents the woman from working or gaining access to economic resources as a way of keeping her in the relationship, and in other cases the battering results in wage loss and even job loss: women are fired for missing work due to injury, and women are fired because their batterers show up at work and harass them. In addition, structural, macro-level factors associated with our economic system in the United States have created a system that is ripe for IPV. This complex relationship between the economy and IPV will be the focus of the remainder of the chapter.

THE ROLE OF CAPITALISM IN PRESCRIBING GENDER INEQUALITY IN THE FAMILY

Capitalism, as a system of economic relations, depends upon the exploitation of one class (or person) by another or, put simply, the uneven relationship between business owners who supply the jobs and the individuals who take the jobs to make a living. This relationship is uneven in that the owner of the store, plant, or corporation often resorts to a strategy of paying the worker less than she or he is worth in order to maximize profits. The classic discussion of this is laid out in volume 1 of Marx's opus *Capital*. After examining the relationship between the economy and IPV I will outline the ways in which Engels (1884) applied the general principles of the Marxist perspective on economic relations to the family.

The Economy and IPV

IPV in the United States occurs within a system of capitalism and patriarchy, a potentially lethal combination for women. Heterosexual women are required to provide sexual access to their male partners—as a result of the erotic property exchange (Engles 1884)—and they are required to reproduce the labor force at home both by having babies and by taking care of the household labor. In addition to the economic dependency produced by this intersection of patriarchy and capitalism (Collins 1992; Engels 1884), women are also subjected to the sexual and physical domination of men. Though I would argue that domination of any sort is not healthy for any relationship, the combination of dominance and economic dependence is doubly dangerous for the victim of battering. Many women living with IPV are unable to leave successfully because they lack the economic means to do so; essentially, they can either choose to stay with the batterer and feed their children or leave and not be able to provide food or, in some cases, even shelter for themselves and their children (Browne 1987). Men remain the head of the household, a status derived from their economic power (Collins 1992; Engels 1884) and male privilege as established and reinforced by patriarchy (Kimmel 1995), and are free to physically discipline their wives or partners when they fail to meet the requirements of their roles as wives and mothers. This was legal in the United States until the 1970s (Browne 1987) and remains commonplace in many couples today.

Disciplining one's wife or girlfriend for failing in her duties is poignantly illustrated in the account from Fred. As he and I were talking about the things in his intimate relationship that make him angry, he pointed immediately to the "duties" of a wife or girlfriend. When I asked him to be specific, he illustrated with the following story. On Sundays, Fred's girlfriend likes to go to church. She normally gets home from church around 1 p.m. He wants his fried chicken dinner *on the table* at 1 p.m. And if it is not, he gets angry. Often he will begin arguing with his girlfriend and verbally abuse her (calling her lazy and no good), and sometimes he hits her.

> And I don't know where it was coming from; I guess I was feeling like trying to put it on her, 'cause I wasn't going [to church], I was trying to make her go or something, and, uh, she come home from church, that's like, well, when I was young [our dinner] should be ready at one o'clock on Sundays, you ain't got started 'til two o'clock!—Fred, forty-something African American man, North Carolina

Fred's reaction can be interpreted as an example of both "rule" and "role" enforcement, as I outlined in the preface. As "rule" enforcement, Fred wants to correct his girlfriend's laziness so that she will get his dinner on the table by 1 p.m. As "role" enforcement, Fred's behavior is an attempt to get his girlfriend to act like a "proper" girlfriend and nurture him.

Perhaps the most troubling illustration comes from Hank who noted that he becomes physically abusive when he feels as if his female partner, Helen, is not holding up her side of the exchange inherent in relationships (Engels 1884). I asked Hank to give me an example of this. At this point in the interview he became very animated, raising his voice and gesturing with his arms.

Helen, Hank's partner, is disabled (he described her as "not right upstairs") and is thus not employed. [At the time of the interview she was in jail serving a seven-month sentence for writing bad checks. Because of her disability she receives a monthly social security (SSI) payment to supplement the household income.] Hank, as the breadwinner, expects that Helen will do the bulk of the household labor. In his mind, this is an "even exchange." This is of course consistent with traditional gender role ideology (Hattery 2001b; Hochschild 1989). Hank indicated that the most common issue over which he and Helen argue is her inattentiveness to household chores and taking care of the children. When he comes home from work and finds that she has not done anything (housework, parenting) all day, he feels she has reneged on her part of the bargain, the exchange (Engels 1884). He becomes verbally and often physically abusive.

> . . . and she let the kids do what the hell they want to do. And they outside, homework ain't done. What are you, what the hell are you doing? Why is you here, basically. You're not helping me raise your kids. See what I mean? These are your kids, but here I am helping you raise your kids and then. . . . Ain't doing nothing as far as I'm concerned. You fat mother fucker you . . . you lazy son of a bitch, this that . . . and I mean I'm . . . especially if I had a drink in me. Oh, then it comes out, I mean, you know, really tell her to turn her ass out. And I did more verbal abuse than anything. Basically, it's just, if you did something for me not to . . . I believe if you, if she . . . . You don't work, I mean. . . . She ain't holding up her part of her bargain, the agreement. I mean, come on now.—Hank, forty-something African American man, Minnesota

I argue that the structures of capitalism and patriarchy at the macro level become real at the micro level when men and women "do gender" (West and Zimmerman 1987) in their intimate partner relationships. This system of gender relations disadvantages women and sometimes leads to IPV. Under patriarchy and capitalism men and women "do gender" based on rigid role expectations and scripts (Acker 2006). Violence in these couples often erupts when men believe their female partners are not adequately playing the appropriate or expected/scripted roles of wife and mother. This is an example of "role" enforcement.

Verbal and physical abuse was not only tied to the failure of women to play their appointed roles, but as I will discuss at length in chapter 4, this often occurred when women accused men of failing at their appointed role under capitalist patriarchy: that of breadwinner. When men felt emasculated by their female partners who earned more money or attempted to exert power in household decisions, they erupted violently. Thus, in an attempt to further our understanding of IPV, the lens produced by combining feminism and Marxism is instructive. This dual Marxist-feminist lens allows us to see how the systems of oppression arising from both patriarchy and capitalism are intertwined to produce a pattern of intimate partner violence that is both gendered and classed, in the traditional Marxian sense (see Acker 2006 for a history of class as a gendered concept). To consider battering without these contexts is to fail to link individual experiences with IPV, as expressed by those men and women I interviewed, with the larger patterns that developed as a critical nexus (patriarchy fused with capitalism) at the very core of capitalism and that exist in the U.S. political economy at the beginning of the twenty-first century.

INTERSECTIONS OF SYSTEMS OF DOMINATION— PATRIARCHY AND CAPITALISM: THE CASE OF IPV

It is important to consider the day-to-day effects of living under an ideological system of patriarchy and a capitalist economy on the gender relations between real men and real women. These systems play out in both structural and individual ways. The stories of men and women living with IPV will be analyzed in order to illustrate this matrix of domination (Zinn and Dill 2005) at the micro level.

The Economy: Household Property

Drawing on the work of Engels (1884), Collins (1992) argued that marriages (or partnerships) were essentially economic exchanges involving property. His first concept, household property, refers to the material property that is exchanged or owned by the household. When economic property, resources, access, and/or opportunity are not equally distributed in a household, the partner with more property, access, resources, and/or opportunity will hold power in the relationship. Collins (1992) is quick to note the gendered pattern of household property within couples in the United States.[6]

As a result of a sex-segregated labor market (Maume 1999; Padavic and Reskin 2002) and strict patterns of motherhood that require women to take time out of the labor market in order to raise children (see Garey 1999; Hays 1996; Hattery 2001a, b; Hochschild 1989) men in the United States tend to have greater control of and access to economic resources and household property, thus wielding more power in the household. This pattern is strongly reinforced by hegemonic femininity as will be discussed at length in chapter 4.

IPV is both an outcome and a cause of this imbalance in economic power in the household. Men's sense of power and entitlement that they derive from economic power contributes to IPV (Browne 1987; Brownmiller 1975; Dobash and Dobash 1979; Finkelhor and Yllo 1982: Gelles 1997; Straus and Gelles 1995). In turn, IPV leaves women economically dependent on men via at least two mechanisms: prohibitions on working and lost wages due to the physical and emotional effects of the violence.

"You Can't Work": A Tool of Control

Because IPV has its roots in anger and control, many batterers seek to control every movement of their partners. Often this includes a prohibition on labor force participation (Browne 1987). I found, in comparing the experiences of both white and African American women I interviewed, that this prohibition was more common in white households than in African American households. This is not surprising given the fact that African American households have historically relied on women's earnings (Hill-Collins 1994). I do note, however, that a few of the African American women I interviewed recounted that they were prohibited from working by men who wanted to "take care of them."

In some violent families, especially in the white community, female employment is threatening to a batterer for several practical reasons: it provides income that would allow a battered woman to successfully leave; it is often the source of friends in whom the victim could potentially confide about the violence; and it often provides interactions with men of whom the batterer is extremely jealous (this will be explored in more depth in chapter 6). Thus, many battered women find that they are prohibited from working outside the home (Browne 1987).

Josie's Story   Now in her early fifties, Josie had worked as a nurse her entire adult life.[7] Josie liked the independence that being employed offered. She also enjoyed the friendships she made at work. But John, her boyfriend, was extremely jealous of these friendships, especially the working relationships she had with men. Many times he showed up unexpectedly at work. One day, after showing up at her job to find that she was out to lunch with a group of her coworkers, including an older man of whom she said "not even Viagra would help," John beat her for the first time. Following this, John forced her to quit her job. He justified this request by saying that he had always wanted to take care of Josie and that he did not want her to have to work so hard.

The rage John expressed at Josie's imagined infidelity was completely consistent with other stories I heard. One young woman, Amy, told me that her partner regarded everyone she worked with as an erotic threat:

> He told me—he gave me a certain day I had to quit my job because he didn't trust me with anybody I worked with. Any guy whatsoever, if I talked to them, I was screwing them. It didn't matter. He accused me of stuff all the time.— Amy, twenty-something white woman, North Carolina

John's attempt to prohibit Josie from working, which was typical of many of the men and women I interviewed, was not really about wanting to "take care of her." In fact, it was one of the many ways in which he was attempting to control Josie's life. After she disclosed the first beating to a friend at work, this friend, whose husband was a police officer, encouraged Josie to search their house. This search revealed significant evidence that John was in fact monitoring all of her phone calls and comings and goings. Josie received her second and final beating the night that John found job applications she was sending out in the mailbox. Desiring to return to work for both the self-fulfillment and the economic reward, Josie had prepared and mailed several job applications. When John found these he beat her severely, and when she left John she never returned. Ironically, Josie had prepared the job applications with the intention of finding a new place for both herself and John, including a move to a new community. His temporary job was about to end, and she was planning for their future together, not attempting to desert him.

Josie's story illustrates many of the threats batterers feel from their female partners' employment, but it also suggests the power that resources, access, and opportunity afford women who are ready to leave. That is, in both the oppression and the breaking of oppression, sexual and economic property are inextricably linked (Woolley 2007). In Josie's case, it was her (platonic) relationship with a man at work that John indicated was the source of and justification for his jealous rage (a threat to sexual property). And it was precisely these "resources" at work that allowed Josie to leave. Josie had made friends at work on whom she could rely for help. After the second and final beating, Josie's friend took her to the emergency room and helped her to arrange for her escape out of state.

> I went ahead and cooked supper and was waiting on him to come home. He came home and hit that door like a bull in a china shop. He said, "I want you to know I know what the hell you're up to." I wanted to know what he was talking about. Well, he had gotten out of the mailbox some resumes that I was mailing off. I had gotten on the Internet and found out about the hospitals here and in Raleigh, Durham, Charlotte and Roanoke, Virginia. And I was just checking out the job market and I sent in a couple of resumes. I figured this job here isn't going to last very long for him, and maybe if I can pick up—hell, I make $32 an hour easy. That's what started it all. It started it all. . . . And I tried to explain to him—I told him that wasn't how it was [she wasn't planning to leave him]. I told him that if he would sit down, I would tell him why I did it. "Well, you should have told me." "Why should I have told you? I don't have to tell you every damn thing and every thought that's going on in my head." We'd be watching television—I'd be sitting on one end of the couch and he'd be sitting on the other end—and maybe I would look up at something, and he would say, "What are you thinking?" Well, I wouldn't really be thinking anything. I was just kind of looking out the window. And he'd say, "Well, you had to be thinking something." That night he would just throw things or he'd smash things. . . . I have a cat. I've always been a cat person. I had a cat that I had for almost 19 years. She was

a Persian. My husband bought her for me. [Josie had been married for thirty years to another man, and their relationship involved no violence. Her first husband died of cancer.] I used to show her. Now she was just a little bundle of love. That's all she was. He kicked my cat out the door. And when I went out to get her, she had blood coming through her little nose and her little mouth, and you could feel where her ribs were crushed. And he come behind me and he kicked me. He told me to put the G.D. [God-damned] cat down. And the more he kicked, the harder I held on. I left and I haven't been back since. . . . He kicked me, and the more he kicked me, the more I held on. When I got here Friday [to the shelter]—I wasn't an idiot, but I wasn't all together. . . . He finally got tired of kicking me. He kicked me almost unconscious. But Libby said when she and the next door neighbor came over, I was still holding the cat. . . . I went to the hospital. . . . You could see the boot prints on my side. The heel print with the logo.—Josie, a fifty-something white woman, North Carolina

Leaving with just the clothes on her back, the income Josie had earned at her job allowed her to relocate out of state, thus escaping the violence that threatened her life and health. And it is her nursing credentials that will allow her to find a new job and thus successfully and permanently leave John.

I called the 800 line. . . . And the lady asked me if I had any money. I told her I had about 60 bucks. This is what I had in my pocket. I called Libby and I told her to meet me at the bus station. I asked her where he was at. She said he and Al went down to have a few beers. So I told her to go to my house and get this and that for me. I told her to meet me at the bus station. She asked me where I was going and I told her I didn't know, but I knew I had to go. I said whatever bus leaves first, that's the bus I'm on. And the bus that left first was for here to Winston-Salem. . . . When I got to Winston some lady that was at the bus station had come to drop off somebody—an older lady—I guess I really looked pitiful and pathetic. She come up to me and said, "Are you all right dear?" And when she came up to me, I guess I jumped at least 20 feet. And I told her, "I'm fine." She said, "No, you're not. What happened?" And she went to put her arm around my waist and she told me somebody has beat the hell out of you. I'm calling the police. I told her that I called the 1-800 hot line number and this is the number that they gave me. She said she would call them because I looked like I would stand there for hours trying to figure out what to do. So she called and the police came and brought me here [to the shelter]. . . . The only reason I lucked up on this job that I have is because the doctor that I interviewed with liked me right away. And I told him I lost my wallet [social security card]—I told him I did have numbers that he can call. And here's the name of the doctor that

I worked for 32 years. And if he wanted to know anything about me, this man has known me since I was 17 years old. Call him. And that's what he did. He called him. —Josie, fifty-something white woman, North Carolina

Finally, it is important to recognize, as Browne (1987) and others highlight, other significant barriers to leaving, among them the presence of young children. Josie has never had children, and thus she had fewer connections permanently binding her to John than many of the other women that I interviewed.

Because employment represents women's freedom from economic dependency on men and is thus threatening to a batterer, he will frequently restrict her employment opportunities (Browne 1987). This is normative in the white community where hegemonic masculinity is adhered to most closely (Smith 2008). As noted previously, prohibitions on working are less common in African American families who have historically depended on women's labor force participation. However, I did hear many stories from African American men and women who reported that the men controlled the women's paychecks, where they could work, and whom they were allowed to befriend at work. Thus the issue of *control* crosses race/ethnic and class boundaries. Stella notes that often the abuse that Will perpetrated on her was triggered when she would not hand over her paycheck to him.

He didn't become abusive to me until I quit [using crack]. And then, I wouldn't give him any more money. And when he was coming down [from a high], he'd get violent and I'd go to work and have choke marks on my throat. He fractured my shoulder blade once 'cause he threw me in the bathroom and I hit the towel bar. Hitting my head against the wall. His favorite one was the choking though.— Stella, twenty-something African American woman, Minnesota

In addition to these restrictions, in a beating or repeated beatings the batterer essentially destroys his victim's freedom by ruining her career and her physical health in one blow. Symbolically this is consistent with a variety of the accounts I heard from the women I interviewed. Many of them changed jobs, either to accommodate their partner's wishes or to get away from their abuser. Most of the women also reported having to call in sick on the days following a beating. Josie recalled that after the first beating her jaw was so swollen that she called in sick and missed a couple of days of work. In some cases the women were just too physically injured to work. More frequently, however, they were too embarrassed to show up at work with bruises and cuts that they had sustained at the hands of a man who claimed to love them.

When I got home, I hit that door like a hurricane and got all up in his face. I told him to not tell me what to do or who I can and can't speak with. I told him, "One other thing, you are not my father. You don't give me orders. I am not some pedigree dog that you have papers on. Ken (her deceased husband) would never have even dreamed about doing me this way." And that's when he hit me. I mean, he doubled up his fist and he hit me. And I mean I hit that floor so hard. My teeth rattled. And I had star bursts in front of my eyes. And I thought I had to hang on and not pass out. If I did, I would be dead. That's all I could think about was that if I pass out, I'm dead. I knew he was going to kill me. I knew he would. Because I had made him that angry. But he walked away. He said, "If you say another word to me, I'll kill you. I swear I'll kill you. You just don't know when to shut up." I just got up and went in the kitchen and put ice on my face. I sat there and thought maybe this was one time I should have kept my mouth shut. And then I heard a voice. It was my grandfather saying, "No, don't ever keep quiet. You don't have to keep quiet." I was shocked. I had never had a hand raised to me. I didn't go to work the next day. I called in sick and told them I had to go to the dentist. That was the most logical explanation that I could think of to explain the swollen jaw.—Josie, fifty-something white woman, North Carolina

Many battered women are beaten so frequently that they cannot afford to miss work every time they are assaulted. Several with whom I talked shared their secret techniques for covering up the cuts and bruises, techniques that allowed them to go to work following a beating. In fact, on the day I interviewed Candy (mid-September 2001), she was volunteering at a Red Cross blood drive in order to help the victims of September 11. She was bruised and battered from a beating a few days before and showed me, almost with pride, how skillfully she had masked the bruises with makeup. Over a long period of time, however, the loss of wages and the potential loss of their jobs due to truancy leaves many battered women, even those who remain employed, economically dependent on their male partners.

"He Showed Up at My Job Brandishing a Gun": Women Fired because of IPV

Though injuries account for most absences from work, the action of men showing up unexpectedly at work, as Josie's partner John did, is also a problem. Browne (1987) argues that this type of intrusion is yet another form of control and emotional abuse in which batterers engage. This type of intrusion allows batterers to monitor the actions and interactions of their partners, and because it is random and unannounced it allows them to create a situation in which battered women are in a constant state of alert or fear, never knowing when or where their abusive partners might show up unexpectedly. The random nature of this activity makes it a successful strategy for batterers to indirectly control their partners, who must be always on their best behavior so as to avoid being "caught" doing something "wrong"—defined as anything the batterer disapproves of—and then being beaten for it later.

> I asked him what he was thinking. That was my job. I told him that if he went in there and showed his ass, people were going to think that I get off work and this is what I go home to and this is the way she probably really is. And I told him that I'm a professional at my job. I'm still funny and I'm still mouthy, but I'm professional. I do my job and I do it damn well. And I told him he couldn't go up there and show his behind. I told him I wouldn't put up with it. He would say, "I'm sorry, baby, I'm so sorry." Then three weeks later, everything started coming to a head.—Josie, fifty-something white woman, North Carolina

Gus, an African American man who was arrested for beating his wife, told of the day he was arrested. Gus believed that his wife was having an affair. They had an argument and she admitted that she was in love with another man. In addition, she told Gus that she wanted a divorce and that she was moving in with her new boyfriend. Soon after, she did move out and move in with her new boyfriend. Gus could not believe the relationship was over, he could not believe that she had cheated on him, and he continued to believe that he was the best person for her. He wanted her back. Unable to convince her with words, he showed up at her office—she was a receptionist in a local pediatrician's office—with a gun and insisted that she leave with him. She was unwilling, so he kidnapped her at gunpoint and drove her across state lines to her mother's house, hoping that her mother would talk some "sense" into his estranged wife.

> Yeah, she went and stayed with him that night. Yeah, since he, that's the night she went and stayed. We went over there—me and my friend Mike went over there. He said, she wasn't there and she had parked her car somewhere else. She was in there. We didn't, we knocked on his door to go see if she was there. He said she wasn't there. And so, we didn't know where she was. Come to find out, yes . . . she was there. So, that's, that would have been different. That would have been a whole nother thing, you know, like, so . . . but its good it didn't, I didn't know she was in there. So I knew she was going to be at work the next day, so I was at her job the next morning. You know, when she got to work. And then, she was, like I don't want to. . . . I said, come and talk, so she got in the car. And I said, I, you know, I was trying to talk to her and talk to her, but at any rate, the conversation

wasn't going good, so she went. She got out of the car, went upstairs to her job. And so I followed her up to her job and then, I said, well, I just want to read you something. Some poetry or something that I had wrote or something. I do everything to make some kind of excuse, but since I was at her job, she was so embarrassed, she said okay. And then she came back down. You know, came back down. And got in the car, and then she went and shut the door. And I said, well, let me just go pull around the car and she waits at the door. But finally, I said, whatever I said, I said I can't quite remember. She shut the door. And when she shut the door, I took off. And I took, I pulled around. And instead of going where, I said I took off and hit the road, and then she was like . . . that's when all, that's when I got in trouble 'cause that was like attempted, that was kidnapping or something. Yeah, 'cause she was hitting me, trying to say let me out and I just kept driving. I kept driving, you know. I wouldn't stop 'cause if I stopped, she would get out and then I could get her to her mom. But any time I saw . . . it was about getting her to her momma. I did. I did that. I mean, I did not . . . when I stopped for gas, we were about an hour away from her home in West Virginia. I mean, I hit the highway. I hit the highway, I did not stop. I ran red lights. Kept moving. I just kept going and wouldn't stop.—Gus, forty-something white man, North Carolina

In and of itself, a woman's partner showing up unexpectedly at her workplace can be understood as emotional abuse. An angry and loud partner showing up is not only embarrassing to the woman but also disruptive to the workplace. Brush (2006) refers to this as "domestic violence spilling over into work."

Even if the partner is not angry, as was often the case with the abusive partner of a woman named Amy, who would show up at her job crying, apologizing, and begging to be taken back, such erratic behavior is highly unprofessional. No woman, battered or not, wants her partner showing up unexpectedly at her job demanding to know what she is doing and to whom she is talking. It would be absurd.

Josie reported that her abusive partner frequently showed up at her nurses' station demanding to see her or be informed of her whereabouts. Though Josie quit this job soon after this behavior began, another battered woman in this situation may be censured or even fired for the disruptive behavior of her abuser, whose presence may impede her from doing her job. Indeed, Gus's wife was fired after he showed up at her office and kidnapped her at gunpoint. And being fired often leaves a woman even more vulnerable to her batterer.

In a practical way, then, battering not only creates a situation in which one class of people finds itself economically dependent on another, but it

serves to reduce the opportunities of the oppressed class to compete effectively for scarce economic resources. Batterers' prohibitions on work remove thousands of women from the labor force, and those that do remain
typically limit their work to part-time so that they can attend to the care
of the home and the children, for not doing so will result in the type
of beatings Hank admitted to. In addition, battered women work less
effectively—due to injuries—leaving them less able to advance. Thus battering not only advantages the men who engage in it, but profits all men by
reinforcing gender inequality in the workplace. As Collins (1992) notes,
this unequal access to economic goods and opportunity structures helps to
shore up men's power at home. Examining IPV through the lens provided
by Collins (1992) and Engles (1884) and Browne (1987) helps to link the
micro experiences of the individual abuser and victim with larger, macro
level patterns that oppress some and benefit others, including the majority
who never participate in IPV.

In interviews with many battered women I found that these inequalities
are compounded and more problematic for African American women in part
because they earn lower wages at less stable and desirable jobs than white
women (Hattery and Smith 2007; Maume 1999; Padavic and Reskin 2002).

Women and Economic Dependency: The Case of African American Women

One of the key issues central to IPV in all types of families is women's economic dependency on men. As I will expound on at length in chapter 4, Rich

Table 3.3. Women's Earnings by Race

Earnings	Race	
	White	Black
<25K	40.0%	47.4%
	(10,329,615)	(2,128,607)
25–35K	24.8%	25.2%
	(6,399,898)	(1,133,261)
35–50K	19.4%	17.0%
	(4,996,444)	(764,463)
50–70k	9.5%	7.0%
	(2,460,044)	(313,112)
70–100K	4.0%	2.4%
	(1,022,609)	(108,639)
100K+	2.3%	1.0%
	(583,334)	(46,264)
All	25,791,944	4,494,346
N = 35,423,475		

Source: DeNavas-Walt, C., Bernadette D. Proctor, and R. J. Mills (2004).

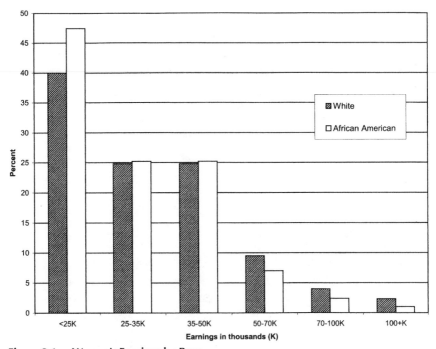

Figure 3.1. Women's Earnings by Race

Source: Analysis based on U.S. Census 2000 data. Analysis performed at www.ssdan.net/ida_resources.shtml

(1980, 1995) argues that one of the strongest compulsions for women to marry (or cohabit) is the fact that their economic standing is almost always enhanced by the economic contributions of their male partners. This dependency on men as breadwinners creates a sort of glue that prevents women from leaving their abusive partners. This barrier to leaving is especially profound for African American women in that they earn less than their white counterparts and are more likely to be unemployed.

Thus, African American women are in greater need for the financial contributions of their male partners, which for a variety of reasons they are far less likely to receive. Specifically, African American men face higher rates of unemployment and incarceration, thus a much lower percentage of African American women receive economic support from their male partners and/or the fathers of their children as compared to white women. As a result, more than two-thirds of African American women and children live in poverty (see Hattery and Smith, 2007a for a lengthy discussion of the impact of unemployment and incarceration on African American families).

Therefore, African American women who lose their jobs—due to violence or any other factor—are more likely to find themselves homeless and unable

Table 3.4.   Unemployment Rates by Race

Whites:	4.4%
African Americans:	10.4%

Source: U.S. Bureau of Labor Statistics, http://data.bls.gov/cgi-bin/surveymost.

	16+ Years Old	*16–19 Years Old*
White men:	5.5%	
White women:	4.6%	
White teens:		15.0%
African American men:	11.0%	
African American women:	9.3%	
African American teens:		29.0%

Source: U.S. Bureau of Labor Statistics, http://www.bls.gov/opub/gp/pdf/gp02_01.pdf.

to meet the daily needs of their children (Brush 2000, 2001; Brush, Raphael, and Tolman 2003; Renzetti 1989). This situation creates more dependency on men such that many battered women return home to their abusers after only brief stints on their own. Furthermore, many of the women I interviewed who did not return to their abusers felt *obligated* to establish sexual relationships with other men in order to survive fleeing their previous abusive relationships. Often these men also turned out to be abusers.

Many of the women I interviewed talked of moving out of the shelter (in North Carolina) and into an apartment with a man they had met at the mall only a few days or weeks before. Recall Andi's story, detailed in chapter 2, of moving hundreds of miles from Chicago to Minnesota with a man she had known less than twenty-four hours. She saw this as her only way out of the shelter where she had been living.

This form of economic dependency is brutal and sometimes lethal for women, especially African American women, because they have less education and lower wages, hence they are particularly vulnerable to this type of economic dependency. This type of dependency creates a situation in which women find that their only option is the selling or trading of their sexuality in exchange for basic needs. I turn now to a discussion of the role that race plays in shaping African American men's perpetration of IPV.

The Unique Situation of African American Men

African American men face a different set of challenges and barriers than their white counterparts. Nearly three centuries of slavery followed by a century of Jim Crow segregation has had long-lasting effects on African American men (and women). It is often difficult to identify root causes of social problems, but with regard to IPV, one of the critical issues is the continued overt and covert racism and discrimination that limits access by African American men to the opportunity structure—to education, political power, job opportunities, leadership in all fields, and economic self-sufficiency. When the unemployment rate runs at 4 or 5 percent for the U.S. population at large, it is often three to four times higher (15–20 percent) for African American men. In fact, in 2006 the *New York Times* reported that 50 percent of African American men in New York City faced bouts of unemployment. The inability to earn a living wage has direct implications for IPV (such as "failure as provider" that I will discuss in depth in chapter 4). It also has indirect implications for IPV (see Hattery and Smith 2007a for a detailed review of this).

In particular, in addition to inequality in the opportunity structure, African American men also face at least two other barriers to successful breadwinning: poor health and incarceration. Two young men I interviewed (at the time of the interview Ronny was 27 and Demetrius was 20) are faced with such serious health issues, including HIV, that neither is capable of working, and neither expects to work again in his lifetime. Because HIV/AIDS now constitutes the sixth leading cause of death for African American men, and because HIV/AIDS is a disease that involves a long period of decline, more and more African American men, as a direct result of serious and chronic health issues, will find it difficult to meet the first requirement of masculinity: breadwinning.

The second major obstacle in meeting the requirements of the breadwinning role is a direct consequence of incarceration. The impact of incarceration on African American men's employability is substantial. With a quarter to a third of all African American men being incarcerated for a period of time, mostly when they are young (age 18–35), it is fair to say that incarceration is a major life stage in the lives of African American men (Hattery and Smith 2007a). In addition to its many outcomes, it prevents them from ever making a living in the legitimate economy.

I note here that incarceration may be replacing other markers of masculinity (such as breadwinning) for African American men. This is logical for several reasons: (1) going to prison is common, (2) it is often related to making money—in the illegitimate economy—and (3) it is the mark of a "tough guy." However, regardless of the commonality of incarceration for African American men and its contribution to a masculine identity, the power of hegemonic constructions of masculinity continue to create a standard (breadwinner) against which all men (and their female partners) judge their success. Furthermore, both the men and the women I interviewed identified "failures" as a breadwinner as a "trigger" to IPV. Indeed the breadwinner role is perhaps the most significant identity for the typical American man. Most men that were interviewed indicated that their identity as a "provider" was central. They identified this as their main contribution to their intimate relationships and to their households. I turn now to a more in-depth discussion of both HIV/AIDS and incarceration and their impact on African American families and relationships.

HIV/AIDS in the African American Community

One of the fastest-growing health risks to African Americans is HIV/AIDS. Especially among young African American men and women, AIDS is a leading cause of premature death that robs communities of productive citizens (Hattery and Smith 2007a). African Americans are disproportionately likely to have AIDS as compared to their white counterparts. Specifically, African Americans make up 12 to 13 percent of the U.S. population, but they make up *nearly half* of all the AIDS cases in the United States (Centers for Disease Control 2004).

Intravenous (IV) drug use is known to be a significant risk factor for acquiring HIV. A common assumption is that African Americans are more likely than their white counterparts to use IV drugs and that this behavior puts them at greater risk for acquiring HIV. However, data from the CDC demonstrate that this issue is more complex than meets the eye: although African American *men* are more likely than white men to acquire HIV via IV drug use (40 percent of HIV cases among African American men compared to 10 percent of HIV cases among white men[8]), among *women*, African American *and* white, about 30 percent of HIV cases are a result of IV drug use.[9]

African American women are most likely to acquire HIV/AIDS through having sexual contact with infected male partners (Hattery and Smith 2007a).

Ronny   I conducted my interview with Ronny in the hospital in Minnesota. He is a 27-year-old African American man with serious health issues. He has had quadruple bypass surgery, has eight bullet holes in his body, and was in the hospital having most of his foot amputated as a result of uncontrolled diabetes. He is also HIV positive. Not only will Ronny most likely die young (at age 27 he has the body of a man forty years his senior), but his potential is already destroyed. At the end of the interview I asked him what he planned to do in the next few years with regard to employment—he had worked for ten years in the fast-food industry, eventually holding assistant manager positions at two different restaurants. He indicated he will probably not be able to work again. As a result of his amputation he cannot even stand up. Even after extensive physical and occupational therapy it is unlikely that he will ever be able to stand for the extended periods of time that are associated with the kinds of jobs he is qualified for in food service or perhaps retail.

Ronny (and his wife Tammy) acknowledge that his unemployment, his failure as a breadwinner, is a "trigger" for violence in their relationship.

> Sometimes we didn't even have food to eat, so you know, we was eating like food she would bring home from work, or scrapping food like everyday or something like that. And then you know, as them problems like that, we started to get into fights.—Ronny, twenty-something African American man, Minnesota

Thus, the risk for IPV continuing in Ronny and Tammy's relationship is further exacerbated by his chronic health conditions, especially his HIV status and the impact of his health and HIV status on his employability.

Incarceration in the African American Community

Incarceration in the African American community is a serious and insufficiently studied problem.[10] The United States incarcerates more citizens than any other industrialized nation in the world. In fact, the number of Americans incarcerated for drug convictions alone is higher than the entire incarcerated population in the European Union (a set of nations with a higher population than the United States).

The data on incarceration reveal a substantially more dismal picture for African Americans. Men of all races are far more likely to be incarcerated than women, but race differences hold by gender. African American men and women are many times more likely to be incarcerated in their lifetimes than are men and women of other races and ethnicities. African American men are seven times more likely to be incarcerated than their white counterparts.

In terms of the total prison population, though African Americans make up only 12 percent of the U.S. population, African American men make up nearly *half of the total prison population, male and female*. On any given day, 1 million African American men are in prison and many more are in jail or under the supervision of the criminal justice system (e.g., parole, probation, electronic monitoring, etc.). Using the most conservative estimates, at least 25 to 30 percent of all African American men will be incarcerated in their lifetimes (Mauer and Chesney-Lind 2002). On any given day, thousands upon

Table 3.5. Incarceration Rates for African American and White Men

All men:	90 out of every 1,000 will be incarcerated in their lifetimes
White men:	44 out of every 1,000 (4.4%)
African American men:	285 out of every 1,000 (28.5%)

Source: Bureau of Justice Statistics.

thousands of African American families are destroyed forever because of incarceration (Hattery and Smith 2007a; Mauer 2001, 2002; Mauer and Chesney-Lind, 2002).

The effects of incarceration are devastating to the African American community. My interviews with African American men and women living with intimate partner violence allowed me to identify a strong and important relationship between incarceration and battering. All but two of the African American batterers I interviewed had been to jail or prison, and these periods of incarceration as well as the difficulties a felony record creates for sustainable employment (Mauer 2001; Pager 2003) were significant "triggers" for violence in these families.[11]

One of the most serious consequences of incarceration for ex-convicts is the inability to get sustainable employment that provides a living wage. I note here the work of sociologist Devah Pager. Professor Pager designed a study to test the employability of men by race and incarceration status. In sum, she sent out fake job applications to companies and measured the likelihood of getting "called back." The applications were identical except for two factors: she varied race and felony status. Her findings are illustrated in figure 3.2.

Not surprisingly Pager found that white men *without* a felony record were the most likely to be called back than any other group, and African American men *with* a felony record were called back only 3 percent of the time. In-

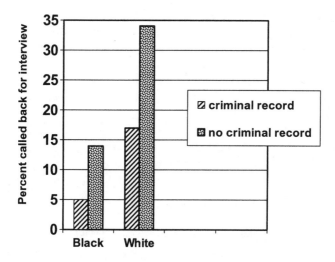

Figure 3.2.   The Effect of a Criminal Record for White and African American Job Applicants

Source: Pager, D. 2003. The Mark of a Criminal Record. *American Journal of Sociology* 108:937–75.

credibly disturbing was her finding that *white men with a felony record* were more likely to be called back than *African American men without a felony record* (Pager 2003). Thus, the impact of incarceration on African American communities is complex and leads to devastating consequences.

Chris   During the course of his five-year relationship with Wanda, Chris has repeatedly been incarcerated. He is unemployable because of his felony record and his stints in jail and prison. During his periods of incarceration, Wanda makes friends with other men who continue to call her and come by after Chris is released back into the "free world." During Chris's stints out of jail or prison, on a typical evening or weekend other men call and drop by "their" house to see Wanda. (Wanda admits that she "hangs out" with other men while Chris is incarcerated.) This is a major trigger for Chris. He is jealous. When he tries to physically assert what he sees as "his right to his woman," Wanda "reminds" Chris that he is not the breadwinner in the household and therefore has no claim to enforce the "rules."

> My house. I'm paying all the bills. I'm talking about rent, gas, light, phone, cable, everything. Everything. Everything. I even buy his deodorant, okay? So who are you? "I don't want nobody around my woman." All this and that, this and that. "What you want with my woman? Don't be calling my house!" But this is his house he say. I'm like, I said, "motherfucker, this ain't your damn house. This is my motherfucking house! You can get the fuck out!" So now I'm mad. Now I'm like get the hell out.—Wanda, forty-something African American woman, Minnesota

Wanda's accusation that Chris is a failure as a provider is interpreted by Chris as a threat to his masculinity. In an attempt to reassert his masculinity the argument escalates and often becomes physical.

> This nigga got the biggest knife it is in the house laying on the counter. So I looked at him, so I eased right? I eased back to the back door and I seen him walk toward the front door. I comes up in the house and I grabbed the knife. And I take the knife and I puts it behind my back in my panties right here, like this right, put my T-shirt over it. I say, do it make any sense for you to act like a fool like you do? Calling that lady house, acting a fool. I said, Chris, it don't make no sense. I said, you know what you need to do? You need to get your shit, get together and get your shit out of here. I said, cause you got exactly two hours. If your shit ain't gone, you ain't got a place to go, far as I'm concerned, it's garbage. I'm not putting up with your shit no more. I'm just through. "Oh, you just talking that shit, goddamn, 'cause you been over there drinking all night with Angela. She fooling your head full of bullshit." I said, no, you got my head full of bullshit. I said, I'm tired now. So, but no, he ain't listen. "You

is my wife til death til we die." So now that's when you start. That don't mean til death do you die like we done took no marriage vows. Til death do you die—either you're going to be, woman, or one of us going to be dead. You see what I'm saying. That's how I interpret it. Okay, so now wait a minute. So then, should I kill this motherfucker?—Wanda, forty-something African American woman, Minnesota

This imbalance of economic power was a key justification from Chris's perspective that entitled him to beat his girlfriend (they were not legally married). He recognized Wanda's economic control as a threat to his masculinity, his sense of himself as a man. In short, Chris beat Wanda and threatened her with the knife when he felt his masculine identity, specifically his economic power in the household, was threatened. Chris engages in this type of violence as a means of reasserting his power in the household.

As these stories point out, the struggles that African American men face in their roles as breadwinners are somewhat different, at all socioeconomic levels, than those faced by their white counterparts. Thus the impact of unemployment, illness, and incarceration on African American families also differs from their white counterparts in many ways, including as a conduit for IPV (see Smith 2008 for a lengthy discussion of race and IPV).

The Economy: Sexual/Erotic Property

Collins's (1992) third proposition is that a marriage or partnership includes an exchange of sexual property whereby women must sign over access to their sexuality to their male partners in exchange for men's economic support. This exchange of sexual or erotic property is illustrated in many rituals and practices such as the white wedding dress, the honeymoon, and the advice to women that men will remain faithful when they are satisfied sexually at home. Women are constantly reminded that they have an *obligation* to meet the sexual demands of their husbands. I would argue that in many relationships, abusive ones in particular, this exchange of sexual or erotic property whereby women give up access to their sexuality and men agree to pay the rent, serves to structure sexual abuse, rape, and other forms of violence in relationships. And, as suggested by some noted rape scholars, this "exchange" is well entrenched in our ideology of dating and marriage (see Hattery and Kane 1995; Pirog-Good and Stets 1989).[12] Collins (1992) further argues that this exchange of sexual/erotic property is among the most important in any intimate relationship because it is the exclusive, sexual nature of the relationship that sets marriages and partnerships apart from other intimate relationships. Sexual infidelity is perhaps the most severe threat to the relationship.

Yet, this too is gendered. Women have been divorced (even in societies in which divorce is rare) or, worse yet, stoned to death (for contemporary cases, see Isaacs 2002; for biblical references see Graetz 1998) for a single breech of this portion of the marital contract. Brides have been burned or stoned for failing to prove their virginity at the time the marriage/partnership is consummated. Yet, sexual infidelity is more readily tolerated and in many cases even encouraged for men. Just as this sort of inequality in access to economic and household property results in household power for men, such is also the case with sexual or erotic property. When women exchange access to their sexuality at the time of marriage or commitment, men gain power, both at home and in the outside world. This power, too, is both a source and a cause of IPV. I will explore this issue at much greater length in chapter 6.

CONCLUSION

The stories presented in this chapter suggest that the combination of capitalism and patriarchy creates a culture that is ripe for IPV. These structural forces create differential access to resources for men and women and provide different degrees of power for both. Under strict patriarchy, norms require that men be the breadwinners and that they control women's sexuality. This set of mores creates a situation in which women are economically dependent on men, thus leaving them vulnerable to IPV. Men hit because they can, and women often believe they can do nothing about it. Similarly, men enjoy greater sexual freedom than women. Men are expected to have more experience, and even when they engage in infidelity it is considered a less serious offense—if an offense at all—than when women do the same.[13] Thus, men feel that jealousy and suspicions of infidelity are justifications for IPV, whereas women are left tolerating the same from their male partners.

At the macro level, battering (a patriarchal vestige) reinforces men's advantage in the labor market. Batterers restrict or prohibit women's labor force participation. Battered women often struggle to advance or even remain employed because in many cases they must miss work due to the physical, psychological, and emotional injuries they experience at the hands of their male partners. Another way of seeing this is that battering reduces the threat of female competition in the labor force. In this way, all men, even those who do not batter, benefit from the ways in which battering eliminates women as competitors in the tight labor market.

The effects of IPV on individual women are well documented (Browne 1987; Dobash and Dobash 1979; Finkelhor and Yllo 1982; Walker 1979).

And, though some research has focused on men who batter, most of the attention has been directed toward predicting which men will batter and which intervention programs are most successful. Even fewer attempts have been made to examine the ways in which IPV operates—at both the micro and macro levels—to produce a model for family and the workplace that rewards male privilege (even for men who do not batter) and limits women's access to the opportunity structure (even for women who are never battered).

This chapter moves us beyond individual explanations for IPV and analyzes these data with attention to the systematic and structural oppression created by both patriarchy and capitalism that is further enhanced or exacerbated by their intertwining. As a result, a clearer picture of both the micro and macro causes and effects of IPV emerges herein. These findings suggest that to reduce or eliminate IPV in the United States will take more than simply teaching individual men not to hit or instructing individual women on how to escape. We must recognize the role that power and privilege, derived from patriarchy and the capitalist economy (Acker 2006), play in perpetuating the epidemic of IPV with which we all must live. In the concluding chapter I will outline policy recommendations to address this structured inequality.

This chapter has also focused on the intersection of these two key systems of domination as well as a third: racial superiority. What is perhaps most intriguing about studying a phenomenon such as IPV in different racial and ethnic populations is the opportunity this provides to see clearly the differential effects of race and social class on gender inequality.

For example, African American men are exploited by a system of capitalism that sets them in an antagonistic relationship with other racial and ethnic minority men and women and to a lesser degree with white women. Perhaps the best illustration of this is the implementation of affirmative action. A policy designed to open doors of opportunity for African Americans in fact actually benefited white women more than any other "underrepresented" group. This is true in education, business, politics, indeed in virtually all areas of social life. It is an example of the continued oppression of African Americans by the system of capitalism, specifically the practice of establishing dual labor markets (Acker 2006).

Similarly, African American men (and women) are subjected to oppression within the system of racial superiority that has dominated the U.S. landscape since our very beginnings in 1610. The examples of health disparities and incarceration served to illustrate this point.

However, African American men benefit and are privileged by the ideology that sets the rules for gender relations that dominate the U.S. landscape: patriarchy (Epstein 2007). And, though the "triggers" African American men identify for IPV vary somewhat from those identified by white men (Smith 2008), the bruises, broken bones, mutilated and raped bodies, and abused psyches feel the same no matter what the racial identity of the woman being beaten. When any man, white, African American, Latino (Hispanic), Asian, Native American, or of any other group, engages in IPV he is taking advantage of the system of patriarchy that allows him to dominate and control his female partner.

Understanding the ways in which various systems of domination interact and are played out in various phenomena, including IPV, is critical if we are to prevent and interrupt this (and all) forms of gender inequality, including and especially violence against women. This is precisely where the race, class, and gender paradigm helps us to make visible the complexities of the social problem (Zinn and Dill 2005; Davis 1983; King 1988).

In the next chapter I will examine the cultural supports for IPV, namely the ways in which constructions of masculinity and feminity create rigid gender roles that almost inevitably lead to IPV.

NOTES

1. Sociologists often use "micro" and "macro" to distinguish between individual experiences or explanations and structural or institutional experiences and forces.

2. Most research on battered women notes that access to a job and/or financial resources is directly linked to their ability to exit battering relationships (Browne 1987; Brush 2000, 2001; Tiefenthaler, Farmer, and Sambira 2005).

3. For a fuller discussion of the Moon case see especially Benedict and Yaeger (1998, 130–33).

4. It is important to point out that this is true in most, if not all, battering relationships. Push and pull factors always complicate staying or exiting decisions.

5. In contrast, most of the poor women I interviewed were from poor families who were not in a financial position to help them. If they were to move in with family, as some of them did, this often resulted in two or three whole families living in two- or three- bedroom apartments.

6. This discussion of exchange reminds me of the classic work by Mauss (2000, 10): "They had a kind of exchange system, or rather one of giving presents that must ultimately either be reciprocated or given back."

7. Josie had a healthy, thirty-year marriage that ended when her husband died of cancer. She worked throughout this marriage. Her relationship with John lasted only a few years.

8. I note that the most common mode of transmission for white men is male-male sexual contact.

9. These data continue to change, especially in the way the CDC recently conducted HIV studies in North Carolina on African American college students. See

Morbidity and Mortality Weekly Report (August 20, 2004), "HIV Transmission among Black College Student and Non-Student Men Who Have Sex with Men, North Carolina, 2003."

10. Recitation is usually reporting on the *number* of African Americans in prison.

11. I note that incarceration is no justification for intimate partner violence, but it is one of the factors that contribute to an increased risk for battering and being battered.

12. It is important to note that the exchange works both ways. Though not the topic of this book, it is widely known that women will trade sex for access to money. The classic example is that of the much younger, fertile, sexual woman entering into a partnership (or marriage) with a much older, wealthy man. In addition, anecdotally we hear about women who are willing to perform a particular sexual favor in exchange for a shopping trip or use of a credit card.

13. The most famous case being former president of the United States William Clinton. If nothing else, he had to admit to the American people and to his wife Hillary and daughter Chelsea that he had an adulterous affair in the White House with a woman who was a White House intern about the same age as his daughter.

Chapter Four

Cultural Supports
for Intimate Partner Violence

Constructions of Masculinity and Femininity

"When I'm old and getting gray, I'll only gang-bang once a day."

—Fraternity ditty

A good wife always knows her place.

—*Housekeeping Monthly* "Guide to Being a Good Wife," 1955

In the first chapter of the book, I outlined the data on Intimate Partner Violence (IPV). I have argued thus far that IPV is a gendered crime: women are by and large the victims and men are by and large the perpetrators. In this chapter I examine the ways in which American culture, particularly definitions of masculinity and femininity, contribute to a culture of violence, especially violence against women. I argue that femininity and masculinity can be conceptualized as mutually exclusive and binary and oppositional. In other words, they are two sides of the same coin. Any quality attributed to men—masculinity—will have its opposite attributed to women—femininity. Men are aggressive, women are passive. Men are dominant, women are submissive. When we understand not only the social constructions of masculinity and femininity but the way in which they are pitted as binary and oppositional we can begin to see more clearly, as I argue, that IPV is an almost inevitable outcome of masculinity and femininity as defined in the contemporary United States. I begin with a discussion of masculinity.

BOYS WILL BE BOYS: CONSTRUCTIONS OF MASCULINITY AND INTERPERSONAL VIOLENCE

What do you envision when you think of a man who beats up his wife or girlfriend? Is he a factory worker who comes home, puts on a "wife beater," drinks a beer—an Old Milwaukee—and socks his wife in the mouth when the meatloaf she cooked for dinner is not ready on time? The truth is there is no description of a batterer. Men who batter are of all races/ethnicities, all ages, all levels of education, all different occupations, and they live in all regions of the country. I will argue here that if anything distinguishes batterers from men who do not batter, it is that batterers are (1) well socialized into hypermasculinity and (2) they respond to perceived threats to their masculinity.[1]

Masculinity

What does it mean to be a man in our society? Masculinity refers to a particular set of characteristics that our society often associates with men. From an early age, most children raised in the United States will ascribe qualities such as strength, power, height, and financial power to boys and men (Connell 1990, 1995). Kimmel (1995, 2005) traces the origins of the fusion of these masculine traits with being male. The sheer correlation between these qualities and being a man in this country illustrates the path through which masculinity has come to be exclusively associated with being male. Men are "essentialized" by the traits, such as physical strength, that are associated with masculinity. Despite differences by race, ethnicity, sexual orientation, social class, and a variety of other factors which suggest several types of "masculinities" (Connell 1990, 1995; Kimmel 1995, 2005), the image by which most men judge themselves and are judged can be boiled down to a few qualities or statuses as suggested by Goffman (cited in Kimmel 1995, 5):

> In an important sense there is only one complete unblushing male in America: a young, married, *white*, urban, northern, heterosexual, Protestant, father, of college education, fully employed, of good complexion, weight, and height, and a recent record in sports. . . . Any male who fails to qualify in any one of these ways is likely to view himself—during moments at least—as unworthy, incomplete, and inferior.

But are there alternative constructions of masculinity for men of other racial/ethnic backgrounds? Some say "yes."

African American Masculinity: The Cool Pose

Therborn (1980) argues that marginalized groups often develop alternative ideologies that are more in line with their lived realities. The most cited attempt at understanding African American male masculinity is attributable to the work of Majors and Bilson (1992) who make the argument that "Cool Pose" is an attempt to make the African American male visible. They argue:

> Cool Pose is a ritualized form of masculinity that entails behaviors, scripts physical posturing, impression management, and carefully crafted performances that deliver a single, critical message: pride, strength, and control. . . . It causes the worry and pain of blocked opportunities. Being cool is an ego booster for black males comparable to the kind white males more easily find through attending good schools, landing prestigious jobs and bringing home decent wages. (1992, 4–5)

Majors and Bilson argue further that African American men are on a disturbing roller coaster ride through black male pathology. It is here that one finds not only failure in school but also extreme violence and criminality, hyper drug use and abuse, and an illogical connection to parenting that preferences one night stands to taking care of children. They conclude that African American men construct their masculinity behind masks, worn to survive not only their second-class status but also their environment (Majors and Bilson 1992).

Therborn (1980) also contends, as do others (see Hattery 2001b) that the behavior of members of marginalized groups is shaped by both these alternative ideologies but also by the hegemonic ideology. Thus, the construction of black masculinity is shaped not only by the lived realities of African American men but also in response to the more general constructions of masculinity (read "white" masculinity) and in response to institutionalized racism.

Duneier (1992) articulates the differences between white men and African American men and the masculinity issues that African American men face on a daily basis. Billy Black—a regular at Valois Cafeteria where Duneier did his ethnographic work for *Slim's Table*—articulates his perception of "black masculinity":

> People fight all the time. It's the only way to iron out your disagreements. I never mistreated my wife once in all the years we was married. . . . Men have to be tough-skinned. You white folks are apologetic and intelligent with women. But that is the problem the white man has with women. And Black folks have trouble then they try to be like White folks in this way. Women like to think they are needed but that you have taken control of them. They don't want an understanding like "He's gonna be nice to me in this way and I'm gonna be nice to

him in that way." Emotions don't run like that. Through all his education, the White man has dulled the edges. When it comes to women and man relations, White people have a tendency to be too damn intellectual. Now that is one of the true prerequisites of making love. It's the emotion, the passion. You don't have time to ask a woman what kind of degree she has. You see what I'm saying? . . . But we is not savage Mitch. Hit my wife, never. When we would have a fight, I would just lock the bedroom door, lock all the windows down, and then I go to sleep. (Duneier 1992, 44)

Duneier's capture of Billy Black's perspective on masculinity (as well as others who frequented the cafeteria on a daily basis) demonstrates that at least some African American men, including many whom I interviewed, adhere strongly to the tenets of patriarchy and hegemonic ideology even though they may be simultaneously on the margins: poor, unemployed, in bad health, and/or in prison.

The power of patriarchy coupled with constructions of hypermasculinity put families and especially intimate partners at peril for hurt, mayhem, and even death. Though the particular constructions of masculinity may vary across race and ethnic groups, what is interesting about IPV is the degree to which it is remarkably consistent across all lines of demarcation and social status locations.

Discourses of Masculinity

Certain well-known men in our culture would be readily identifiable as "men's men," or "manly men." Most of the exemplars or "ideal types," as Weber would call them, come from the realms of sports, entertainment, politics, and occasionally from the world of big business. What do these men have in common? They are successful, affluent, "strong," good-looking, mostly white, and according to popular discourse, they have multiple female sex partners. Regular men, masculine men, have access to images of these quintessential men by watching ESPN, CNN, or most other cable television shows. For example, recently we saw the CEO of Tyco, Dennis Kozlowski,[2] spend a million of his company's dollars on a birthday party for his wife. In the video images what we saw was a successful American businessman flanked by beautiful women.

We saw America rally around Kobe Bryant as he endured a public rape charge. Many American men (and women) just wanted Kobe to be allowed to play in the NBA championship, reasoning that the "player" status is legendary among NBA players: witness Wilt Chamberlain and Magic Johnson. Wilt Chamberlain bragged throughout his career that he had sex with at least twenty thousand women, and Magic Johnson contracted HIV as a result of having unprotected sex with countless women he did not know. The public shunned him because of HIV but embraced his masculinity (as did his wife, Cookie, who stood by him). Or even James Worthy (also a former Los Angeles Laker), who got caught propositioning a prostitute, did not fall from grace. In this regard, Kobe Bryant is just one more example of the sexual exploits of successful American men, especially those who are athletes.

These images bombard us from the twenty-four hours a day, seven days a week broadcasts on CNN, ESPN, as well as in the images that are created for music videos and broadcast on MTV, VH-1, and BET, just to name a few networks. The important point here is that a specific construction of masculinity is being transmitted to the young men (and women) who are watching. Men are supposed to be tough, strong, unfeeling, and most important, especially for African American men, a "player" (hooks 2004; Satcher 2001).

No matter that these real men whose images bombard our living rooms are different—their races, occupations, education—they all share at least two traits: financial success and sexual prowess. Kimmel (1995, 2005) and Messner (2002) have argued that these two traits have come to *signify manhood* in contemporary America. With remarkable consistency, the key issues that both batterers and battered women—who have not necessarily had the luxury of being exposed to masculinity theory—identified as "triggers" to battering are men's successes in breadwinning and the bedroom—the two Bs.

Ya she does. She um, challenges my masculinity a lot, she uh, well you know a real man uh, blasé, blas, a real man uh take his wife to like you know, like, oh just use the thing, I don't fly a lot, I don't fly a lot of places before, you know, fighting and you know, different places. I flew to New York here recently. She never flew so you know, a real man will take his wife on a plane and she ain't never been there you know, a real man uh do this for her, tote his wife to bed.—Eddie, thirty-something African American man, North Carolina

Table 4.1.   Triggers for IPV by Race

White Men	African American Men
Failure at breadwinning (not earning enough)	Female partners refusing to work but wanting to spend money; failure at breadwinning
Jealousy	Jealousy

Source: Interviews.

Breadwinning

The first "B" is breadwinning. Breadwinning has long been defined by both popular discourse and sociological theory as one of the key roles that men in our society must play.

Structural-functionalists such as Parsons and Bales (1955) argued that men and women have evolved both biologically and socially toward distinct spheres of specialization. Based on this perspective, men and women are believed to be *biologically* suited for different tasks. As a result, men have come to dominate the *instrumental* sphere while women have been relegated to the *expressive* sphere (Hattery 2001b). The instrumental role, according to Parsons and Bales (1955), refers to the activities associated with providing for the basic needs of the family. In contrast, the expressive role refers to meeting the emotional needs of family members. Parsons and Bales (1955, 23) trace our current division of labor back to our earliest roots as humans.

> In our opinion the fundamental explanation for the allocation of the roles between the biological sexes lies in the fact that the bearing and early nursing of children establishes a strong and presumptive primacy of the relation of mother to the small child and this in turn establishes a presumption that *the man who is exempted from these biological functions should specialize in the alternative* [occupational] *direction.* [emphasis mine]

Parsons and Bales argued, for example, that a man's greater ease at being away from his children for forty-plus hours per week, and even traveling away from home as part of his job, have evolved out of the time in human history when men went on long, extended hunting trips in search of meat. According to Parsons and Bales (1955), these hunting excursions encouraged a more detached masculine character (Hattery 2001b).

With regard to the contemporary American family, the perspective of Parsons and Bales has been used to conceptualize appropriate roles for men and for women. The man is the breadwinner, he provides the economic support for the family, usually in the form of a paycheck. The woman, in contrast, takes care of the children, nurtures them, and comforts the man by providing a loving, quiet home, good food, and clean clothes in order to rejuvenate him before he heads back off into the stressful world of work.

The perspective of Parsons and Bales (1955) is important for several reasons. First, they offer a sociobiological argument for the rigidity of gender roles that we see perpetuated even into the twenty-first century (for a review, see Hattery 2001b; Padavic and Reskin 2002). Biological arguments for gender roles imply immutability. Second, Parsons and Bales's argument is often incorporated into discussions of IPV. For example, I argue that masculinity (and femininity) is constructed around these rigid gender roles, and it is this narrow and rigid construction that contributes to a culture of violence against women. Third, Parsons and Bales's argument can also be extended into the arena of IPV in that it can be used to construct an understanding of men as violent and aggressive and women as passive and submissive—thus IPV is a "natural" outgrowth of the biology of men and women rather than a "natural" outgrowth of a system of patriarchy. Finally, Parsons and Bales's belief that gender roles are based in biology is the underpinning for beliefs among biological as well as social scientists in genetic sex differences. This general belief that men and women are *biologically different* and thus suited to different tasks is hegemonic and pervasive today. It is a part of the dominant ideology that shapes patriarchy (Epstein 2007).

I illustrate the point with a well-publicized example. In the spring of 2005 Harvard president Larry Summers argued that women were underrepresented as tenured and promoted faculty in departments such as math, physics, and engineering because they were *biologically inferior* in math (2005; Bombardieri 2005). Biological and genetic explanations for gender differences perpetuate the beliefs that men beat up women because they are biologically programmed to do so and that women need to be disciplined for the same reasons—because they are biologically inferior and like children need to be trained and "corrected." This becomes a convenient and popular explanation for IPV that treats it as immutable, inevitable, and individual, rather than structural. In other words, as long as battering is a result of individual men getting "out of control," then one never has to examine the role that male superiority, power, and patriarchy play in IPV. This is akin to Larry Summers's explanation (2005; Bombardieri 2005) for the underrepresentation of women in the sciences: women's lack of innate ability at math remains an individual problem rather than a result of structural barriers such as the well-documented inequities in funding, salary, and lab space in studies of gender equity at technology universities, including the infamous MIT.

Breadwinning in the Current Economic Climate

Kimmel (1995, 2005) argues that one outcome of the contemporary political, economic, and social climate, replete with declining real wages for men (Padavic and Reskin 2002) and soaring unemployment, is that men's attempts at establishing a masculine identity vis-à-vis their success in the labor market is tenuous at best and leaves men feeling threatened by the possibility that they are not masculine enough. "At the grandest social level and the most intimate realms of personal life, for individuals and institutions, American men have been haunted by fears that they are not powerful, strong, rich, or successful enough" (Kimmel 1995, 8). As a result, "American men try to *control them-selves*; they project their fears on to *others*; and when feeling too pressured, they attempt to *escape*" (Kimmel 1995, 9).

Kimmel (1995, 2005) argues that this history of using economic success to establish a masculine identity—an experience that leaves men feeling threatened—created a landscape in which to develop norms of masculinity that persist today. In many ways, he argues, the social world has become more threatening for men as women gain more and more ground on men in the labor market.

> American men feel themselves beleaguered and besieged, working harder and harder for fewer and fewer personal and social rewards. Women have not only entered the workplace but demand entry into men's social clubs. There are even women Boy Scout troop leaders and scoutmasters. The criminalization of sexual harassment and date rape has left some men angry, and frightened of demonstrating manhood through sexual conquest. . . . What's a man to do? (Kimmel 1995, 299)

Kimmel (1995, 2005) calls into question a dilemma for men in the United States. As they are struggling to define themselves as "real" men through economic success and having the right kind of woman, they see the rules changing. Suddenly they are competing *against* women for jobs they once monopolized. They are working side by side with women who have no interest in dating them. Furthermore, they believe that the rules of sexual conquest have changed; men no longer have free sexual access. Many feminists would argue that, in fact, women have made relatively few strides in the labor market—still earning only 70 percent of what men earn. Similarly, feminists and many women note that they do not have control over their sexual or reproductive lives—a quarter of women are likely to experience rape in their lifetimes—as the men Kimmel describes believe. However, Kimmel's (1995, 2005) point is clear: the advances women have *actually made* and the threat they *actually pose to men* is not important. What matters is if men *perceive* these threats to be real, especially threats to their manhood and masculinity. And, Kimmel (1995, 2005) argues convincingly, this is in fact the social landscape of the contemporary United States.

Given Kimmel's (1995, 2005) argument that in this economic, political, and social landscape masculinity is already at risk, it seems that threats to masculinity—especially those related to the two Bs (breadwinning and the bedroom), the organizing principles of intimate partner relations—especially threats coming directly from men's intimate partners, will be particularly powerful and, according to Kimmel (1995, 2005), would leave men feeling particularly vulnerable.

If this is true, and men's reaction to feeling humiliated is "invariably violent," or—in a less extreme interpretation—as Kimmel notes, if men's reaction to vulnerability is to *control*, then it seems that battering is a logical and probable outcome of threats to men's masculinity and power in a patriarchal system.

I turn now to the men's own explanations for their violent episodes. These are not justifications for battering and should not be seen as such. What they do provide is a unique opportunity to examine battering through the lens and words used by men who batter. These are *their* explanations for their behavior. I argue that though men who batter rarely offer a critical perspective, nor do they often recognize the position of privilege they occupy in a patriarchy, listening to the voices of men who batter offers insights that are important to incorporate into broader proposals for radical social transformation.

Threats to Breadwinner Role

Threats to this provider or breadwinner role came in several different forms: men's own failure as providers, not being able to keep up with the demands of their wives or girlfriends, and frustration with wives and girlfriends who wanted to be "kept" when this was really unrealistic.

Women as "Nags"

The majority of men I interviewed indicated that their wives and girlfriends failed to recognize their *efforts* in the provider role. Put in their terms, these men felt "nagged." These men reported that their wives and/or girlfriends nagged them about not earning enough money, about not being able to provide the standard of living they believed they deserved, and not providing them with the means necessary to keep up with their girlfriends and coworkers.

Eddie is an African American man in his late thirties who lives in North Carolina. In addition to owning his own painting company, he is a professional boxer. He has been involved in several violent relationships with ex-girlfriends as well as with his wife. When I asked Eddie to talk about conflict in his marriage he indicated that they frequently argued about money.

> Small stuff, you know. She's always complaining about that I don't treat her like a wife, because I don't buy her what she wants, things like I can't afford, she always throw up in my face like what her friend's husband, what kind of car he bought her and what kind of gifts he bought her. Of course he can buy her a brand new car when he, the assistant chief executive at Wachovia. And uh, she a RN, got a master's degree at Wake Forest, you know, and she complain about, oh and he just bought this 160 thousand house and you know you

married me and you supposed to do this for me and my children, well what
you, what you gonna do for yourself, and she always just nick-nagging at
me.—Eddie, thirty-something African American man, North Carolina

From Eddie's perspective not only is this nagging unwarranted—he sees
himself as a good provider who is doing the best he can[3]—but his wife is not
contributing financially to the household. "My wife hasn't worked, man, right
now she don't even work. She, we don't get no kind of assistance, we don't
get no kind of assistance, I make the money. She just get a little small child
support check from their father, that's it?"

Eddie and his wife have had numerous arguments about her spending
habits, the fact that she does not work, and her perception that he is not an ad-
equate provider. These arguments often involve yelling and sometimes physical violence that is not limited to pushing and shoving.[4]

Failure as a Provider

Many of the men and women[5] I interviewed identified unemployment or underemployment as significant sources of conflict in their relationships.

Darren is a white man in his mid-forties who resides in North Carolina.
When I asked Darren to describe the incident in which he hit his wife[6] and
was subsequently arrested he described an argument about money. During the
summer of 2000 the conflict in Darren's marriage escalated. The couple had
a particularly heated debate over a vacation and his perception that his wife
had foolishly paid too much for what turned out to be a disastrous airline
flight. The argument lasted for a week during which time Darren attempted to
discuss the issue with his wife and she refused to even speak to him. This
eventually erupted into a heated debate. While he was yelling at her, his wife
ran into the kitchen. Then, Darren says,

I went into the kitchen. I grabbed my wife around the neck. I layed her on the
kitchen floor. She rose up. I slapped her. She rose up again; I slapped her again.
And then I made some threats. . . . And I told her, listen, let's go sit down in the
living room and we're going to talk about this and you're going to listen to me.
Ok? I'm taking control of the situation, is how I felt. I'm going to take over.
You're going to listen to me, regardless of whether you want to or not. You're
not going to turn your back on me, you're not going to give me a sneer, you're
not going to make a snide remark, you're going to listen to what I have to
say.—Darren, forty-something white man, North Carolina

Darren puts his reaction into context. Rationalizing their violence is extremely common among batterers:

I was making a lot less money than I was in Washington State. And I was contributing a lot less to the household. I didn't have all the great benefits that I had in Washington. I didn't feel like I was the man of the house, you know. I was kind of hurting here. She had made a couple of cracks, you know, about the way things are different. And about if I was single, I could barely get by [laughing] on what I make, and all this stuff. In the past, she had said these things, and it stuck. We lived in a nice neighborhood—a really nice neighborhood. There was a president of a company next door, a psychiatrist across the street, a business owner down the street. It was a really nice neighborhood. And here I was; I'm a pipe fitter, a pipe welder. I worked refinery maintenance in Washington. And when I moved out here, I took a job in Concord at a synthetic fiber mill at their pipe and maintenance department. I came home dirty and I worked with my hands. I've been a pipe fitter welder for 24 years. That's all I've ever done, you know. I started . . . [laughing] . . . the neighbors were really clean when they got home . . . and I started having these, gee . . . , self-esteem issues. So, when my wife would reject me and when she would resent me, showed resentment, I'm thinking, well, gee, you know, maybe the money thing is a problem because she inherited a million dollars, more or less. She bought a 625,000-dollar house with it, and furniture and all that stuff. And here I am working at the mill in Concord. I'm contributing maybe 525–40 dollars a week to the household. And she's making all the major purchases. Things were out of balance financially.—Darren, forty-something white man, North Carolina

This imbalance of economic power provided Darren with a justification for beating his wife. He interpreted his wife's economic power as a threat to his self-esteem. In short, Darren beat his wife when he felt his masculine identity vis-à-vis his economic power in the household was threatened. I turn now to a discussion of the second measure of masculinity: sexual prowess, otherwise known as the second "B": the bedroom.

THE BEDROOM

The "bedroom" really encompasses several issues, including men's ability to satisfy their partners (sexual prowess) and to be "players" by gaining access to multiple sexual partners—over their lifetimes, or in the case of many of the high-profile athletes I mentioned previously, over a twenty-four-hour period—often through sexual conquest (see Sanday 1990/2007).

As old as America, perhaps most of the world, is the double sexual standard for men and for women. This double standard proscribes that men should or can have more sexual experiences and more sexual partners than women. The evidence for this is overwhelming and far reaching. Consider for example the fact that polygyny (having more than one wife) was the dominant marriage form throughout history and across the globe (see the Human Relations Area Files, www.yale.edu/hraf/) and continues to exist in parts of Asia, Africa, and the Middle East (Sanday 1981). Typically the only prohibition against multiple wives in these cultures is the ability to provide economically for them. Furthermore, in the United States, despite a thirty-year trend of declining age at first intercourse and a decline in the percent of newlyweds who are virgins at the time of marriage, American boys become sexually active a year or more earlier than their female peers who are more than twice as likely to be virgins on their wedding day (Alan Guttmacher Institute 2006). Finally, compare the language we use to describe men who have multiple sex partners to the language we use to describe these same women. Virtually all the words for men are positive—*player, stud, sugar daddy*—and all of the terms for women are negative—*loose, whore, slut*.

When taken together, the sexual double standard, a history of polygyny, and the acceptance and praise awarded men who engage in sexual conquest, it is clear that sexual prowess is an important part of masculinity in the contemporary United States—if not in the world more broadly. Given the importance of sexual prowess in constructions of hegemonic masculinity, men were reluctant to discuss their failures in this area—though they were happy to share their successes in the bedroom. However, wives and girlfriends were not so closed-lipped on this issue.

In some cases wives and girlfriends admitted to me that they were dissatisfied with their sex lives, and they talked about how they expressed this dissatisfaction to their male partners. Charlotte is a woman in her early fifties who is married to Perry, also in his fifties. This is Charlotte's second marriage and Perry's first. They married each other when they were well into their forties. Charlotte and Perry are both white Americans who live in North Carolina.

In discussing their relationship Charlotte talked openly about her dissatisfaction with Perry as a "lover." From Charlotte's perspective, their sexual relationship, the second measure of a masculine man, was unsatisfying. Charlotte indicated that she had to beg Perry to have sex with her and that his lack of attention to their sex life contributed to her feeling badly about herself.

A lot of times I would say, why? Please. What is your problem? It would be like two weeks, three weeks. I'm thinking, you know, I'm going to go get sewed up. I told him I was going to go have it sewed up. I did. I would actually tell him that. I said, I might as well just go to the doctor and have it completely . . . .

And he looked at me like, well, can you do that [laughing]?—Charlotte, fifty-something white woman, North Carolina

Though few men admitted to having problems in their sex lives, Eddie, the boxer, had this to say:

We don't have a healthy sex life, because you have damage in the relationship, it takes the desire away from me. I sometimes come home and she touches me. Oh you can't hug, I say, I don't want to hug. Why, you got somebody. What she don't understand, she had damaged me so much. There's so much that's been said and done until I just sometimes I don't even want to be bothered or talked to, I just want to come home, take a little shower, put on my stuff and go to the gym. I don't want to talk, because maybe that morning before I left, she done told me you can just take your stuff with you. She been said something so damaging [unclear] when I come home from work, she can just lovey dovey with me, like nothing never happened or said, and it just be so damaging to me.—Eddie, forty-something African American man, North Carolina

Though not as forthcoming as Eddie, Chris also talked openly about the problems in his sex life. Chris blames Wanda's drinking problem for tension in their sex life as well as for the violence in their relationship. Chris claims that Wanda becomes sexually demanding and physically aggressive when she drinks, and it is at these times that he must "put her in her place."

That's when I had to throw the jabs at her and stuff. But, I got in here the first time, the mess with me and her. We was in the basement and she wanted more sex or whatever, and she was drinking her E&J [brandy]. She definitely, when she drink her E&J, that's when she gets physical.—Chris, fifty-something African American man, Minnesota

One of the clear advantages to interviewing both members of the same couple is that the researcher gets to hear both sides of what is undoubtedly a very complicated story. Wanda was clear about her own dissatisfaction with their sex life. She has very clear desires and she feels that Chris often fails to meet these needs.

[Chris] don't appreciate nothing. Don't appreciate nothing, you know. There living free, eating good, got a nice, I mean, a real nice hot water running in the shower in the bathtub. I mean, you know what I'm saying? But you know, a woman get tired. A woman get tired and then and I tried my best to figure out, why do we keep taking these men back? [*AH: He isn't rubbing your feet anymore, is he?*] No! I put my foot up like this here, hmmph. Like they stink or something. Uh-oh, okay. So now you know, you're slacking up on everything, even the sex too now. Like sex, like it's a reward or something. NO way. And you know I'm a scuppy. I'm a freak, you know, I like my groove on when I want it. And you're going to tell me no? Oh, hell no. It's time for you to go 'cause I don't need you. 'Cause I got, I can go over here to Lovin' Fun [a lingerie store], I can buy anything, any toy I need and make love to myself 'cause I don't need you. And suck my own titty and everything. I'm just going to be frank. And so, all hell breaking . . . I am so serious! Ya'll laugh, but I'm so serious.—Wanda, fifty-something African American woman, Minnesota

Taken together, the sexual double standard and the prevalence of male sexual privilege—including rape in marriage—are evidence of a hegemonic sexual ideology that locates sexual prowess at the core of masculinity. To recapitulate, it works this way: men grow up learning that conquest is part of the way that you obtain sex. And the more women a man can conquer the more of a "man" he is. Furthermore, men (and women) are taught that men have a right to seek sex, and they will, and that it is up to women to act as gatekeepers, to decide when to "give it up." This set of antagonistic relationships results in men believing they have a right to sex whenever and with whomever they desire. When women attempt to act as gatekeepers, saying "no," men believe they are being denied what they have a right to. As a result, they will engage in whatever means necessary to have sex, by definition one of the rights and privileges of being a man.

Sexual Conquest, Jealousy, and IPV

Aside from the obvious—marital rape—how does the double standard contribute to IPV? Perhaps the single most common theme in the interviews with both men and women was the issue of jealousy on the part of the men. All or most of the men worried about and/or believed that their female partners were sleeping ("talking") with other men. This constituted a significant threat to their masculinity simply because an integral part of sexual prowess is the ability to keep your woman satisfied and thus not straying.[7] As a result, many men engaged regularly in hypercontrolling behavior meant to prevent their female partners from having contact with other men. This of course is in addition to the violent outbursts and beatings that were dramatic but occurred less frequently.

Each day, when C's partner returned home—he was not working but was out hustling and involved with other women—he would conduct an investigation of the bed sheets, including smelling them, in order to detect the presence of another man. Another woman I interviewed, Sheri, also reported that each day when her male partner returned home from hustling, he would *smell her panties* just to be sure she was not cheating on him.

> He called, he'd come home, stare at the sheets and smell them, trying to see if anybody else been there.—Sheri, twenty-something African American woman, North Carolina

Eddie recounts the night that he caught his former girlfriend with another man, probably engaging in prostitution. That night he admitted to beating her to the point that she was unrecognizable. If the description is not powerful enough, remember that Eddie punched a man in a boxing match, and later that day the other boxer died. Eddie's fists are, indeed, lethal weapons. (In fact, at the interview Eddie shared with us that he had appeared a few weeks earlier on ESPN's morning show "Cold Pizza" to discuss the events that led to the other boxer's death.)

> She was playing that role, you know, so what had happened was, come to find out she had got a hotel room at the Innkeeper on Broad Street, and what had happened was, I used to hang out on the street called 14th street, you ever heard of that? I used to hang out on 14th street a lot, and I seen her coming up and down 14th street, that's a drug area buying drugs. But I would call her and she would keep going in the car. So later on that Saturday night, because I couldn't catch up with her that Friday. Later on that Saturday night she was coming up 14th street and I seen her and her cousin was out there, and we was out there smoking rocks, 'cause we used to just behind trees and hit the pipe. That's how terribly it had gotten, you know, so I told him I would pay him if he would stop her when he saw her coming, when he catch her coming up the street. So he agreed, for a fee, for a small fee [laughter], so she fell for it. I gave him a rock. I gave him a rock. He took and stopped her, and when she stopped, I snuck up behind the car and jumped in the car and gave him the rock and told him to go ahead on and I told her to pull it off, and she was like, no, no get out of my car, and I was like if you don't pull off I will break your face, you know, I told her that. So she got scared and she pulled off. Now I had [unclear]. I didn't know that she had this room at the Innkeeper on Broad Street, so I had scared her so bad when we was in the car, say where'd you been, when I got in the car I smacked her. You know I smacked her when I got into the car, and she said well I been at the hotel, and the [unclear] slipped out of her, and I said, what hotel you been in? She was like I got a room at the Innkeeper on Broad street because I wanted to be by myself, and now listen. Just before he called her, she was riding up the street with a guy on the passenger side. She didn't know that I was out there and I seen her and when she came back down the street she had dropped him off and she was coming back down the street by

herself when he called her. You see what I'm saying? So therefore I said, why did you let him out, who did you just let out. Blasé, blasé, and I knew who the fellow was and he got high [unclear]. When we got back to the room, you see, 'cause I got high with him before, I knew that he used to smoke those rocks inside the cigars, so we, she took me to her room she had cigar butts in the ashtray, and I know she didn't smoke them like that, but I know he did, the one that she had just dropped off. Then I seen her underwear by the shower and her bra, as if she had took a shower and just slipped on something to come out to drop him back off, so when I got in there and seen that I lost my mind man, and I beat her so badly, man. I beat her so bad until, they couldn't hardly recognize her man. Her eyes were swollen, her mouth was busted, I had chipped her tooth, but I didn't know that I had beat her that bad, because I had been up on 4 days straight, I had been on a mission man, and you know I was like out of my misery you know, and so I went to sleep and when I went to sleep she snuck out of the room and went and called the cops, and they was flashing pictures, they were flashing pictures, and when I woke up they was shooting snapshots of me.—Eddie, thirty-something African American man, North Carolina

In summary, in this chapter I have argued that hegemonic masculinity is essentialized by two core concepts: breadwinning and the bedroom, the two Bs. Because masculinity is defined by such a narrow range of behaviors, with the greatest weight resting on these two aspects—breadwinning and sexual prowess—many men construct most or all of their gendered identity—as masculine men—around their success (or failure) at these two roles.[8]

At an individual level, this may not seem so extraordinary. Men must simply get a job, work hard, make money, and satisfy their female partner. However, examining this from a structural or sociological perspective we see that success and/or failure in these arenas is not entirely up to individual effort. As was detailed at length in chapter 3, especially with regard to successful breadwinning, individual performance is heavily structured by external forces such as the economy, returns on human capital, and race and class discrimination (see also Hattery and Smith 2007a).

RACE, CLASS AND GENDER: INTERPRETING DIFFERENCES ACROSS GROUPS

The precise mechanism by which failure in the breadwinner role triggers violence among men is mitigated or shaped by race and ethnicity. In short, as noted by Kimmell (1995, 2005) and others, white men feel threatened when they cannot meet the role of sole provider. This is illustrated best by Darren.

In contrast, as a result of a long history of unemployment for African American men and ready employment (as domestics) for African American women coupled with a long history of sharing the provider role that dates back to slavery (see Hattery 2001b; Hattery and Smith 2007a; Hill-Collins 1994), most African American men *expected* their wives and girlfriends to work outside of the home and contribute financially to the household, as noted by Eddie. For African American men, then, the frustration or "trigger" to violence arose from a situation in which their female partners *refused to work* yet desired a standard of living that the men could not deliver on their own. In other words, for African American men, the "trigger" is set off when their female partners refuse to contribute financially while simultaneously expecting their men to be able to adequately act as sole providers. What is interesting to note is that breadwinning is a significant "trigger" for both white and African American men, but the "trigger" is set off differently—the "trigger" is structured and shaped by race/ethnicity, social history, and the contemporary sociopolitical climate.

Similarly, sexual prowess is experienced differently for men of different racial and ethnic groups. Coming out of a stronger tradition of Protestantism and conservative Christianity,[9] white men are less likely to assess their sexual worth by multiple sex partners but instead focus on their sexual behavior within the context of relationships that demand absolute monogamy. They are particularly threatened when they suspect that their female partners are being unfaithful.

In contrast, African American men, as many scholars including Patterson (1999) suggest, have the lowest marriage rates of all men in the contemporary United States (see also Hattery and Smith 2007a for a long discussion of marriage in the African American community). Popular culture paints a picture of African American men as "players" on a hunt for sexual conquest of multiple female partners (Hattery and Smith 2007b; Smith 2008). Yet, they too are especially threatened when they believe that their wives or girlfriends are being unfaithful. Ironically, in the case of African American men, the majority admitted freely that they had another woman "on the side"—as illustrated by the lyrics of the most popular rap music songs—but they expected absolute devotion and faithfulness from their female partners whom they admitted they suspected of cheating. This suspicion was the primary cause of a great deal of violence in their relationships. As with so many things, interviews with women confirmed this high level of jealousy that African American women were subjected to by their male partners. While the vast majority of these women confirmed that they were not having affairs, all reported that they were aware that their jealous male partners were.

A common phrase in American life is that "it takes two." Hegemonic masculinity and its counterpart, hegemonic femininity,[10] both contribute to a culture that is ripe for intimate partner violence. It is also important to understand that the very nature of hegemonic masculinity requires a particular, specific, compatible construction of femininity. I turn now to a discussion of hegemonic femininity.

HOW TO BE A "GOOD" WIFE: CONSTRUCTIONS OF FEMININITY AND INTERPERSONAL VIOLENCE

A Brief History of Women's Roles

Across the relatively brief history of the United States, the gender role expectations of wives have been relatively stable. This is not to say that the norm of the stay-at-home mother, so aptly illustrated in 1960s television shows such as *Leave It to Beaver* and the *Brady Bunch*, was always dominant. However, as I have argued elsewhere (Hattery 2001b), despite the lack of dominance of this family form, many Americans talk with nostalgia for "the good old days" when men were the breadwinners and women were homemakers, both occupying completely separate and nonoverlapping spheres of social life. Part of the lure of this nostalgia is the widespread belief that "the good old days" were really the way things "always were" until this *preferable* way of life came to an abrupt halt thanks primarily to the sexual revolution— I would actually argue it was more about gender than sex—of the 1960s and 1970s, when women began, in greater numbers, to be educated, to enter the labor market in numbers greater than during the World War II period, and to gain some measure of control over their reproductive lives as a result of the birth control pill that was first introduced in 1960 and legalized abortion (Luker 1985).

Despite the valiant efforts of historians such as Stephanie Coontz[11] (1992, 1997) who uses empirical evidence to debunk many myths about family life, especially the myth of the dominance of the traditional family replete with the breadwinner father and the stay-at-home mother, this nostalgia for the 1950s has seen a powerful resurgence among politicians, the Christian Right, and groups with wide appeal such as the Promise Keepers. For example, during the 1996 Democratic and Republican conventions I was anxiously watching to see how gender and family issues would be discussed by various political figures. (I was doing work for a book on women's roles as mothers and in the labor force at the time [Hattery 2001b].) I was struck by the attention that motherhood and the family received during the speeches of extremely high profile speakers. Bob Dole, the 1996 Republican candidate for the presidency, spoke about the decline in the American family. He argued that the changing American family, specifically women going into the labor market, contributed to a wide range of social problems including teenage pregnancy and juvenile delinquency (*Newsweek* 1996).

Dole's message was consistent with the Family Values rhetoric advanced by groups such as the Promise Keepers. This message is appealing because it is focused on social problems such as teen pregnancy, drug abuse, and school violence, which trouble many (if not most) Americans. Who among us is not deeply troubled by recent episodes of child and teen violence such as school shootings at Columbine High School and Pearl, Mississippi, and Virginia Tech? Furthermore, many Americans do blame families for the problems U.S. children and teenagers experience. At the time of this writing, politicians such as President George W. Bush, public figures such as comic Bill Cosby, and founder of the Promise Keepers and former University of Colorado head football coach Bill McCartney are again promoting this Family Values package. In my estimation it is all rhetoric rather than based in empirical realities. In fact, though most women in the United States across most of our history have been engaged in economic production, this resurgence in an emphasis on the "traditional family" and the norm of the stay-at-home mother demonstrates its continued hegemony (Hays 1996; Hattery 2001b).

The Cult of Domesticity

Across all of U.S. history, the home has been the women's domain.[12] Reskin and Padavic identify the home as the "private" sphere and the workplace as the "public" sphere, though the public/private split—the removal of economic production from the home or farm—does not take place until the industrial revolution (Padavic and Reskin 2002; Reskin and Padavic 1994). During the agricultural era that dominated American history many women *were also involved* in the "economic production" of the farm. And on the typical "family farms" that dominated the Midwest, women were responsible for small animals (chickens), milking (on dairy farms), large vegetable gardens, and farm processes such as milk and egg production. Yet, historical accounts (see Coontz 1992, 1997; Wolf 1992) note that in addition to this "economic" work, women were relegated to the home and to all of the tasks associated with it. Of course African American women were also highly involved in agricultural work, though for centuries their involvement brought no economic advantage to their families as a result of the system of chattel slavery and the system of sharecropping that later replaced it (Hattery and Smith 2007a).[13]

Earlier in the chapter I outlined the functionalist perspective on gender roles as proposed by Parsons and Bales (1955). Women, they argue, are the *expressive* leaders in the household, and with that position comes the work of the home. Engels (1884) wrote at length about the importance of this work by terming it "reproduction." Engels extended the model of the relationship between the bourgeoisie and the proletariat that he and Marx developed[14] to the home. He argued that the role of women in the family was to "reproduce" the labor force, both literally through procreation, and figuratively by nurturing their husbands and preparing them to return each morning to the arduous life of the workplace. Engels identified this nurturing as involving the provision of a home that would be a place of convalescence for the worker. Thus, women were to cook each evening a warm meal. They were to design and decorate a home that was relaxing, and they were to limit the chaos in the home by teaching their young children to be quiet and calm when the man of the house arrived home each day.[15] This ideology was later termed the cult of domesticity. (Note that Engels did not endorse this model of family life but rather was offering the analogy of the antagonistic relationship between the bourgeoisie and proletariat as a mechanism for describing gender roles in family life.)

The cult of domesticity, or the "cult of true womanhood" as it is sometimes called, is an ideology built around the idea that a woman's place is in the home. This phrase connotes the fact that not only did women belong in the home, but successful homemaking was critical in moving from the status of "girl" to that of "woman." Though women had always been assigned the role of maintaining the home and the family, the rise of the cult of domesticity began in the early 1900s and reached its peak in the 1950s and 1960s. Despite a modest decline in importance, which began in the 1970s, it remains at the core of constructions of hegemonic femininity today (Hattery 2001b).

In the early 1900s the industrial revolution was in full force in the United States, and this led to the public/private split Reskin and Padavic (1994; Padavic and Reskin 2002) so aptly describe. This public/private split began the hyper sex-segregation that persists today in the labor market in the United States. The industrial revolution ushered in wage-based, nonagricultural labor for men in the United States. As the men went off to the factories, and later the service industry and the professions, they claimed the public space, and women were thereby relegated to the private sphere: the home. Along with the industrial revolution came the urbanization of U.S. society and increasingly women's work "at home" no longer included working in a garden or tending to small animals. Instead, women had more time to engage in child rearing and in caring for the home. Especially for upper-class white women, the care of the home—decorating, maintaining, even cooking—became an art rather than a simple task. With the completion of the national rail system, for example, access to a greater variety of foods, especially fruits and vegetables, as well as products to decorate the home, was opened up to the middle class, whereas these "luxuries" had initially been available only to the affluent. And, with access to more and more foods and goods—often items that were not "native" to a woman's area of residence and thus not familiar—more and more training was required to teach young women how to make a proper home. Thus, we see the rise of "finishing" schools.[16]

For a variety of reasons, the cult of domesticity, which had become an important part of the construction of femininity in the United States, reached a peak and ultimate hegemonic dominance by the 1950s, following two historical periods when women's involvement in the paid labor force was relatively high. From the Depression through World War II, women began to penetrate the public sphere. Initially women sought work during the Depression in order to offset the wages lost by their husbands. Because it was legal to pay women less than men (the Family Wage Act), during lean economic times women were often hired as they cost less to employ. However, women were primarily hired in low-wage service work. The high-paying union and factory jobs were still off-limits for women. During World War II women's labor was needed in the factories for the war effort, and with many men abroad fighting in either the European or Asian theaters, women became the economic providers for themselves and their children. Along with earning a wage, working provided women with skills and the independence they had previously been denied (Padavic and Reskin 2002; Reskin and Padavic 1994; Wolf 1992).

When men returned from the war, women were displaced from the labor market. A series of laws made it legal to dismiss women from any job and replace them with veterans who had returned from war. Though some women happily left the labor force to return home, many did so reluctantly. In order to ease the pain of this dismissal as well as to meet the needs of this new woman, one who was more likely to have a college degree, one who had learned a trade, or who perhaps even built cars or bombs, several forces coalesced to *professionalize* and *glamorize* the work and the life of the housewife (Wolf 1992). The work of the home was defined as essential to the role of being not just a good wife, but also a good *woman*. Women were warned in television ads, magazine reports, and political rhetoric that their primary responsibility was to their home and the care of their family and that to fail at such would be to doom their entire family to certain failure. Women began to be taught about the dangers of dust in their homes, for example. And one always worried that the white-glove testers might appear on your doorstep to assess not just your skills in dusting but your success as a true woman. Television and print ads for home appliances showed beautiful, even sexy women, who nearly had orgasms vacuuming with a Hoover or doing laundry with a Maytag.

The positive outcomes of doing housework and using these appliances were not limited to the women themselves, but these actions translated into happy husbands and successful children, or so the ads told.

Women had demonstrated that they were intelligent and capable. In the absence of men created by the demands of World War II, women had managed every conceivable industry from factories to health care. But the country was not ready for women to enter these professions permanently. Therefore, entire curricula were designed to educate women on the virtues of the cult of domesticity. It was believed that women were being educated and prepared for lives as housewives, a social location that was even renamed "domestic engineers" in the 1980s as part of the attempt to professionalize it.[17]

Many dispute this claim that women were being prepared for a life at home, rather they argue that women were committing themselves to the difficult and important work of mothering. As many women I interviewed as part of another study would remark, "What could be more important than caring for my children?" (Hattery 2001a, b). Yet, by the 1960s the age of marriage was still young—around 21 for women—as was the age of first childbirth. Fertility rates had fallen to 2.5 children per woman, and life expectancy was longer—around 72 for women. The typical woman in the United States could expect to have launched her children by her early forties and have another twenty-five to thirty years to live. If women were staying home just for the important work of child-rearing, then we would expect to see these women enter or return to the labor force in their forties when their children were "launched." However, this did not happen. Why? Because, the cult of domesticity glorified not just childrearing, but housework. Women were being educated to be good wives, not just good mothers, both of which were essential qualities of good women. The socialization girls were receiving for their future roles as wives was simultaneously constructed as formal education for this "career."

While the boys in high school were taking "shop" class and gaining skills that would serve them in the labor market, specifically in entering the highly paid, unionized trades, women were taking "home ec," learning skills that would serve them as they strove toward the ultimate goal: being a good wife, as defined by the cult of domesticity. I include in its entirety, an illustration of what young women in the 1950s were learning about what it meant to be a good wife (see box 4.1). This kind of course is also depicted in the film *Mona Lisa Smile*.

Setting aside for a minute one's like or dislike of this sort of "advice," let us consider the impact of this prescription on status, power, and ultimately violence.

First, I argue that this is not simply "advice," which implies that one can either take it or leave it. This message was not up for debate. Young women were being instructed by their teachers in regular classes (not clubs or voluntary activities) in how to be a good wife. A young woman could read a magazine such as *Ladies' Home Journal* or watch the television and be bombarded with images of women's success—as wives—being inextricably linked to their use of appliances. And, relaxing in front of popular television shows of the time, which would have included *Leave It to Beaver*, women (and men) were bombarded with a clear, essentializing message that being a successful woman was achieved exclusively by being a good wife. Being instructed in such a message in the landscape of the 1950s would have cemented the importance of adopting the "wife" role in the marriage. This was not optional.

Furthermore, it is important to realize the power of defining masculinity, as was discussed in the earlier part of this chapter, in relation to work, while defining femininity in relation to the relationship. One definition leads to independence and the other to dependence. A man's ability to have a roof over his head and food in his stomach was tied to his ability to work and earn a living. A woman's ability to have a roof over her head and food in her stomach was tied to finding a man, keeping him, and more important, relied on his generosity toward her.

Young women today may no longer be indoctrinated into lives of second-class citizenship through such glaring messages as this, but the cult of domesticity remains hegemonic. While writing this book I saw an ad run several times each day, during the day, on the Cable News Network (CNN). The ad begins with a white man saying "What do women really want?" and a picture of a dozen red roses appears. He then says, "A vacuum cleaner!" and the roses are replaced with an Oreck vacuum cleaner. Perhaps the images are *not* less glaring today. Further evidence for the proliferation of these messages can be found in examining the publications and websites of many conservative, "family oriented" organizations. For example, the Promise Keepers, an organization that influences literally millions of American men, posts the following message on their website:

> The role of women is not a topic we address at our events; however, we do believe husbands are called to love their wives just as Christ loved the church (Ephesians 5:25).
>
> A Promise Keeper is committed to building strong marriages and families through love, protection, and biblical values. This is certainly good news for women.

Box 4.1.   The Good Wife's Guide

From *Housekeeping Monthly*, 13 May, 1955.

- Have dinner ready. Plan ahead, even the night before, to have a delicious meal ready on time for his return. This is a way of letting him know that you have been thinking about him and are concerned about his needs. Most men are hungry when they get home and the prospect of a good meal is part of the warm welcome needed.
- Prepare yourself. Take 15 minutes to rest so you'll be refreshed when he arrives. Touch up your make-up, put a ribbon in your hair and be fresh-looking. He has just been with a lot of work-weary people.
- Be a little gay and a little more interesting for him. His boring day may need a lift and one of your duties is to provide it.
- Clear away the clutter. Make one last trip through the main part of the house just before your husband arrives. Run a dustcloth over the tables.
- During the cooler months of the year you should prepare and light a fire for him to unwind by. Your husband will feel he has reached a haven of rest and order, and it will give you a lift too. After all, catering to his comfort will provide you with immense personal satisfaction.
- Minimize all noise. At the time of his arrival, eliminate all noise of the washer, dryer or vacuum. Encourage the children to be quiet.
- Be happy to see him.
- Greet him with a warm smile and show sincerity in your desire to please him.

- Listen to him. You may have a dozen important things to tell him, but the moment of his arrival is not the time. Let him talk first—remember, his topics of conversation are more important than yours.
- Don't greet him with complaints and problems.
- Don't complain if he's late for dinner or even if he stays out all night. Count this as minor compared to what he might have gone through at work.
- Make him comfortable. Have him lean back in a comfortable chair or lie him down in the bedroom. Have a cool or warm drink ready for him.
- Arrange his pillow and offer to take off his shoes. Speak in a low, soothing and pleasant voice.
- Don't ask him questions about his actions or question his judgment or integrity. Remember, he is the master of the house and as such will always exercise his will with fairness and truthfulness. You have no right to question him.
- A good wife always knows her place.

Note: There is some debate about the authenticity of this particular "guide" but many women I spoke with who were in high school in the 1950s, including my own mother, verified that these guides did exist and were part of the high school curriculum many girls received.

I ask, is this really good news for women? In these posts the Promise Keepers are encouraging men to love and honor their wives. Yet, they are also promoting a form of marriage that is inherently based on inequality and patriarchy. This might be good news for a woman if her husband is a good, honorable man who encourages her to seek equality, but it implies that even in his support of her, he is rendering her to be dependent on him.

A tour of Amazon.com or a stroll through Borders reveals a plethora of books instructing women on the benefits of giving over power to their husbands, or these days, "partners." And, lest you believe these ideas are simply relics from a time gone by, Laure Doyle authored several books in the late 1990s and early 2000s that offer women advice on how to become submissive to their husbands. For example, her book, *The Surrendered Wife: A Practical Guide to Finding Intimacy, Passion, and Peace with Your Man*, published in 1999 and released in paperback in 2001, offers just this advice. A careful examination of the chapter titles is revealing: "Give Up Control to Have More Power," "Abandon the Myth of Equality," and "Relinquish the Chore of Managing the Finances." I offer an excerpt to illustrate my point:

Respect means that when he takes the wrong freeway exit you don't correct him by telling him where to turn. It means that if he keeps going in the wrong direction you will go past the state line and still not correct what he's doing. In fact, no matter what your husband does, you will not try to teach, improve, or correct him. That is the essence of a surrendered wife.

Perhaps more troubling than the advice that you should allow your husband to behave stupidly, as this excerpt seems to advise, is the advice to give up management of the finances. One of the critical barriers to leaving that battered women face is lack of access to financial resources (Browne 1987; Gelles 1997; Koss et al. 1994; Tiefenthaler et al. 2005).

It is precisely this power imbalance that Engels had in mind when he compared the relationships in a marriage to those in the economy. "How to Be a Good Wife" and *The Surrendered Wife* are not simply guides to pampering a husband. Read carefully, they say a wife should put her husband's needs above her own, that her problems are less important than his, that he can behave however he chooses, even staying out all night, a right he has earned by working so hard. In fact, these guides to being a good/surrendered wife are guides for women to accept their status as second-class citizens, to accept male domination: the Christlike man, we are reminded, is the master of the house, and you are not to question his decisions.

The Surrendered Wife and IPV

When one reads books like *The Surrendered Wife* or the postings on websites such as the Promise Keepers and similar websites for Christian women, one quickly finds that the rhetoric is justified by a caveat about the "good husband." Women's concerns about giving up power are dismissed by suggesting that a good man will not take advantage. Perhaps this is true, but this approach has several troubling problems.

The Surrendered Wife and the Master of BS

When men and women in America enter partnerships they do so in the social landscape outlined in this chapter. Men are socialized to believe that masculinity means earning a good wage and being the master in the bedroom. And, as both the batterers and the partners of violent men confirm, when some men experience threats to their masculine identity, they engage in IPV. They slap, kick, punch, blacken eyes, break bones, bite, call their partners horrible names, and some even rape their partners. When women enter these partnerships believing they are second-class citizens, that men should have total sexual freedom, that women should serve their men's every need, that they should put men's needs above their own, they remain vulnerable to these slaps, kicks, and blows that injure and sometimes kill them.

Accepting even a *portion* of this inequality leaves women at risk for abuse. Thus structured inequality, and the acceptance of it, creates a set of social arrangements that results in 4 million acts of IPV *reported* per year. Perhaps the most troubling part of this is the pattern—which has increased in the last decade or so—of women encouraging other women to accept this form of oppression and second-class citizenship. Even if your partner never strikes you, what are the outcomes when women in the United States actively *pursue* their own oppression by offering and adopting advice such as this? What kinds of marriages and partnerships develop under patriarchy? Unfortunately the statistics on IPV and the stories of battered women tell us that millions of women in the United States live as second-class citizens not only in the public sphere where they experience sexual harassment (MacKinnon 1989) and wage discrimination (Padavic and Reskin 2002; Reskin and Padavic 1994) but in the private sphere where they are subjected to millions of acts of violence, emotional abuse, and rape per year. Candy's story that was detailed in chapter 2 illustrates aptly that in some cases women accept oppression and abuse in the private sphere in order to avoid it in public.

ECONOMIC DEPENDENCY AND IPV

One of the clearest and most problematic outcomes of these hegemonic constructions of femininity is the high probability for women in these relationships to have limited or no access to the economic resources of the family. Women earn less than men, a situation which many feminists argue leaves them dependent on men and even requires that they be partnered with men (Browne 1987; Engels 1884; Eggebeen and Hawkins 1990; Hattery 2001b; Hochschild 1989; Rich 1980, 1995). This situation is worsened when women are denied access to the household resources, a portion of which they may have earned. When a woman finds herself in a troubled relationship, one that may include emotional, physical, and/or sexual abuse, she may be unable to access the financial resources she needs in order to successfully leave the relationship. Thus, this proscription for women to give over their finances to their male partners sets up a context that is quite dangerous for women.

Anyone who has talked with or interviewed women in a battered women's shelter knows that in many cases they flee with only the clothes on their backs and any possessions they can fit into a duffle bag. Sometimes they drive broken-down cars, like C, whom we interviewed in the shelter, who drove from South Carolina to North Carolina, in the winter, in a 10- to 12-year-old SUV with a broken sunroof. She recalls that the sunroof actually blew off the SUV while she was traveling seventy miles per hour on an interstate highway.

Her young son held a garbage bag up on the roof to prevent the sleet and snow from coming into the car.

Many women who flee violence find themselves with nothing more than the clothes they escaped in. They find themselves homeless, living in a shelter, faced with the challenge of setting up a new life, finding a job in a new city or state, saving up the money for a rent deposit, and all within sixty to ninety days of arriving at the shelter, depending on the policies of that particular shelter. Thus, the outcomes of economic dependency that is engendered by hegemonic femininity can be devastating.

Compulsory Heterosexuality

For a hundred or more years, feminists have been debating the costs and benefits of marriage for women. Among the first marriage "resistors" was Charlotte Perkins Gilman. She argued that marriage required that women give up their identity and their power and become nothing more than cooks and maids for their husbands.[18]

A hundred years later, Adrienne Rich (1980, 1995) argued that hegemonic femininity and wage discrimination required women to seek partnerships with men. Rich argues that according to the tenets of the cult of domesticity women are not "true women" until they are married and mothers. A 35- or 40-year-old man, depending on his social status, may be defined as an "eligible bachelor." Yet, a woman of similar status is an "old maid." Conventional wisdom holds that a woman is better off with *any* man than *no man at all*. Second, Rich argues, that because of the severe wage discrimination women face in the labor market it is virtually impossible for them to achieve middle-class status or better unless they have the benefit of a man's wages.[19] Thus marriage is a virtual economic necessity except for the small percentage of women who either inherit wealth or achieve in the well-paying professions.

Often at the end of an interview with a woman who has spent an hour or two or more telling of her experiences with IPV, frequently at the hands of more than one man, I would ask her, "So, what's next? Are you going back to him? Have you had enough of men for a while?" And so often the answer she gave is that she is going back or already has or has moved on to yet another male partner.

Compulsory Heterosexuality: The Penis

Cheri had been involved in a series of abusive relationships. When I asked her why, after successfully leaving an abusive relationship, she jumped so quickly into another only a few months later, she responded:

I'm a Sunday school teacher. My grandmother says, well, does God approve of going to clubs and just putting all my business out there. And so, I didn't say anything. So the next week came and met my little friend and I'm hanging out with him and my mom's locking me out now. And here it is July, and *I don't go seven months without no penis*, even though I know some people go longer than that. I was like, well, that's pretty good for a 24-year-old who was active every day. That's what I was saying to myself you know.—Cheri, twenty-something African American woman, North Carolina

The desire for a penis, a man with whom she can have a sexual relationship, is really a less sophisticated articulation of Rich's point. Women often define themselves in relation to the men in their lives. They are someone's girlfriend or wife. And, the sentiment expressed by this woman, one that I commonly heard, identifies this constant need to be in a relationship in order to feel complete. Of all the women I interviewed, more than thirty-five, almost none had spent any time "single," not in a relationship with a man, from the time they were in their early teens.[20]

Compulsory Heterosexuality: Economic Dependency

Economic dependency can trap women with abusive men, but it can also be a strong pull into relationships. Many of the women I interviewed indicated that what initially attracted them to their boyfriends/husbands was their ability to "pay the rent" or feed the children. Connie recounted meeting a boyfriend who would later abuse her: She was out in the front yard with several children, some of them hers. It was her birthday. This man drove by and told her she was pretty. He asked if he could get her anything and she smiled and said lunch for the children. He returned a few minutes later with *two buckets* of Kentucky Fried Chicken, enough to feed all the children. That night they went out on a date and within weeks they were living together. Yes, he was paying the rent, but he was also already abusing her.

And then I meet my son's father which is Gary. It was my birthday. And I was feeling—I had, like, fifteen hundred dollars in my pocket and I was stupid and blue and sad and just so depressed. And he walks up. And I'm outside, and I have all my nieces and nephews, there was, like, twenty of them—and he was, like "a pretty girl like you shouldn't . . . "—I was drinking, like, vodka—and he was, like "a pretty girl like you shouldn't be drinking vodka; you should be drinking something else like Courvoisier or Hennessey." And I was, like "well, [I do if] you buy it." And he bought it. And I was like, well, "I'm hungry"— 'cause I wasn't really interested—so I'm like "I'm hungry" he was like "well, that's no problem, I can feed you." And I'm like, "well all of these kids are mine, you know? feed them too." And he went and he got two big boxes of

Kentucky Fried Chicken and he brung me Hennessey [cognac].—Connie,
twenty-something African American woman, North Carolina

When I asked battered women what qualities they hoped or planned to look
for in the next man in their lives, the most common was that he be employed,
that he have a J-O-B. This underscores, especially for many of the African
American women I interviewed, the relationship among wage discrimination,
unemployment, and IPV.

Perhaps the saddest of all the stories I collected was that of a young woman
named Sally. The abuse in her life began with her father who molested her
and prostituted her out in the drink house[21] he owned. She lived in several
abusive relationships including her most recent. When I interviewed her in
the shelter, only a few weeks after she had successfully escaped the violence
her partner perpetrated against her, I asked her about her plan for the future.
She told me that she had no money, no job, and had lost custody of her three
older children (the youngest lived with her in the shelter). In order to regain
custody of these three young girls she needed to have a "home." Therefore,
she had already moved in with a man she met "in the neighborhood." He was
paying the rent, and this allowed her to move out of the shelter. Given that she
has never been in a relationship that does not include violence, I suspect that
she has once again traded her personal safety for a roof over her head. A
choice no woman should ever have to make.

RACE, CLASS, GENDER ANALYSIS

As I have argued elsewhere (Hattery 2001b), hegemonic ideologies, by definition, dominate the ideological landscape for all people living in the United
States, and yet many individual actors, especially racial and ethnic minorities
and the poor, may resist the hegemonic ideology and/or develop noncon-
forming ideologies (see Hattery 2001a; Therborn 1980).

I would argue that acceptance of and resistance to hegemonic femininity
varies across race/ethnicity and class groups. For example, the degree to
which women adopt the culture of domesticity has varied. In fact, historically,
white middle-class women have employed African American women and
Latinas as domestics (see Romero 1992), enlisting them as "partners" in fulfilling the quest for domestic success. These women, who were working long
hours for low wages, had very little time or energy left to focus on their own
homes or children. Furthermore, as many scholars have noted (see Hattery,
2001a; Hill-Collins 1994; Romero 1992; Segura 1994), the opportunity to be
a stay-at-home mother has eluded most women of color and poor whites, even

during the 1950s and 1960s when this traditional family form dominated in the white middle-class community.

Some might look at the gap in marriage rates, especially between African American and white women, as further evidence that African American women are more likely to resist the cult of domesticity than are their white counterparts. However, based on interviews with both African American and white women,[22] I argue that though marriage rates differ (and there are many explanations for this (Burton 1990; Hattery and Smith 2007a; Patterson 1999), *heterosexual partnering* did not vary. In other words, despite the fact that very few of the African American women I interviewed were legally married (10 percent), and almost all of the white women I interviewed were, no difference existed in the likelihood of being in a partnership or committed relationship; African American women were simply less likely to *marry* their intimate partners.

The second part of compulsory heterosexuality, economic dependence on men, does vary by one's membership in various social categories. Women with little education, few job skills, few resources in their families of orientation, and poor women of all race/ethnic groups are more likely to remain with men or move in with them shortly into the relationship than are middle-class and affluent women. And because African American women are more likely to have less education, less human capital, less education, and less accumulated wealth[23] than their white counterparts, they are more vulnerable to IPV than are white women (Tjaden and Thoennes 2000).

In contrast, white women, who are less likely to be employed, experience a different vulnerability to IPV. White women may be less likely to seek out a man for economic support initially, but once they are involved in the relationship and have begun childbearing, they are more likely to be out of the labor force as stay-at-home mothers and thus may be forced to *stay* with an abusive partner longer. In contrast, African American women, who are more likely to be employed but earning low wages, may seek male partners in order to meet their basic financial needs. But because African American women have always had and continue to have overall higher rates of employment (see Hill-Collins 1994) despite the fact that these jobs are most likely to be low-wage, by virtue of being employed African American women have more access to opportunities such as contacts, friends who will intervene or help, even their own wages, all of which are necessary to leave abusive relationships. Thus, as illustrated previously, African American women may be more likely to leave abusive relationships than their white counterparts, but because by and large they have limited access to jobs that pay a living wage and accumulated wealth, they will frequently bounce from one abusive relationship quickly into another.

In other words, just as threats to the breadwinner role exist for all men even while being shaped by race and class, economic vulnerability is experienced by all women, though the form this vulnerability takes is significantly shaped by race and social class.

CONCLUSION

Intimate partner violence is a cause of great injury to many women and even becomes fatal for some. It is easy to argue that "bad" men batter and that "weak" women submit to it or will not leave. These explanations are compelling because they focus on individual explanations and because they suggest that as long as women marry "good" men and not "bad" men, they will be fine.

As I argued at the outset of this book, one of the most powerful contributions and advantages of the research design I employed is the fact that both men and women were interviewed about their experiences with IPV. Very few actions that occur in relationships are completely one-sided. And this is true in many violent intimate partnerships as well. I would never engage in an argument that in any way resembles victim-blaming. Nor will I argue that IPV is primarily "mutual" as Gelles and Straus suggest. But to deny that women who are battered are part of the IPV equation is to rely only on the analyses and proposals for change that our foremothers (Lenore Walker, Susan Brownmiller, and others) and to a lesser extent forefathers (Richard Gelles and Murray Straus) offered. A higher level of understanding can be reached only when the experiences of both members of the couple—the battered woman and the man who batters her—are considered and understood. This philosophy is no better illustrated than in these discussions of hegemonic masculinity and hegemonic femininity.

Rule Enforcement and Role Enforcement

I offer here a more complex way of understanding battering through the framework of hegemonic masculinity and femininity. First, consider the assertion that Murray Straus made that the marriage license is a hitting license, that men batter because they can. I extend this argument by suggesting that men also batter because it works. I refer to this as rule enforcement. I refer the reader to chapter 2 and the description Fred gave of wanting his Sunday dinner on the table at 1 p.m. When his wife was running late and failed to get dinner on the table at 1 p.m. Fred would sometimes beat her. This can be interpreted as rule enforcement. When Fred's wife failed to do what he expected, he disciplined her in an attempt to change her behavior. This analysis of battering is very similar to the argument Straus and others in the family violence tradition have made, for example, that parents spank their children in order to change their behavior.

However, Fred's behavior can also be interpreted as role enforcement. When Fred's wife fails to deliver dinner at 1 p.m. Fred can interpret this as an insult to his masculinity and a failure on his wife's part to meet the role expectations associated with the duties of the wife. Fred's wife is not only failing to provide his meal on time, but she is failing to treat him with the respect he deserves as a man. Her role, as Engels described it, is to provide an environment of rejuvenation for her husband, and a major part of that rejuvenation is to nourish him. When she does not deliver his meal on time she is disregarding her role as a good wife. We can interpret Fred's battering as an attempt to remind his wife of her proper place in the home and her obligations as his wife. I argue that acts of battering can be understood as both rule enforcement (discipline) and role enforcement (the reinforcing of appropriate gender roles), and sometimes as both simultaneously (as in the case of Fred). Applying this more complex framework to men's battering behavior moves our understanding of IPV forward.

Synthesizing the arguments regarding hegemonic masculinity with those regarding hegemonic femininity leads to the conclusion that elements of ideologies of masculinity and elements of ideologies of femininity are mutually reinforcing and together they work to maintain a system of gender oppression—an inequality regime (Acker 2006)—that leaves women vulnerable to IPV and lets men off the hook when it occurs. Thus, both systems will have to be unseated before we can expect to see a dismantling of this serious form of gender oppression. I return to a much more in-depth discussion of this as well as a discussion of recommendations in the concluding chapter. I note here, however, that a clearer and more precise understanding of these constructions of masculinity and their racial/ethnic variations will, if employed, lead to more culturally specific and effective prevention and intervention programs for men at risk for battering. These are articulated in chapter 7. In the next chapter I turn to an examination of intimate partner violence and the ways in which it varies in interracial and intraracial relationships.

NOTES

1. Although it is now a part of our colloquial speech, the source of the saying "Boys will be boys" is Sir Anthony Hope Hopkins, who wrote, "Boys will be boys. And even that wouldn't matter if only we could prevent girls from being girls." —Anthony Hope (1863–1933), British author. *The Dolly Dialogues*, no. 16 (1894).

2. Dennis Kozlowski is currently serving a prison term of eight to twenty-five years for spending Tyco's money for his personal pleasure.

3. Not only does Eddie own his own company, but he has accomplished this without a high school diploma and with a criminal record.

4. I assert that even a push or a shove from a professional boxer can cause injury to a woman much smaller than he.

5. In this case the women were talking about their perceptions of their male partners.

6. The majority of men I interviewed initially insisted that they only "pushed" their wives or hit them *once*. If I would leave the room and my male colleague (Professor Smith) would continue probing they were more likely to reveal the true extent of the violence.

7. A recent article in the *New York Times* on "genital cutting" summarizes nicely the motive behind this practice, one that remains widespread in Africa and the Middle East: to keep women faithful.

8. It is important to note here that femininity is also rather narrowly defined, primarily by the ability to keep a good house and raise children.

9. See Weber's *The Protestant Ethic and the Spirit of Capitalism*.

10. R.W. Connell (2008) notes the relationship between masculinity and femininity arguing, among other things, that femininity cannot be "hegemonic" (he prefers the term "emphasized") because ideologies of femininity are created and dictated by the power structures of men. I chose to use the term "hegemonic femininity" in order to emphasize the power that the dominant ideology of femininity has in shaping women's behavior. Second, I do not believe that my use of the term "hegemonic ideology" implies necessarily that it is created by women. Nor do I believe that the term "hegemonic femininity" assumes any sort of dominance by women or by femininity over masculinity. Rather, I use the term in order to underscore the power that dominant ideologies of femininity have in shaping the lived realities of women. I argue that "emphasized" implies that one form of femininity is preferable to others, that one form is emphasized to young girls as they are being socialized into young women. Women have less agency in defining themselves and their roles, and in many ways they have less ability to resist dominant ideologies. Using Therborn's (1980) notion of hegemony, one that is necessarily located within power structures and cannot be resisted, I argue that indeed hegemonic femininity exists: it is an ideology of the feminine, of gender roles, that is narrowly constructed by men, that men (not women) benefit from this construction, that it cannot be easily resisted, and it is so pervasive that women are not even aware that they are being socialized into a set of roles that privileges men and oppresses women.

11. Coontz demonstrates that across most of the history of the United States most women were engaged in economic production. Black women were slaves for two-hundred-plus years, and in the one hundred years following the Civil War they worked as sharecroppers, field hands, and domestics. Rural white women worked on small family farms or doing piece work in their homes. Poor women and single mothers (through most of U.S. history this status was a result of being widowed) of all races have always worked. Rather than being dominant, Coontz shows that the era of

the stay-at-home mother, that era for which so many Americans pine, was a mere blip in U.S. history. Economic, social, and political forces combined in a unique pattern to produce a brief period, lasting no more than twenty years, when many white, middle-class women could afford to stay at home and dedicate themselves entirely to home-making and mothering. See both Coontz (1992, 1997) and Reskin and Padavic (1994) for an in-depth discussion of this.

12. This is not to contradict the adage, "A man's home is his castle." I do not imply here that women *own* their homes, but that they are responsible for all of the work associated with the home and the children.

13. Women of true leisure would have been limited to those in the upper class and women on large plantations in the antebellum South.

14. Reference to the Communist Manifesto.

15. Note: Engles did not *endorse* this construction of femininity, but rather identified it as a predominate social form and argued that it was linked directly to women's oppression.

16. It is also important to note that the exclusion of women from education and the professions meant that finishing schools and "professionalizing" the care of the home were the only options available for women who had intellectual and/or professional goals.

17. I would like to find an actual reference to the origin of this term, but will say that when I typed it into Google, thousands of sites came up and 90 percent referred to "housewives." In addition, I remember my mother and the other women in the neighborhood talking about this term and the degree to which it professionalized housework. Around this same time, white middle-class women began a fad of "striking" as a way to motivate their children and husbands to take on more responsibilities at home.

18. She eventually succumbed to social pressures and married, but later divorced.

19. For an update see Richardson (1996).

20. Though it is also true that many/most men seek long-term committed relationships, an alternative status, that of "player," which is not a negative or stigmatized status, exists for men, yet no counterpart exists for women.

21. A drink house or liquor house is an unregulated club, usually in a public housing project. The proprietor, usually a man, lives in or rents out the bedrooms in the apartment and runs an unregulated drink in or carryout service in the main rooms. See chapter 2 for a lengthy discussion of liquor houses.

22. The marriage rates of Latinos and whites are similar except among the undocumented who live in common-law marriages but do not seek legal marriages out of fear of deportation.

23. See Dalton Conley (1999) for a description of accumulated wealth.

Chapter Five

Race and Intimate Partner Violence

Violence in Interracial and Intraracial Relationships

According to the 2000 Census, interracial marriages account for only 1.9 percent of all marriages. The overwhelming majority of these marriages are white-Asian couplings (1.2 percent), while marriages between Blacks and Whites still remain least common (0.06 percent). As Rockquemore and Brunsma (2001, ix) argued, Blacks and whites continue to be the two groups with the greatest social distance, the most spatial separation, and the strongest taboos against interracial marriage. Previous research has also documented that African American–White interracial couples are viewed more negatively than other racial combinations. (Childs 2005, 544)

In the United States the racial-sexual boundaries that have historically been most strictly and violently upheld are those between African-Americans and Whites. (Steinbugler 2005, 426)

In the previous chapters I examined the roles of individual factors, structural factors, and cultural factors in creating an environment ripe for IPV. In this chapter I examine a particular aspect of intimate partner violence: that which occurs in interracial relationships.

Why study IPV in interracial relationships? First and foremost, most of the men and women I interviewed for this book were involved in intraracial relationships, while a few were involved in interracial relationships. This sparked my curiosity about the ways that race dynamics shape IPV. Second, I had interviewed both intra- and interracial couples and could compare their experiences. Third, this book is framed by the race, class, and gender paradigm, which allowed me to examine the paradigm's utility in understanding IPV as it occurs in couples of different racial composition.

This chapter is different from the previous chapters in its content but also in its approach. Because I interviewed very few men and women in interracial relationships, I rely much more heavily in this chapter on analyses of national level data, based on a phone survey conducted with more than eight thousand male and female respondents. Despite the very low rates of interracial marriage in the United States, such a large sample produced enough interracial couples for analysis. In order to provide a context for my analyses I begin with a discussion of patterns of interracial relationships in the United States.

INTERRACIAL RELATIONSHIPS

Looking at the big picture, an examination of trends confirms an overall steady increase in the rates of all interracial marriage (Wilson 1987). In 1960 fewer than four in one thousand married couples in the United States were interracial couples. Currently (based on the 2000 U.S. Census), 5.7 percent of married couples and 10.2 percent of cohabiting heterosexual couples were interracial (Simmons and O'Connell 2003). Although still modest overall, interracial marriage has become particularly pronounced among some segments of the population while it remains very uncommon in others. For example, it is important to note that among all interracial marriages, the highest rate by far is white-Asian marriages, most commonly between white men and Asian women. In fact, currently 50 percent of Asian women are now "marrying out" (U.S. Bureau of the Census 1999).

With respect to African American–White marriages, these unions are also strongly shaped by the intersection of race and gender. Those involving African American men and non–African American women, for example, have become increasingly more common since the U.S. Supreme Court ruled that laws prohibiting interracial unions are unconstitutional (Kalmijn 1993). In 1970 fewer than 1.5 percent of married African American men were married to non–African American women, and only 1.2 percent of African American men were married to white women (U.S. Bureau of the Census, 1972). In comparison, according to census data, by 1990 about 4.5 percent of the nation's married African American men had non–African American spouses, with the majority of these being white women (U.S. Bureau of the Census, 1999).[1] In contrast, marriages between African American women and non–African American men, especially white men, have historically been much less common than intermarriage between African American men and non–African American women. Census data indicate that in 1990 fewer than 2 percent of the country's married African American women had non–African American spouses (U.S. Bureau of the Census 1999), up from just 0.8 percent in 1970 (U.S. Bureau of the Census 1972).

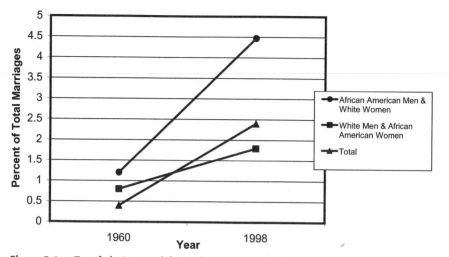

Figure 5.1. Trends in Interracial Marriage in the United States 1960–1998
Source: Data from the U.S. Bureau of the Census.

In addition, Qian (2005) notes other differences in marriages between African Americans and whites. Though overall African Americans receive less education than all other race/ethnic and gender status groups (Hattery and Smith 2007a), when they do attain high levels of education they are more likely to marry outside of their race. For example, when white women marry African American men the women effectively "marry up" in terms of educational attainment. In other words, educational differences in marriages between African American men and white women are more pronounced than in *intraracial* marriages of either African Americans or whites (Qian 2005). Qian goes on to suggest that this difference in educational attainment can lead to the presumption that white women are taking the "best" African American men out of the marriage pool, which is consistent with the beliefs that many African American women report (Qian 2005).

African American–White Intermarriage

Because of the contentious nature of interracial dating and marriage in American society—from early on to now—particularly the African American/white variant of these relationships (Steinbugler 2005), a sort of "odd" curiosity about these couples persists (Johnson 1970). As a result, we have decades of opinion poll research that examines Americans' attitudes about interracial dating and marriage (Datzman and Brooks 2000).

For example, in 1948, when the Supreme Court of California legalized interracial marriage (it was the first state to do so) about 90 percent of American adults opposed interracial marriage. In 1967 about 72 percent of Americans were opposed to interracial marriage. This was the same year that the U.S. Supreme Court, based primarily on the case of *Loving v. Virginia* (388 U.S. 1 [1967]), declared unconstitutional all state laws that banned interracial marriages.[2] Based on experiences with school desegregation and other major shifts in social life which provide examples of attitudes lagging behind court decisions, it stands to reason that it was not until 1991 that the percent of Americans opposed to interracial marriage became a *minority* for the first time. Yet, research shows that despite the liberalizing of Americans' views on African American–white unions, a big gap remains between what white Americans say ("I Am Not a Racist, But"), and what they do.

> A very high proportion of Whites claim to approve of interracial marriage, friendship with Blacks, and with people of color moving into predominantly White neighborhoods. . . . However, results based on two non-traditional measures of social distance from Blacks indicate something different. (Bonilla-Silva, E. Forman, and T. Forman 2000, 55)

Bonilla-Silva and Forman (2000) conclude, based on data from their in-depth interviews, that contrary to the color-blind attitudes of their respondents, most of them actually held very color-conscious views.

It is true that interracial marriage rates, particularly those between African Americans and whites, are still extremely low (less than 5 percent). Yet, the "strict and violent" (Steinbugler 2005) upholding of the boundary of African American–white sexuality coupled with the "central role" that African American–white sexuality has played in the history of both African Americans and whites (Childs 2005) results in African American–white relationships occupying a unique space that calls for an examination of the intimate lives of these couples. Furthermore, because these couples often experience negative reactions to their unions—violence on the outside (Steinbugler 2005)—I examine the violence that comes from within.

EXPERIENCES WITH IPV IN INTERRACIAL RELATIONSHIPS: THE STORY

In order to carefully examine the role that the racial composition of the couples plays in rates of and risk for IPV we must first break the issue down and look at each individual component separately. In other words, we must first examine the ways in which race shapes victimization and perpetration of IPV.

Race Differences in Victimization

Most, if not all, researchers who pay attention to rates of IPV across racial and ethnic lines note that IPV knows no boundaries. Women of all racial and ethnic groups are at risk for being the victims of IPV, "Domestic violence is statistically consistent across racial and ethnic boundaries" (Bureau of Justice Statistics 1995, 3). And, yet, when I analyzed the data from the National Violence Against Women (NVAW) survey (Tjaden and Thoennes 2000), I found that though the overall rates for experiencing IPV were the same, that African American women are more likely to report certain forms of IPV. Furthermore, the types of violence that African American women are more likely to experience are the more severe, near lethal forms of IPV (Hattery and Smith 2003).

In summary, the data in table 5.1 compare the percent of African American and white women who reported experiencing different forms of physical IPV during the past year. First, we should note that more than 25 percent of all women, regardless of race, report some type of physical IPV. The most common types of violence reported, regardless of race, are "being pushed, shoved or grabbed" by one's partner and "being slapped." Second, we should note that for half of the measures of physical IPV there is no statistically significant difference between the experiences reported by African American and white women. However, for six of the most serious, most lethal types of violence African American women are *more likely* to report experiencing these forms of IPV than are white women. Specifically, African American women

Table 5.1.   Intimate Partner Violence by Race of the Victim

Types of Physical Violence	White	African American
Partner throws something at woman that could hurt her	10.1	9.3
Partner pushes, grabs, or shoves*	22.2	27.3
Partner pulls woman's hair	10.8	10.8
Partner slaps woman*	19.9	25.2
Partner kicks or bites woman*	6.2	8.6
Partner chokes or drowns woman	6.5	7.9
Partner hits woman with an object	6.8	7.9
Partner beats woman*	9.8	14.7
Partner threatens woman with a gun*	4.9	7.7
Partner threatens woman with a knife	4.2	5.7
Partner uses a gun on woman	2.0	2.8
Partner uses a knife on woman*	2.2	3.8

Note: Analyses were performed using the data collected as part of the Violence and Threats of Violence Against Women survey, a national probability sample of men and women. Descriptions and data can be found at http://www.icpsr.umich.edu/cgi-bin/SDA.

*Indicates physical violence that is significantly *lower* among affluent women than middle-class and poor women. All other forms of physical violence are not significantly different by household income (social class). Chi-square p-values <.10.

are 1.5 times more likely to report being "beat up" by their partners, "being threatened by a gun," or "having a knife used on them" by their intimate partners. Thus, I conclude that though race does not predict one's likelihood of experiencing IPV, race shapes the types of violence that victims experience.

One of the strengths of quantitative survey data like that reported above is that it allows researchers to assess the prevalence of various types of violence among all Americans. One of the weaknesses, however, is that it does not always paint the picture of the violence in a manner that is compelling to the reader. The compelling stories are one of the strengths of qualitative interviews. When I talk about the fact that African American women experience more severe, near lethal forms of violence, it often helps to hear the stories. When I began these interviews I knew the statistics on violence and I knew that some of the women I would meet and interview would tell me of the horrors of IPV. Admittedly I was struck by how commonplace these stories were. Stella's story of being hit with a baseball bat—which appears in the introduction to the book—was typical of the violence the women I interviewed described. Lara describes the night she was beaten up and hit in the head with a ball-peen hammer.

> He thought I had went somewhere. When he came here, I wasn't here, so I guess he thought I was out somewhere else. And he came in and we argued, and then, the pushing started. He grabbed me and hit me with a *hammer* . . . right here. And like across my head, whatever. . . . They [her kids] heard it. They didn't see it, but they heard it 'cause they were in the room. It was terrifying. So I went in the other room, locked myself in there, called the police and whatever, and they came. By that time, he was gone. And they came, and I was just hysterical, I mean, bleeding everywhere, and the kids screaming and hollering. And it was just a terrible night. It really was. And I went to the emergency room and I had to get maybe twelve or thirteen stitches, 'cause they were in different spots. I had like six up here, I had maybe three over here, and like maybe half on my ear. It was like hanging down, ripped off, so a plastic surgeon had to come in and sew it back up. I called her [a friend] and she came to my house and picked them [her kids] up.—Lara, twenty-something African American woman, Minnesota

In sum, the qualitative interviews I conducted for this book complete the picture that the national data tell; namely that, though violence, even severe violence, crosses all racial/ethnic lines, African American women were more likely than their white counterparts to report severe violence that required medical attention in the emergency room and even hospital stays. Furthermore, the analysis guided by the race, class, and gender paradigm reveals that race/ethnicity shapes women's *experiences with*—though not their risk for—victimization.

Race Differences in Perpetration

Next I examined the rates of physical IPV that men reported perpetrating. The data in table 5.2 indicate a relatively high degree of consistency with the data reported by the women (table 5.1). Approximately 25 percent of the men, regardless of race, report engaging in at least one act of physical IPV during the last twelve months, with the most common types of violence they report being "pushing, shoving or grabbing" their partners, "slapping" their partner, or "beating up" their partner. These are also the only types of physical IPV that African American men report perpetrating more frequently than their white counterparts.

The fact is that very few statistically significant differences exist in the rates of physical IPV perpetrated by African American and white men, which is especially important given the widespread beliefs among whites that African American men are violent and dangerous (Davis 1983; Glassner 2000). In fact, the same basic trend holds on both sides of the IPV experience; just as few racial differences exist in the experiences women have as victims of IPV, few racial differences exist in the violence that men report perpetrating against their intimate partners.

Table 5.2. Rates of IPV by Race of Male Perpetrators (Percent of Men Reporting)

| | Race of Men | |
Types of Physical Violence	White	African American
Partner throws something at woman that could hurt her	8.8	10.0
Partner pushes, grabs, or shoves*	20.1	25.1
Partner pulls woman's hair	9.2	11.1
Partner slaps woman*	17.5	25.4
Partner kicks or bites woman	5.1	7.2
Partner chokes or drowns woman	5.3	6.8
Partner hits woman with an object	5.7	6.8
Partner beats woman*	8.5	12.8
Partner threatens woman with a gun**	4.5	2.8
Partner threatens woman with a knife	3.8	4.8
Partner uses a gun on woman	1.8	1.4
Partner uses a knife on woman	2.0	2.8

Note: Analyses were performed using the data collected as part of the Violence and Threats of Violence Against Women survey, a national probability sample of men and women. Descriptions and data can be found at http://www.icpsr.umich.edu/cgi-bin/SDA.
* Race differences are significant at P-level <.05.
** Race differences are significant at P-level <.1.

Racial Composition of the Couple

In sum, few racial differences are found in either the perpetration or victimization experiences of physical IPV, yet those that do exist occur among more dangerous, near-lethal forms of violence. When we consider these differences alongside the myth that African American men are more violent and the concern many Americans continue to express about African American–white intimate relationships, I decided to examine rates of physical IPV in interracial couples and compare these to rates in intraracial (both African American and white) couples.

African American Men and White Women

The data in table 5.3 indicate the rates of physical IPV reported by women whose partners are African American men (the perpetrators).[3] In order to compare intra- and interracial rates of IPV, data for both African American women (intraracial) and white women (interracial) are included. With the exception of "partner using a gun on woman," African American men are statistically significantly more likely to perpetrate every other type of physical IPV when their partners are white than when they are African American. Nearly half of all white women in relationships with African American men report they were "pushed, shoved, or grabbed." And, for most forms of phys-

Table 5.3.   Rates of IPV by African American Men by Race of Their Partners (Percent of Women Reporting)

	Race of Victim	
Types of Physical Violence	*White (43)*	*African American (308)*
Partner throws something at woman that could hurt her	25.6	7.8
Partner pushes, grabs, or shoves	46.5	22.1
Partner pulls woman's hair	32.6	8.1
Partner slaps woman	41.9	23.1
Partner kicks or bites woman	20.9	5.2
Partner chokes or drowns woman	18.6	5.2
Partner hits woman with an object	9.3	6.5
Partner beats woman	25.6	11.0
Partner threatens woman with a gun	4.7	2.6
Partner threatens woman with a knife	11.6	3.9
Partner uses a gun on woman*	0.0	1.6
Partner uses a knife on woman	4.7	2.6

Note: Analyses were performed using the data collected as part of the Violence and Threats of Violence Against Women survey, a national probability sample of men and women. Descriptions and data can be found at http://www.icpsr.umich.edu/cgi-bin/SDA.
Race differences for all types of violence except (*) are significant at P-level <.05.

ical IPV, white women are *more than twice as likely* to report at least one incident of violence than their African American counterparts. In other words, white women who are in relationships with African American men face a higher probability of experiencing physical IPV than African American women in relationships with African American men. Put another way, African American men are significantly more likely to engage in physical IPV when they are in interracial rather than intraracial relationships.

White Men and African American Women

Finally, I turned to an examination of the likelihood of women experiencing physical IPV when they are in relationships with white men. Again, this is based on the reports of African American and white women who are in relationships with white men (the perpetrators). The data in table 5.4 indicate that African American women report almost no incidents of physical IPV when they are in relationships with white men. In contrast, the data for white women are nearly identical to the data reported in table 5.2. Clearly, in part this reflects the fact that more than 97 percent of the white women who report physical IPV are in relationships with white men. Though the number of African American women in relationships with white men is very small, the data here suggest that African American women's probability for experiencing physical IPV is very, very low when they are in relationships with white

Table 5.4.   Rates of IPV by White Men by Race of Their Partners (Percent of Women Reporting)

	Race of Victim	
Types of Physical Violence	White (441)	African American (11)
Partner throws something at woman that could hurt her	8.8	0
Partner pushes, grabs, or shoves	20.1	9.1
Partner pulls woman's hair	9.2	0
Partner slaps woman	17.5	0
Partner kicks or bites woman	17.5	9.1
Partner chokes or drowns woman	5.1	0
Partner hits woman with an object	5.3	0
Partner beats woman	5.7	0
Partner threatens woman with a gun	8.5	0
Partner threatens woman with a knife	4.5	0
Partner uses a gun on woman	3.8	0
Partner uses a knife on woman	1.8	0

Note: Analyses were performed using the data collected as part of the Violence and Threats of Violence Against Women survey, a national probability sample of men and women. Descriptions and data can be found at http://www.icpsr.umich.edu/cgi-bin/SDA.
Race differences for all types of violence are significant at P-level <.05.

men. Put another way, white men are significantly less likely to perpetrate physical IPV when they are in interracial relationships (with African American women) than when they are in intraracial relationships.

RACE, CLASS, AND GENDER: ANALYZING THE DATA

The data presented in this chapter have demonstrated several important relationships. First, women's risk for experiencing physical IPV and men's likelihood of perpetrating physical IPV are *not* shaped by race. In other words, approximately 25 percent of women and 25 percent of men, regardless of race, report experiencing or perpetrating physical violence in their intimate partner relationships. However, as the data in tables 5.1 and 5.2 demonstrate, race shapes the *types* of physical IPV that women experience and men perpetrate. Furthermore, I note that the role that race plays in shaping physical IPV is *stronger* for women than for men. African American women report significantly higher rates of near-lethal violence than do their white counterparts, whereas fewer significant differences are found in the types of violence that white and African American men report perpetrating.

However, when I examined physical IPV in interracial relationships—as compared to intraracial relationships—the results were highly significant and quite perplexing. In sum, African American men's probability for perpetrating violence is two to four times higher when they are in interracial relationships than when they are in intraracial relationships. In contrast, the reverse is true for white men; almost no instances of physical IPV were reported in relationships between white men and African American women.

I turn to the race, class, and gender paradigm to explain this intriguing finding, and I offer two possible explanations for this difference: (1) the access to institutional power that individuals in the couple have and (2) the perceptions outsiders have of the appropriateness of the union.

First, I suggest that when white men are in intimate relationships with African American women (a relatively rare interracial combination), the race and gender composition of the couple mirrors the race and gender hierarchies present in the United States (Zweigenhaft and Domhoff 2006) and thus white men have no reason to use power and violence to assert dominance in their relationships. White men hold power imbued to them by patriarchy, and white men hold power imbued to them by the system of racial domination in place in the United States (Zinn and Dill 2005). Because the power in their intimate relationships is in line with the structures of societal power in which these relationships are embedded, white men in interracial relationships are more likely to feel comfortable with the gendered distribution of power in their relationships and therefore do not need to use violence to assert their masculinity and power over their female partners. Finally, because relationships between white men and African American women are so rare (as noted above), it is possible that a selection factor is at work; specifically, the types of white men who enter relationships with African American women may be different in ways that are linked with a lower likelihood of engaging in physical IPV.

In contrast, when African American men and white women are in intimate relationships the result is a relationship that combines power and oppression in ways that may be inherently more egalitarian. African American men are imbued with power they draw from patriarchy, but this is balanced against the power that their white female partners draw from the system of racial domination. In these relationships the power is balanced, overall, but it may seem out of balance with regard to the rigid gender roles Americans prescribe to intimate relationships, dictating that men be the "head of the household" (Hattery 2001b; Hochschild 1989; Kane 2006). For example, we might ask, can an African American man be "head of the household" when he is in a relationship with a white woman who has access to racial power and privilege which may allow her to earn more money, for example, than he does?

Masculinity studies and studies of men who batter provide insight to unraveling this question (Smith 2008). Hegemonic masculinity is historically and culturally bound. Yet, according to Kimmel (2005) and Messner (2002), for most of the history of the United States masculinity has been constructed around several key concepts: breadwinning, sexual prowess, and physical strength, which I explored at length in the previous chapter.[4]

When we consider the issue of breadwinning, for example, it is important to note that unemployment, a common experience for African American men, throws off the gendered pattern of wage earning in intimate partnerships. Furthermore, as noted in chapter 4, men who batter report that they beat their partners specifically as a show of masculinity in order to reestablish the gender roles dictated by hegemonic masculinity, femininity, and heterosexuality (Hattery and Smith 2007a). A man has many ways to assert his masculinity, thus one might ask why he engages in violence. Simply put, because an act of physical IPV—a demonstration of physical power—may be interpreted as the most potent demonstration of masculine identity. Furthermore, because the victim of this violence (physical or sexual), his female partner, is the very being who is the *perceived cause* of the power imbalance—she appears to have power that she is not entitled to—through a single act of violence the man is able to vindicate his masculinity. Furthermore, his act of violence creates a power vacuum that restores the balance of power to the gendered state in which it "should be" under a system of patriarchal oppression.

What is particularly interesting about the use of violence to create and re-inforce power is that the batterer believes that his female partner is the cause of the power imbalance, when in fact, as a sociologist, I note that it is the in-equality regimes of patriarchy and racial superiority that create power and in-equality in the first place. It is the particular configuration of these inequality regimes in interracial relationships between African American men and white women that creates the egalitarianism that violates the gendered "marital" contract. Ironically it is the state of egalitarianism itself—which might seem to provide protection from IPV—that can be perceived as a threat to African American men's sense of manhood and power, which in turn can provide a "trigger" for IPV (see Hattery and Smith 2007a; Smith 2008).

A second possible "trigger" to IPV may be found in the dissatisfaction, dis-approval, resentment, and even violence that is expressed toward interracial couples. I note, as Steinbugler (2005) suggests, that of all interracial relation-ships, it is those between African American men and white women that cause Americans the most discomfort and which are the most likely to draw vio-lence from the outside.[5] Perhaps the resentment that is expressed to and ex-perienced by African American men who choose to be in committed relation-ships with white women is somehow turned by these men on their female partners. Much like the example of the "breadwinner," this might be yet an-other example of the ways in which men, in this case African American men, respond to antagonism against a misidentified "offending party"—the women they choose to partner with—rather than toward the real source of the antag-onism: disapproving outsiders. This phenomenon is similar to the oft-invoked belief that men come home frustrated with their boss and kick the dog. Thus, I suggest that more research on interracial relationships focus on the dialectic between "inside" and "outside" violence.

CONCLUSION

In this chapter I have examined the ways in which the racial/ethnic com-position of a couple shapes the likelihood of relationships including IPV and the types of IPV that are most likely to be experienced. Analyses of na-tionally representative data indicate that IPV is significantly shaped by the racial/ethnic composition of the couple. Specifically, African American men are significantly more likely to engage in physical IPV when their partners are white than when their partners are African American women. In contrast, white men are significantly less likely to engage in physical IPV when their partners are African American than when their partners are white women. Thus, African American–white interracial relationships are more violent than intraracial relationships *only* when the male partner is African American; in contrast, white men are more prone to violence in intraracial rather than interracial relationships.

Myths about the violent tendencies of African American men (Davis 1983; Hill-Collins 2004; Hill 2005; hooks 2004) would have us conclude that the problem is that African American men are just more violent than white men. Yet, these data, specifically the data in table 5.2 (men's perpetration of IPV) indicate that white and African American men are equally violent, but that their rates of engaging in physical IPV are shaped by the race of their intimate partners. This finding alone moves us beyond the simplistic analysis that relies on the old assumptions of African American male violent behavior. The second finding, that white men are significantly less violent in interracial relationships, raises several important questions about the appropriate explanation. Because this cell is so small and these relationships are so rare, it is possible that the findings reflected here are a result of a statistical artifact—the small cell size for white male–African American female relationships—and/or a selection factor (as noted previously). Yet, neither of these explanations undermines the theoretical argument made in this chapter, which remains supported even when limiting the discussion to the statistically significant finding for African American men who perpetrate physical IPV. These findings force scholars to analyze the roles that race, gender, and couple composition play in the complexities of IPV.

Utilizing the race, class, and gender paradigm as a lens through which to interpret these findings, I argue that systems of race and gender domination and oppression are experienced and "performed"[6] in individual relationships and that one expression of this is IPV. I argue that understanding these systems of race and gender domination and oppression helps us to explain the ways in which IPV is shaped by race and gender as well as by the racial/ethnic composition of the couple. These findings also have particular policy implications. Specifically, I suggest that in order to design successful prevention and intervention programs, these must be tailored not only to the race of the victims and the offenders but also the racial/ethnic composition of the couple.

In the next chapter I will explore the ways in which ideologies of romance establish norms of behavior that contribute to IPV. I will specifically examine jealousy, possession (sexual property), intrusion, and isolation. I will also explore a concept that continued to emerge in the interviews: that of destiny. Both batterers and battered women, when asked why they stayed with their partners, indicated that they were "made for each other."

NOTES

1. Wilson (1987) explores these trends using a different technique, examining marriage license data. His analysis confirms the same trend.

2. We note that these laws were referred to as antimiscegenation laws.

3. Because of such a high rate of correlation between the reports of men and women we analyzed only the data reported by the women in the sample.

4. Furthermore, this construct of masculinity is so pervasive that it is socialized early on. For example, Kane (2006) documents, using qualitative interviews, the mechanism by which parents teach their children "gender" and notes that fathers in particular are quick to "discipline" their sons when they behave in "nonmasculine" ways.

5. We note that "relationships"—often nonconsensual—between white men and African American women were common during slavery and Jim Crow and were an accepted part of white male privilege.

6. See West and Zimmerman's concept of "doing gender" (1987, 125–51).

Chapter Six

We Were Made for Each Other

*Definitions of Romantic Love
and Ties to Intimate Partner Violence*

But by the time I had found that out [that he was a crack addict], I was already madly in love with him. I mean, he was my world. . . . He was my world. He was everything.—Stella, thirty-something white woman, Minnesota

I love the hell out of her.—Hank, forty-something African American man, Minnesota

One of the most frequently heard comments by scholars and practitioners who work with battered women is that they didn't see the first assault coming. Yet, as discussed in depth by Angela Browne (1987), many violent relationships include what she terms "early warning signs." In this chapter I will explore the presence (or absence) of these early warning signs in the relationships that I analyzed, and I will then extend this discussion beyond Browne's to an important issue that emerged in my interviews: destiny, two people "made for each other" and thus envisioning themselves together forever, despite severe physical violence, sexual abuse, and severe emotional abuse.

I DIDN'T SEE IT COMING! THE EARLY WARNING SIGNS

In her interviews with battered women, Angela Browne (1987) noted that although the first assault often seemed to come out of the blue, that in fact there were patterns of behavior in the relationship that were so consistent in their prediction of violence that she termed these "early warning signs." The early warning signs that Browne identified are: intrusion, isolation, possession, jealousy, prone to anger, and unknown pasts. Here I will briefly summarize each warning sign and then I will analyze the data from my interviews in order to determine if these relationships exhibit the same general patterns and trends as those identified by Browne.

Intrusion: "Popping Up at Work"

Browne identifies intrusion as the need for the batterer to monitor the comings and goings of his partner.[1] Many battered women report that they feel as if their partners "check up on them" all the time. For example, many women report that they are required to call and check in when they are not in the physical presence of their male partners. Women report being berated and often beaten when they are late or take longer than expected on a chore or a commute home from work. These outbursts of verbal venom and/or physical abuse can be set off by being fewer than five minutes late in arriving home. In a highly publicized case that came to my attention in the spring of 2004, a battered woman who had finally escaped after ten years of abuse reported that she was required to stay inside the house all day long. Her husband would call at all times of the day, and if she did not answer the phone on the first ring he would come home and beat her severely. This type of control significantly restricted her movement inside the house and rendered impossible any chance that she could step out of the house, even for a breath of fresh air.[2]

Another example comes from Josie, whose situation I discussed at length in chapter 3. Josie's boyfriend installed wire-tapping and recording technology in their home so that he could monitor each and every telephone conversation Josie had. In addition, he opened her mail, and on several occasions when she was out shopping with a girlfriend, she caught him spying on her and trailing her.

Browne notes that "popping up" is a form of intrusion. As I detailed extensively in chapters 3 and 4, many women and men reported this sort of behavior. Josie recounted how her partner would come by the nurse's station looking for her, and when he found out she had been at lunch with her colleagues, he beat her after she got home from work.

This type of control is a form of abuse. Intrusion reflects a lack of trust on the part of the batterer. It is also closely linked to jealousy; it is motivated primarily by the worry that when he cannot see his partner she is probably with some other man.

If you have never been battered or the victim of emotional abuse and controlling behavior then you may wonder: what woman would put up with this level of intrusion and control? How does this type of behavior become part of a long-term relationship? As is the case with all of the other early warning signs, Browne (1987) argues that what is truly insidious about these early warning signs is that in new relationships, early on, these behaviors appear to be simply expressions of love, and these acts are interpreted by the women as "romantic." Most Americans, upon reflection, will be able to identify experiences in the early stages of their relationships that include patterns of intrusion. In healthy relationships these forms of intrusion diminish over time; in violent relationships they increase.

Intrusion as Part of Romance

"Intrusion" in many ways is part of the romance typical in new relationships. For example, a new partner may call his or her new love during the workday, just to say hello or leave messages when one or the other is out with friends or traveling. Most women would consider it romantic if their new boyfriend popped up at lunchtime for a surprise lunch or at the end of the day to whisk her off to a romantic dinner. In many new relationships, these examples would be considered romantic, and they would not raise any "red flags."

> I would come out from work—I worked 3:00 to 11:00 at the hospital. I would come out from work and I'd see his truck parked there. Then when I would get to the house, I'd ask him, "What were you doing at work?" And he'd say I was seeing things. "That wasn't my truck. I was at this person's house and it couldn't have been me." Then just so many things that when you think about it, it's like "duh." Why didn't I see it?—Josie, fifty-something white woman, North Carolina

For many battered women, these patterns begin early on, and the women, many of whom have never been in a healthy relationship and/or lacked models of healthy relationships in their families of orientation (see Browne 1987; Lawless 2001), reported that this attention made them feel like a princess. They felt swept off their feet.

Though many of us may have similar experiences and feel equally wooed by them, these experiences amount to the early warning signs of potentially violent relationships. As I noted above, and as most of us can probably confirm, this sort of "popping up" and calling just to say "hello" usually declines precipitously in healthy relationships. As the couple moves into a more advanced relationship and trust is in place, reassurance is less needed—often the real source of the constant phone calls and messages—and thus romantic behavior or gestures, including surprise visits, become less common and may be reserved for special occasions such as a birthday or anniversary. Yet in battering relationships, these forms of intrusion increase dramatically. Calling just to say hello becomes calling to check up. Popping up as a romantic surprise turns into a way to be sure that the woman is where she said she is; it is a way of controlling her movement, and it serves to satisfy the batterer that she is not with other men. As noted in chapter 3, this sort of intrusion is experienced as highly controlling behavior by battered women and can lead to reprimands from supervisors or even being fired from their jobs. Because these abusive patterns of intrusion begin as something that seems romantic, they are often overlooked by women until the level of intrusion is severe and their relationships have already become abusive.

Isolation: Married in Thirty Days at His House

In Browne's (1987) study of battered women, she found that over time, many batterers isolated their partners from family and friends, and this had several negative outcomes for the women. For example, many batterers prohibited their wives and girlfriends from working and required them to stay at home, usually in the house, all day long. This resulted in complete economic dependence on the batterer, it eliminated any chance for the women to amass the financial resources necessary to leave, and perhaps most important, it severely impacted the social networks of the women (see chapter 3 for a lengthy discussion of this). In many cases battered women were cut off from all family and friends. This served to keep the battering a secret, and it significantly decreased opportunities for the women to leave, as they had no friends or family who knew where they were or who could pick them up and help them to leave the relationship.

Just as I noted in the discussion of intrusion, what woman (or man) would put up with being isolated from friends and family? Yet, as with the patterns of intrusion, isolation begins slowly. It is similar to common expressions of romance, and for many battered women who are leaving abusive family environments, this isolation from family may seem desirable at first.

Most women will remark that their girlfriend disappears when she starts dating a new man. It is not uncommon in new relationships for the couple to isolate themselves almost 100 percent from others. Going out with friends is quickly replaced by private, intimate, one-on-one dates. In our culture, this seems "normal," it is just part of the "getting to know you" period in new relationships.

In healthy relationships, as the couple gets to know each other better, a pattern of mixing intimate one-on-one dates and group dates or outings with friends and family emerges. Most couples arrive at a "mix" that works for their relationship. In battering relationships, however, what begins as a preference for one-on-one, intimate dates becomes an exclusivity of the relationship such that the couple rarely, if ever, socializes with others—friends or family—and the woman is typically prohibited from any socializing on her own with friends or family. In contrast, the man often continues to have "guys' nights out" with his friends and perhaps his family. As Will explained,

> Monday through Thursday are "family" nights, dinner with the family, being around the house. Friday night is the night you take your woman out to the club. To show her off. Saturday night, well that's men's night out. To do what he wants.—Will, forty-something African American man, Minnesota

When, I wondered, was women's night out?

In extreme cases, as discussed in chapter 3 as well as in Browne's (1987) book, women report that they are prohibited from working, they are required—by various mechanisms such as random phone calls that must be answered on the first ring, nailing windows shut, locking doors from the outside, covering the windows with tinfoil—to stay inside the house and see no one while their partners are out: at work, running errands, even socializing or on dates with other women.

Furthermore, in the case of many battered women, this isolation began early and was supplemented by forced commitments. Rose, an African American woman I interviewed in North Carolina, grew up in a terribly dysfunctional family. Her father was never in her life, and her mother abandoned her and turned custody of her over to her own mother (Rose's grandmother) when she was just a young girl. When I asked her about her relationship with her mother she indicated that she had not seen or talked to her in years and she was not sure she would even recognize her.

Rose indicated that her grandmother was a good maternal figure, caring for her and nurturing her. But it is obvious that the scar of abandonment remains in Rose some forty-five years after her mother left (Rose is now in her early fifties). When she turned 18 she moved away to attend college. She met her husband on a blind date and things progressed quickly, based on his wishes, not Rose's.

> He was just nice. I guess I should have realized he was too possessive or something then. We hardly knew each other. He always thought I should be in my dorm. He was in the Army and he came home on weekends and I would be gone. He would act like that's okay if I wasn't there and stuff like that. Once we got married, that changed. Then I had to be in a room or in the house all the time.—Rose, fifty-something African American woman North Carolina

Within a month or so, Rose was married. She skipped over this part so quickly that at one point in the interview I asked her to return to this major event in her life. She spoke candidly, saying that her husband never asked her to marry him. In order to keep her away from other men, whom he clearly identified as potential suitors, he began telling people that they were married.

> We never even talked about getting married, really. I just know he was telling people that we were getting married. But he never asked me. I was only seeing just him. His cousins and friends and people were saying that they heard we were getting married. We never had a wedding or anything. The next thing I know. . . . I don't even think of it as a real marriage. I don't even know what I was thinking. It was only his mother, his grandmother and uncle. They were the witnesses..We were at their house. She preached and signed the papers and that was it. We were married. [*AH: Would you have wanted your grandmother to be there?*] Oh, my gosh. They probably wouldn't want to come. They wouldn't have let it happen. I wish I would have told somebody. I don't have any family here.—Rose, fifty-something African American woman, North Carolina

This "marriage" seemed quite unusual to me. The more and more Rose and I talked about it the more it became clear that Rose's husband used marriage as a way to both isolate Rose and possess her.[3]

I do not view Rose's experience as unique; I heard similar stories in interviews with other women. As I noted in chapter 3, in some cases battered women on the run moved in with men they hardly knew in order to avoid being homeless. They understood this as an *economic* decision or exchange. Though these stories reflect more about economic dependency than isolation as the motive, the resulting isolation—even if an unintended consequence—is often as severe as the type of isolation Rose's husband intended to create.

I return to a discussion of Andi, whose story was presented in chapter 3. Andi moved from Chicago to Minnesota within twenty-four hours of meeting a man outside of the homeless shelter. She and this man shared a bedroom and soon became sexually involved. In a short time the relationship became emotionally, verbally, and physically abusive. Andi found herself isolated, by her choice and her actions, from any family or friends who could come to her aid; she was literally five hundred miles away.

Why do women make these sorts of choices to enter into committed relationships, in some cases even marriages, so quickly? The answer lies, I think, in two places: living on the economic margins and fleeing abuse or neglect in their families of orientation. In the case of Rose, for example, she married her husband because she was looking for something better, something to replace the relationship she never had with her mother or father. In the case of Andi, she moved across state lines with a man she did not know because she was living on the economic margins. Fleeing a toxic environment, facing homelessness in a huge urban area, and faced with what she perceived as very limited choices, she made a dangerous choice.

No clear pattern to becoming a victim of IPV is evident. The best predictor of being a victim of battering is one's gender—being female. However, as the cases of Rose and Andi point out, and as I noted in chapters 2, 3, and 4, certain women, especially African American women, are much more vulnerable to IPV because they live on the economic margins, a place where access to the opportunity structure is severely constrained. Backed into a corner, many women, especially those with childhood and adolescent experiences with abuse, make dangerous choices that frequently leave them vulnerable to abusive partners.

Possession: You Belong to Me

Another "early warning sign" that Browne identified in her study of battered women who have killed their abusers (1987) is a behavior she terms "possession." For Browne, possession describes the sense of ownership that many batterers exhibited toward their female partners. As noted in the discussion of erotic property in chapter 3, the United States has a long history of viewing women as the property of men.

Since the beginning of time in this country, as I noted in chapters 1 and 3, the crux of gender relations has been men's ownership of women. This is codified in both legal and religious codes. Violence toward women dates back centuries. "Throughout Euro-American history, wife beating enjoyed legal status as an accepted institution in western society" (Weitzman 2001). When John Adams was attending the Continental Congress in 1776, his wife Abigail wrote to her husband, whom she addressed as "Dearest Friend," a letter that would become famous: "In the new code of laws, I desire you would remember the ladies and be more favorable than your ancestors. Do not put such unlimited power into the hands of husbands" (Compton and Kessner 2003). But John Adams and other well-meaning men were no more able to free the women than they were their slaves. When the founders of our country signed the Declaration of Independence, their own wives were still, in every legal sense, *their* property. Upon marriage, a woman forfeited the few rights she had, and her husband owned her just as he owned his horse. Another example that illustrates the point: the rape of a woman was considered a "property" crime, not a personal crime. A typical punishment involved the rapist being indentured to the woman's husband.

Men's ownership of women is ritualized in a tradition that continues into the third millennium: at a typical American wedding the father of the bride walks the bride down the aisle and "gives her away." This ritual symbolizes the transfer of the woman from the ownership of her father to the owner-ship of her husband. As one of the central scholars on intimate partner violence, Murray Straus, notes, the marriage license is a "hitting license" (Straus and Gelles 1995).

Based on this belief that men own their female partners, if a woman engages in any interaction with another man (it need not be sexual), her husband or partner is likely to interpret this as a threat. Just as we are justified in shooting a prowler who attempts to enter our homes, men feel justified in reacting violently if they think another man is about to "steal" his woman. It is interesting to note here that most often his rage is executed against his female partner—the possession—but not against the other man—the intruder. This is much like a man setting his house on fire when a prowler approaches instead of attacking the prowler. Similarly, a man will only hasten his loss when he holds the preposterous—but common—notion that beating his female partner is an acceptable and reasonable response to his fear that she will leave him for another man.

Browne's (1987) discussion of possession refers to something more, though. It also refers to the belief that when you own something, you can use it at your own discretion. This applies, according to Browne, particularly to sexuality. The battered women in Browne's study recalled many experiences in which they felt that their male partners tried to "possess" them sexually.[4] This is a nice, and very polite way of saying that battered women, as noted by scholars such as Browne (1987) and Lawless (2001), reported being raped by their male partners.

The issue of marital (or partner) rape is, in itself, contentious. One of the outcomes of the belief that men owned their wives that was clearly reflected in the U.S. legal system was the "marital rape exemption." The "marital rape exemption" was a provision in the rape statutes that essentially made it legal for men to rape their wives. Husbands were legally exempt from claims of rape made against them by their wives. These exemptions were part of the legal code well up into the 1980s, when the last of the states, among them North Carolina, finally dropped this exemption. Though the marital rape exemptions are now gone from the legal code in all fifty states, their sentiment continues. In reality, rape is a very difficult crime to prosecute, especially when the victim and the offender know each other.[5] It is nearly impossible if the victim has had consensual sex with the man she is accusing (see Hattery and Kane 1995). It will take much more time before women in our society will be able to successfully charge their intimate partners with rape.

In addition to directly articulating rape within their partnerships, many more women, in order to please their husbands and avoid further violence, reportedly had sex when they did not want to or participated in sexual acts that they did not want to do.

Rose, whose dating and swift marriage were recounted in the previous section, described the way in which her husband possessed her. I asked Rose: "When you were in college and you were dating him, there are a variety of ways that you can feel and react to someone wanting to know where you are. Do you remember how it felt? Did it make you angry? Did it make you feel flattered that he paid you that much attention?"

> It didn't make me feel flattered. I didn't like it. I used to tell him I didn't like it. It seemed to aggravate him. He seemed to think that I should be flattered, but I wasn't. I remember when we got married, as soon as a week or so, he said something like, "Now I was his" or something like that. And then I was pregnant within a month after we got married. It was just awful.—Rose, fifty-something African American woman, North Carolina

Many battered women recount instances of feeling as if they are possessions, that their male partners treat them as such. An example from the HBO film *The Burning Bed* illustrates this point well. The battered woman in the film, Fran, whose character is based on the real-life story of Faith McNulty and is portrayed by Farrah Fawcett, is on the stand at her trial for murdering her abusive husband, Mickey. She is asked to describe the night of the murder. She recounts a night filled with violence when she was beaten severely and then raped. As she describes the rape she notes: "It was like he wanted to possess me." Browne (1987) also notes that rape in battering relationships can be experienced as attempts at possessing a woman by possessing her body. The women I interviewed also used this language. Interestingly, Browne (1987) notes that women who are raped, possessed in their relationships, are *more likely* to leave or kill their partners than women who are not raped. The stories I heard from battered women confirm this. Many women reported that when rape became a regular part of their experiences with their intimate partners, it was like the proverbial straw that broke the camel's back: they knew they had to leave.

Other Forms of Possession: Molding Her

Browne (1987) focuses primarily on sexual possession in battering relationships. However, I interviewed many women (and men) who talked of other kinds of possession and controlling behavior. In the context of these relationships, men described having to shape their female partners to be the way that they wanted them to be. And, for their part, the women acquiesced, at least temporarily, until they realized that the acquiescence was dangerous for them.

Though I heard this story repeatedly, perhaps the most dramatic example came from Will and Stella whom I interviewed in Minnesota. Will is an unemployed crack addict. According to Stella, he has been using crack for thirty years or so. He is a hardcore addict, which was evident when he arrived for his interview, at 8:30 one morning. The social worker who arranged the interview had told me in advance how excited Will was about doing the interview and that he would be dressed for the occasion. Will arrived dressed like a lower-class pimp. His hands shook throughout the interview, and he appeared to have been up all night. He was a few minutes late to the interview because he had asked the social worker, who picked him up and brought him to the interview, to stop for coffee on the way.

Addiction is a way of life for Will. He managed to keep the addiction under control for twenty years, holding down jobs in the fast-food industry, but for the last ten years he has relied exclusively on Stella for the financial support for his habit. His addiction is so out of control that not only is he unemployed, but his driver's license has been revoked for repeated DUI. Finally, he has done several stints in jail for drug use, and at the time of the interview he was awaiting trial on a drug charge that could send him to prison for the rest of his life under the "Three Strikes You're Out" drug laws (see Hattery and Smith 2007a for a lengthy discussion of the impact of this law on African American families).

At the beginning of their relationship Will decided to make Stella into the woman he wanted her to be, to mold her.

When I met her, *I had to mold* her into the ways, into the things that I like. Ok, like with the cooking and stuff. Now she can, boy, she can put some dishes together now. I had to show her, look, this is where I like to eat, this is how I like, you know, how I like my pants folded. She used to doing laundry and would pop them out like this, instead of putting the seams together. She'd just pop them and then fold 'em like that. I'd grab them, I'm like, wait a minute. You got to fold my pants like this. "Well, I did fold 'em like that. Yeah, they folded, but you didn't put the seams together. They're easier to iron this way. So you know, and then the same thing with me, you know.—Will, fifty-something African American man, Minnesota

Will and Stella's relationship started when he "saved" her from G. W., her previous boyfriend, who was also abusive. (Stella's beating by G. W. is detailed in the introduction.) Stella saw Will as a knight in shining armor who rode in on his white horse to save her from G. W. Despite Will's addiction that was spiraling out of control, Stella loves him and even began using crack and getting involved in a life of drugs in order to be with him.

And I, to stay with Will, because I don't know why, if it was my upbringing or if it was from being with GW or what, I just, I had to be with him. I couldn't, you know, and to fit in with his friends, I started using. And, but for some reason, it didn't click in with me like it did with him because I lost everything. . . . It got to the point where I ended up losing my driver's license because he had been driving and I was the passenger and he was actually smoking cocaine in the car and he hit another car. And by that point, he had me so mentally . . . to conform to him, you know what I'm saying . . . before the police came, he made me get into the driver's side, so I . . . And he took off and left me there, so I took the blame. Another time, then another time, and this was kind of like the drawing point. He had used my car and when he came back, he had a bunch of clothing and TV and stuff in it. I asked him where he had got it from and he had said he bought it at the Salvation Army. I said, alright. And he's like, well, can you give me a ride over to my friend's house? I said, sure. Got stopped by the police. It was a breaking and entering. It was all stolen. He took off again. Left me there with it. Plus there was stuff in the car at that time.
—Stella, thirty-something white woman, Minnesota

I posit that sexual exchange—reinforced in our cultural idiom as a woman "giving herself" to a man—cues abusive men to view "their" sexual partner as property. One can liken this to how buying a car or a house can generate feelings of ownership. However, abusive men fail to see the difference between such objects and their human partners. In a culture that devalues women's sexuality through pornography and prostitution (Brownmiller 1975; Griffin 1979; MacKinnon 1989), men feel entitled to controlling sex both inside their relationships and with anonymous women whose bodies they use for sexual arousal and gratification. These separate spheres of control and power further men's power based on the sexual/erotic property exchange that I discussed in chapter 3, noting that these relationships of ownership and exchange exist in abundance in heterosexual relationships under both patriarchy and capitalism.

Jealousy/Sexual Infidelity: Smelling Her Panties

Jealousy, a signal of an actual or perceived violation of the sexual/erotic property exchange, was a similarly common and a particularly threatening aspect in the relationships I studied. This finding reinforces Browne's work (1987). Virtually every man interviewed suspected his female partner of infidelity, yet fewer than 20 percent of the women I interviewed admitted to having an affair. In fact, though it was the men who expressed extreme jealousy, it was often they who were actually engaged in infidelity, and most often their female partners were aware of the flings with girlfriends and/or with prostitutes.

How can we understand this double standard—that the batterers reportedly accused their partners of infidelity and often beat them for affairs they were not having, while the batterers were, in fact, sleeping with other women themselves? This is precisely the kind of question that an intersectional approach helps to explain. If for a moment we consider Kimmel's (1995, 2005) work on masculinity, Browne's (1987) work on jealousy and the need to control one's partner sexually, and Engels's (1884) and Collins's (1992) discussion of erotic property, a clearer picture of the role of infidelity in intimate partner violence emerges. First, let us consider Kimmel (1995, 2005). As I have repeatedly noted, and in fact highlighted in chapter 4, a primary component of masculine identity is sexual prowess, and one way in which to establish this is to be a "player"—to have sexual relationships with many women at the same time. Thus, one interpretation of men's sexual infidelity is that they are simply seeking to establish their identities as "real men." Though their female partners may not like this behavior, the women I interviewed seemed to be somewhat tolerant of it, and the reality of male infidelity was absolutely taken for granted by a number of the men interviewed. One man, Akim, who had multiple affairs during his marriage, reflected that he had learned his attitude toward women from his older friends on the street:

> And they always, influenced—you know—I used to watch them. They got girls, girls girls girls. So I, I basically, picked that up . . . and actually, what they were teaching me and showing me, and the uh examples that I was getting from them, it was not right, but it was real, you know what I mean? Yeah.—Akim, fifty-something African American man, North Carolina

The majority of women I interviewed knew their male partners were involved with other women. In the case of Betty, Akim's wife, she knew that he was involved in a long-term relationship with another woman. For most of the women interviewed, the infidelity they lived with was a series of one-night stands their male partners had with other women.[6]

Though men do not expect their female partners to be jealous of other women, Browne (1987) notes that jealousy was extremely common and severe among men who battered, and that it began early in the relationship. In fact, she cites its importance as an early warning sign of intimate partner violence. Additionally, as suggested by Kimmel (1995, 2005), a significant way in which men exert masculinity is by controlling women, and this can be seen profoundly in men's control of women's sexuality (Browne 1987; Kimmel 1995, 2005; MacKinnon 1989; Rich 1980, 1995). Batterers are extremely jealous of *any interaction* between their female partner and any other man. Batterers were jealous when their partners flirted, but they were also jealous when it was other men doing the flirting. As Josie's case points out, batterers were even jealous of any platonic or working relationship their female partners had with other men. This extreme jealousy, even when it was unfounded, was often the trigger of violence.[7]

Male Perspectives on "Cheating"

Evidence of the double standard was particularly trenchant among couples living with IPV. Not only did the men freely admit their own "cheating" and that their jealousy was a primary trigger for their rage, but in fact, many of the batterers *defined* their "outside" relationships differently than they defined such relationships that their wives or girlfriends might engage in. Typical of batterers, Hank was jealous of his girlfriend and used this unsubstantiated jealousy as a justification for emotional and physical abuse. Hank's girlfriend was in jail when I interviewed him, and when I asked Hank if he was being faithful to his girlfriend while she was serving a seven-month sentence for parole violation, he smiled and said he had some action going on the side. Here is how he put it: "I gotta get my thing thing on, you know."

When I pressed him, forcing him to deal with the apparent inconsistency that he was admitting to cheating and yet would not tolerate any suggestion of the same by his girlfriend, he clarified things for me:

> Oh, while she in prison. Nah, nah, she know about it you see. It ain't cheating when she know about it. Hey, go ahead and do what you got to do baby, just as long as you don't . . . send me some money and you don't leave me.—Hank, forty-something African American man, Minnesota

Now things were clearer for me, thanks to Hank. Hank articulates what is the most common theme in these relationships: women know about the "outside" relationships of their male partners, and the knowing about it makes it OK in the minds of the men. Of equal importance is the attitude on the part of the women that the cheating is OK as long as the men continue to pay their expenses and not leave them for the other woman. In contrast, men's fear of "outside" relationships on the part of their female partners, which is hardly ever true, provides the primary fuel for their rage.

Women's Experiences with Jealousy

Most of the women I interviewed reported that they were accused by their male partners of having "outside" relationships. The frequency and severity of these accusations varied from rare to every day. Many women reported that their male partners rifled through their pocketbooks or cell phone directories. More than one woman told of her male partner engaging in extreme behavior in order to be sure they were being faithful to them. I refer the reader to the discussions in chapter 4 of women who reported that their male partners conducted inspections of their bed sheets and smelled their panties.

Though the reader might find these inspections almost humorous in their absurdity, jealousy was often the trigger for severe violence. Cindy describes the situation with her boyfriend—she was 17 and he was in his late twenties. They had been to McDonald's—Cindy's first-ever trip to the ever-present fast-food restaurant—for pancakes. After they had pancakes, he took Cindy into the woods and had sex with her against her will. Then, in a fit of jealousy, he beat her up.

> He, umm, beat me . . . he just got my nose and was like, beating me in my back, you know what I'm saying. It wasn't . . . I don't think . . . I don't even know that I was bruised 'cause I didn't want him to see. But see, he would be . . . he never checked my panties. But he checked other ones' panties. But I was in love with him.—Cindy, thirty-something African American woman, North Carolina

Employing the concept of erotic property (Collins 1992; Engels 1884) helps to unlock the power of jealousy. As noted by Kimmel (1995, 2005), establishing one's sexual prowess is critical to establishing a masculine identity. However, this is not the case for women. In fact, based on the principles of erotic property, women exchange access to their sexuality for the financial support and protection of the men they partner with and marry. Further, this exchange is exclusive. Thus, a woman who is unfaithful is committing perhaps the greatest violation of the sexual contract. Under this contract, men have a right to control the sexual lives of their female partners because the women have *become their erotic or sexual property*.

Furthermore, an act of infidelity committed by a woman is perceived as an act of theft committed by the other man involved, aided and abetted by the woman. Women who are viewed as property can be owned by only one man at a time. Thus, infidelity is akin to other property violations. Just as we uphold the right to defend our property, violence—at least against a man's female partner—is understood as a "reasonable" reaction to a woman's infidelity.

Infidelity is threatening on another level as well, as it suggests that a man is unable to keep his partner satisfied. This double threat to masculinity makes infidelity a potent act and one which can be avenged by violence. The fact that in our culture we "understand" when men go into a violent rage and beat either their female partners or assault the "other" man—we term these acts "crimes of passion"—further indicates the potency of this violation: a violation of the sexual contract is a direct threat to masculine identity.

As with the other early warning signs identified by Browne (1987), jealousy is common in the early stages of intimate relationships. Before a couple makes a commitment to each other, each member often has anxiety about the level of commitment and exclusivity of the relationship. Jealousy often signals the insecurities typical of early relationships. Over time, however, in healthy relationships, as commitments are solidified and the level of trust increases, jealousy decreases. In contrast, in violent relationships, jealousy becomes more intense and more frequent as time goes on. And, as noted both here and in chapter 4, jealously often becomes the trigger for violent outbursts.

Prone to Anger: Other Assaults and Prior Records

Many scholars who study battering report that batterers often are "serial" abusers, moving from one relationship to another, battering each of their partners along the way.[8] As a result, battered women often report that at some point they learned about their partners' previous wives and girlfriends and the violence they experienced. Among the women that Browne (1987) interviewed, most of their abusive partners had previous experiences, and in some cases even criminal records, for interpersonal violence such as fighting and assault, though few of the women knew about these histories prior to their partners' deaths.

Many of the men I interviewed had a history of violence, and nearly all—90 percent—of the African American men I interviewed had served time in prison, mostly for violent offenses and/or drugs. Certainly this time in jail and prison added to these men's experiences with violence even if their sentences were for drugs, robbery, or breaking and entering (B and E). The reader will recall that Eddie is a professional boxer whose punch killed someone in the ring just months before I interviewed him.

I interviewed many battered women whose male partners had violent pasts, but Cindy's story illustrates this particularly well. Cindy is an African American woman whom I met in the shelter where she was seeking asylum from her abusive partner, Leon. When I asked Cindy how she met her partner, she told me that he was the younger brother of her first love, her true love. Her first relationship, which began during her teen years, was with a man named Sam, somewhat older than she. They were involved for a few years and early on had a child together. Sam was abusive toward Cindy. He beat her several times, including hitting her with a closed fist in the face when she was a teenager and pregnant with their child—I refer the reader to

Cindy's description above of her rape and battering after Sam took her to McDonald's for her very first McDonald's pancakes.

Sam went to prison for dealing drugs, but Cindy kept in touch with him while he was locked up.[9] One day Sam called Cindy and told her that his mother had died. He asked Cindy to pick up his younger brother Leon and take him to the funeral. Cindy agreed. She picked up Leon and took him to the funeral, and they were "hanging out" by the end of the day. She and Leon began what would be a long-term, on-and-off, violent relationship. Soon after she and Leon moved in together, Cindy went to visit Sam in jail. She told him that she was dating one of his brothers. He asked if she was seeing this one and that one and she repeatedly responded "no" to each inquiry. Finally Sam said, "You're not seeing Leon are you? He's got a lot of problems, including being violent!" She admitted that she was, in fact, involved with Leon.

After ten years and six children with Leon, Cindy admitted in her interview that she should have listened to Sam's warning. She chose to ignore it and lived a decade with this horribly abusive man.

Furthermore, knowledge of his previous violent relationships could have been an early warning sign for Cindy. She recalled that when she left Leon the first time and entered a shelter in another town, the social worker asked her who the man was who had beaten her so badly and cut her face with a knife. When she said it was Leon, the woman showed her a long scar on her own cheek and said that many years ago he had done the same to her. She was indeed one of his past partners.

> I can't explain I let him do it you know what I'm sayin' 'cause I thought he was in love with me but society ain't got shit to do wit it you know what I'm sayin' I can't even blame it on 'cause his mama used to beat his daddy [and his daddy] used to beat his mama he ain't no mama's boy he mean he too mean to be a mama's boy I ain't the first woman that he hit I might not be the first one that he raped you know what I'm sayin' . . . he ain't go rape me no more you best believe that shit 'cause I was in the counselor's and like I wrote my kids' name down this lady very educated pretty woman got a big ol' scar right there she was doing financial at one of the shelters I was at before financial care and she looked at me she seen my kids' name (touches the scar on her cheek) she said Leon Allen did this.—Cindy, thirty-something African American woman, North Carolina

Unknown Pasts: I Moved with Him the Next Day/Married in Thirty Days

Finally, Browne (1987) notes that among the battered women she interviewed, this lack of information regarding their partners' previous experiences with violence extended as well to other aspects of their lives. The truth is that most battered women knew almost nothing about the past experiences of the men they partnered with.

Browne argues that this is typical of battering relationships and is difficult for victims-to-be to detect because it is masked as romance. Battered women reported (Browne 1987; Lawless 2001) that early on in their relationships with their abusers the men were focused on learning about them, paid them a great deal of attention, wanted to hear about their lives and pasts and hopes and dreams, and at the same time revealed very little about themselves. Many of the women interviewed by both Browne (1987) and Lawless (2001) noted that while growing up, no one had paid them this kind of attention. They were not used to being the center of attention, to being listened to. Therefore, when these men made them the center of attention and listened attentively they did not notice that the men said very little about their own past experiences.

This sort of imbalance in information sharing has many important outcomes for the individuals involved. One outcome is that the women experience an unrealistic sense of emotional intimacy with their partners. They have shared a great deal about themselves, they feel close to their partners, without recognizing this imbalance in emotional sharing. Thus, they make what appears to outsiders to be very unwise decisions, but which feel very natural to them. For example, as I noted in the discussion on isolation, Andi moved from Chicago to rural Minnesota with a man less than twenty-four hours after they met. Most, if not all, of us would consider this an unwise decision, but as noted by Browne (1987) and Lawless (2001), the level of intimacy created in this new relationship may be greater than she had experienced in *any* relationship before, and thus she inaccurately assessed how much she could trust this new partner. Consequently, she made an unwise decision to move with him across the country, isolating herself from outside influences and contacts, thus leaving herself extremely vulnerable to the ravages of IPV.

WE WERE MADE FOR EACH OTHER

I conclude the discussion in this chapter by focusing on one of the key factors that inhibits battered women from leaving their abusive partners: the notion that they belong together. Most people who have never been in an abusive relationship wonder why battered women stay. And, most women will remark that if they were struck even one time, they would leave.

This book has not focused on why battered women stay, rather it attempts to tell their stories and analyze them using a more complex framework than the common "why doesn't she just leave" perspective.[10] Yet, throughout this book, I have tackled issues regarding staying and leaving and the reasons that battered women stay: they believe that in the balance they will lose more if they leave, and/or their personal history of abuse leaves them "handicapped" in their ability to respond to adult violence, but most often they stay because they love the men who batter them. They do not like what those men do or the way they behave, but they love them.

Seldom have I read accounts that ask batterers why *they* stay. Perhaps the question seems less relevant in light of the fact that most batterers work so hard to control their female partners and literally "posses them," as noted above, that one never considers the possibility that it might be healthier for the batterer—as well as his victim/survivor—to exit the relationship. However, in talking at length with many batterers in a nontreatment environment, I learned that batterers may not only rationalize their violence as a reasonable response to the behavior of their wives and girlfriends, as noted in chapters 3 and 4, but further rationalize the violence as a way of expressing love and concern for their female partners. This is similar to the way in which some parents who physically abuse their children rationalize the abuse by indicating that "it was for their own good," they needed to "be taught a lesson," and so forth.

Returning to Hank, whose story was presented at length in chapter 3, the reader will recall that Hank describes a situation in which he would return home from a long day at work—he worked as a security guard—and the house would be a mess and dinner was not ready. His girlfriend would begin nagging him about something and he would explode. He would call her a "motherfucking lazy bitch." She would attempt to run out of the house and he would grab her and beat her to keep her from leaving.

> Right, I got a fifth-degree assault with her, as far as . . . she I don't . . . I get mad at her. And then I cuss at her. I call her out a name. . . . But I, she provokes me, for me to put my hands on her. Now say for instance, I want to walk out that door. She'll run in front of that door and tell me I ain't going nowhere. Get the hell out of the house, get away from her for a little bit 'cause I'm steamed, I'm mad. She done pissed me off. I'm mad. I want to walk out that door. She stand in front of the door and won't let me out. I try to move her. Pulling her, get away from the door. She holding the door, no, no. So I have to put hands on her to try to move her. She won't move, so I don't just hit her or anything, I try to get her out of the way. I try to . . . look, let me out. And she, that's a provocation to me. She throw things at me. She just pick up shit and she'll just throw it at me.—Hank, forty-something African American man, Minnesota

After listening to Hank complain about his girlfriend for over an hour, I asked him, "Why do you stay with her?" He responded immediately:

I love the hell out of her. And it got to be love because we separated one time, and it just fucking hurts like hell. And like, somebody reached into my heart and just tried pulling it out. But I got over it. I moved on. I had another girl. Then all of sudden, she want to come back in my life. She's doing bad now. She can't get these kids together. You was the only one who knew how to keep my life together.—Hank, forty-something African American man, Minnesota

Andi, whose story is detailed in chapter 3, moved with a man she barely knew from Chicago to Minnesota. They moved in with his family and became sexually intimate. Their relationship has been like a war zone filled with constant violence. When I asked Andi how she interprets the violence, she, like Hank, talked about love. She loves him because he is good to her kids. And, after he beats her up, he justifies the violence by claiming that he hits her because *he loves her*. If he didn't love her, she would not be worth hitting.

Well, first he had just grabbed me, and like, slammed me into the wall; and me, I'm not gonna just stand there—so, like, I try to shove him off me. And I grabbed his shirt up, like, roped it up—like that—and then I kept telling him "get off me," and stuff and, no, he steady slinging me around and stuff and he ended up hitting my face against the wall. And so I called the police on him as he was walking out the door, and all this other crap. And so the police came to my house and while they were there he had called but I didn't know he was on the phone because my phone was off of the hook . . . and so he had heard everything I was saying to the police. So he decided to call the police and tell the police that I assaulted him. But the police weren't going for it. So the police went and got him because he had ended up going back to his mom's house. So the police went and arrested him and everything. And that same night he called me from jail and he was like, *"The only reason I hit you is because I love you."* I was like, "That doesn't make sense to me." He was like, *"If I didn't love you, then I wouldn't have cared, I just would have walked out on you, like, "F you and 'bye."* I was like, whatever. But, I mean, I still love him, I mean he's good to my kids and everything.—Andi, twenty-something African American woman, Minnesota

Many women stay because the men are "good" to their children. In these cases the women believe they are putting the needs of their children above their own needs.

No. I pay everything. I pay . . . and I even said that out loud in front of him. I said, I said it to one of my friends. I said, why should he leave? He doesn't contribute anything to the house. I said I pay the rent. I pay the rent. I pay the utilities. He drives my car. I put the gas in. I pay everything for the kids. I do the cooking and cleaning. Why should he leave? He's got it made. You know. And it's sad that I can realize that and I know I'm being used, but I just can't take that final step and I think it's because of the kids. They love him so much, but it's even gotten to the point where they'll say, Dad's not here again. He's out with his friends. Or why can't Dad do something with us? You know.—Stella, thirty-something white woman, Minnesota

Equally as powerful and intimately connected is the fact that in many cases the man a woman is with, the man who beats her, saved her from violence in a previous relationship. Returning to Stella and Will, Stella was in a horribly abusive relationship with G. W. when she met Will. Will confronted G. W., telling him to leave Stella alone. Despite the fact that Will is more violent with Stella than G. W. ever was, she views Will as her savior.

But by the time I had found that out [that he was a crack addict], I was already madly in love with him. I mean, he was my world. [*AH: But he had saved you.*] Yeah. He was my world. He was everything.—Stella, thirty-something African American woman, Minnesota

Because I love her. When I questioned other batterers, many of whom were separated from their partners, about where they thought their relationship would end up, they often responded that they would stay together, that they knew their female partners would come back to them—some were living in the shelter, others had moved out and were on their own—because, in their words, "they were destined to be together." Wells is an African American man I interviewed in North Carolina. He was charged with assault and child endangerment for holding his wife and daughter hostage at gun point. The trigger for the event, according to Will, was finding out that his teenage daughter was sexually active. At the time of the interview his wife was living in the battered women's shelter, and his daughter had moved in with her boyfriend. Despite a restraining order that prevents Wells from coming in physical contact with his wife, he fully expects to reconcile with her. Note in his comments that he talks only about *what she does for him.*

But I enjoy life with my wife. I always tell her that if she go before I go that I wouldn't have anybody else. Not that marriage has been bad but I've been with her so long now I'm set in my ways and there ain't nobody else gonna respect me the way she respect me and what I mean by respect is that ain't nobody gonna do for me like she has done you know.—Wells, fifty-something African American man, North Carolina

I would argue that this sense of destiny, derived from the notion of possession, is part of the unhealthy nature of these relationships. These men seek to literally possess their wives and girlfriends, to own them, to control them, to treat them as they wish, and they are completely unable to imagine that these women would ever leave them. Many studies of battered women who are killed by their abusive partners note that the riskiest time for being murdered is at the time of separation (Browne 1987). Women are killed as they are trying to leave, they are stalked and killed after they leave, and they are killed at the courthouse as they file for divorce. Thus this notion of possession woven together with the concept of "destiny" is an extraordinarily dangerous combination for battered women.

This notion of destiny is not limited, however, to batterers. Many, if not most, battered women I have interviewed speak in similar terms. Over and over I talked with battered women in the shelter or in their apartments out on their own, and I always concluded the interview by asking them what would happen next. In some cases I would say, "Maybe you want to be alone for a while, without any men?" All admitted, sometimes reluctantly, that though it might be good for them to give up men, they anticipated or were already engaged in new relationships with men or had returned to "talking" with their abusive partners.

Some women reported that they were with new men because they needed a place to stay (see chapter 3). Others indicated that they were already or would soon be looking for a new man. But the majority admitted that they would probably end up back with the same men they had struggled to escape. This scenario was extremely common. But, perhaps the most interesting example to illustrate this point is what I call "the Leon syndrome."

One of the most important aspects of reporting on IPV is keeping the identities of the men and the women confidential. The following illustration *requires* that I use the batterer's real name. Therefore, I will change the details of the story so as to keep confidential the identities of those involved, while using the real name to illustrate a point I found impossible to illustrate effectively with a pseudonym.

Earlier in this chapter I talked about Cindy, whose first love—Sam—was in prison when she got involved with his younger brother Leon. Cindy and Sam had a child together, and subsequently she and Leon have had five children together. As a young woman in her mid-thirties she has six children.[11] I began to see Cindy's obsession with Leon when she talked about her children. She named her first child by Leon, Leon Jr. She proceeded to name the other four children she bore by Leon various names that are created by rearranging the letters in Leon's name. I was so confused that she finally had to write her children's names down: Leon Jr., Noel, Elon, Nelon—I had never heard anything like this. When I asked her about it she said that she loved Leon, that it was simple, she was obsessed with him.

> His name is Leon so I got a Leon Jr. stupid then I'm creative 'cause I'm so smart my second son is Noel [Leon backward] . . . so mind you my mama told me before she died that Leon want to keep me with my hair cut which it was it's cut now this is a wig I have a big head he want to keep me with my he go keep me fat with my hair cut and pregnant mama no ma he love me I had another son 2001 guess what his name is (pause) Elon. I was just so clever. And Leon doesn't have a middle name he just Leon Hadley so none of my kids have middle names neither 'cause I'm just stupid.—Cindy, thirty-something African American woman, North Carolina

CONCLUSION

IPV often seems to sneak up on its victims. Many battered women report that they did not see it coming. Browne's (1987) work illustrates that, whereas the women might not have recognized them, distinct patterns, or "early warning signs," can be detected in potentially violent relationships. The problem is that the romantic landscape of the United States, which is heavily influenced by the media—especially romance novels and movies—serves to mask the early warning signs. A great deal of attention focused on the woman (by her new boyfriend), private dates, talking about her all the time, wanting to be with her all the time, her boyfriend showing up unexpectedly to surprise her, and jealousy are all within the typical range of "romance" in early relationships. In most healthy relationships, as the relationship becomes more committed and trust is built, these patterns decline and are replaced by other patterns. Couples spend more time apart, and they integrate, as a couple, into their personal social networks. In violent relationships, these patterns escalate rather than diminish. Typically this escalation coincides with the onset of violence, thus women feel caught off guard.

I certainly do not advocate that we remove romance from courtship. However, given the importance of these early warning signs in violent relationships, women ought to be aware of these patterns and learn to take a more critical look at the behavior of new boyfriends.

I closed this chapter with a discussion of obsession. Being obsessed with another person to the point of wanting to possess them is typical of both men who batter and the women they batter. This obsession inhibits leaving on the part of battered women and sometimes leads to murder on the part of the men. In order to reduce IPV, men must be taught that women are not their possessions to do with as they wish.

But more important—albeit more difficult to achieve—is to address the system of patriarchy that allows men to literally "possess" or own their female partners. Any system of ownership, including slavery, capitalism, and patriarchy, that allows one class of human beings to "possess" another class of human beings will establish and reinforce inequality regimes (Acker 2006) that will inevitably lead to and depend upon violence as a means of keeping the inequality regime intact. In this context, all forms of violence against women—including sexual harassment, rape, and IPV—must be understood as being rooted in not only patriarchy, but more significantly, in that aspect of patriarchy that defines women as the "possessions" of their male partners. Violence is a tool that men in a patriarchal society utilize to remind women of their status as "possessions," much like violence against slaves and later the lynching of freed African Americans was a tool whites used to remind African Americans of their status as second-class citizens, as three-fifths of a person, in a country ruled by a system of racial domination. When understood this way, one recommendation for reducing IPV is clearly the dismantling of all systems of domination, including patriarchy.

In the final chapter I will summarize the tenets and data presented in this book and I will make policy recommendations for intervention, reduction, and prevention of IPV and the factors that contribute to its development and persistence.

NOTES

1. Interestingly both Brush (2006) and I explored this concept independently without being aware of each other's work. Merton and Barber (2004) refer to this as serendipity. The fact that we came upon this same concept without knowledge of each other's work suggests even more strongly the importance of this reality in the lives of battered women.

2. This woman's story of abuse, which entailed being a prisoner in her own home, was aired on ABC's news program *20/20* on August 13, 2004.

3. I will return to Rose's story in the section devoted to possession.

4. Other examples of men "possessing" their female partners were reported. In many cases women had to hand over their paychecks to men, they were treated as servants who had to do all of the household labor (cooking, cleaning, laundry, childcare), and they were treated like objects whose existence was merely for the enjoyment of their male partners.

5. The criminal case against Kobe Bryant was dropped, but the victim was awarded a financial settlement as part of a civil action. This case is an excellent example of the difficulty in prosecuting a rape when the two individuals know each other. Bryant and his accuser barely knew each other, and it was difficult.

6. Although I will not address the subject in this book, I am well aware of the literature outlining infidelities in the lives of affluent men and women, particularly those

in the public view; e.g., Martha Wales Skelton Jefferson (wife of Thomas Jefferson), Hillary Clinton, Vanessa Laine Bryant (Kobe Bryant's wife).

7. Evidence of the double standard is even in the language that we use to describe men and women who have multiple partners. Such men are defined as "players," for example, whereas virtually no "positive" terms exist for women who have multiple partners. In contrast, virtually no "negative" terms exist for men who "sleep around," but they abound for women who do so. Asking students to list these terms in class is an instructive exercise.

8. Incidentally, it is also true that many battered women move from one abusive relationship to another, never able to break the cycle.

9. Sam is still in prison serving another sentence for drugs.

10. A simple search on Amazon.com will produce, in a matter of seconds, a list of literally hundreds of books that offer women advice about how to leave abusive relationships. *Defending Our Lives:Getting Away from Domestic Violence & Staying Safe* by Susan Murphy-Milano (New York: Anchor, 1996) is but one example.

11. Note that one of the five children Cindy bore by Leon died last year, so Cindy is now raising five children.

Chapter Seven

Where Do We Go from Here?

The Search for Equality

In the psyche of the individual man it might be his denial of social power-lessness through an act of aggression. In total these acts of violence are like a ritualized acting out of our social relations of power: the dominant and the weaker, the powerful and the powerless, the passive . . . the masculine and the feminine.

—M. Kaufman (1992, 28)

I began this book with a description of intimate partner violence as a matter of public safety. My argument is really twofold. First, that intimate partner violence is in fact a matter of public safety. Many of the "mass murders" and school shootings that have taken place in the past fifteen years began with a domestic violence homicide. Furthermore, the tragedy at Virginia Tech, though perhaps the most glaring example because of its scale and recency, was typical in that the decision by law enforcement agents and others to treat domestic violence as a private matter rather than a public matter created a very real threat to public safety. Thus, our whole society will be safer when we begin to define domestic violence as a matter of public safety rather than something to be dealt with behind closed doors. Second, as long as we continue to define IPV as something that is someone else's problem, as something that "won't happen to me," as something that affects only women, we will remain in a state of false consciousness. I argued throughout this book that as a public safety issue *IPV is everyone's problem*. And if we are to make advances in dealing with IPV we must begin to articulate the shared self-interest that men and women, indeed all of us, have in eradicating this epidemic.

The men and women I interviewed for this book are in many ways no different from most Americans living in the beginning of the third millennium.

They want to be in a relationship with someone they love and who loves them back. They want a decent home to live in and a decent job. They want their children to attend better schools than they attended and to have better lives than theirs. They want to avoid making the mistakes their parents made. In a word, they want access to the American Dream.

Yet, for a variety of reasons, some of them structural (such as systemic poverty) and some of them a result of bad choices (such as drug addiction), I found them in 2003 and 2004 to be living lives that most of us would describe as horrible. The men and women I interviewed sincerely desired and attempted to create good, intimate relationships. But, so many things went wrong that they ended up living lives riddled with violence and abuse.

I began this book by describing Intimate Partner Violence (IPV) as an epidemic in American families. Data from national studies such as the National Violence Against Women (NVAW) survey report that not only are women being battered and abused at the rate of one in four but that the types of violence are varied and often brutal. This is illustrated by a woman I interviewed in Minnesota (Lara) whose partner had beaten her unconscious with a ball-peen hammer in front of her children, and by the case of a man I interviewed in jail in Minnesota (Chris) who poured gasoline around the house threatening to set his wife and their six children on fire.

IPV takes the form of emotional, verbal, physical, and sexual abuse. In some relationships only one form of violence is present, but in many these various forms of violence and control are mutually reinforcing. IPV is damaging to everyone involved, including the children in the household,[1] and it is devastating to the relationship. All estimates of IPV indicate that a quarter of all American women will experience at least one incident of physical violence,[2] and many more will experience emotional and/or verbal abuse. These women who are our sisters, daughters, and friends need our collective help. When a quarter of women experience IPV it means that most of us, if we are not battered or abused ourselves in an intimate partner relationship, know someone who is.

Though the risk factors for IPV are many, and though every woman is at *some* risk, not every woman is equally at risk. IPV cuts across every conceivable social category. Women of all races and ethnicities experience IPV, though race/ethnicity shapes particular experiences with IPV in that women of certain race/ethnicities are more likely to experience specific forms of physical assault. Women of all social classes report IPV, and estimates from national probability samples indicate that the rates are similar across all socioeconomic levels (see table 3.2). As noted in chapter 3, social class shapes responses to IPV as well as the experiences the men accused of IPV have in the criminal justice system (Weitzman 1998, 2001). Women of all ages experience IPV, though it is most common from the teen years to about 50 years of age. Women of all religious traditions[3] experience IPV, and the majority who seek the advice of a priest, minister, or rabbi report that they are counseled to return to the relationship and to try to please their partners (Graetz 1998). The greatest risk factor for being a victim of IPV is gender: women are far more likely to be on the receiving end of IPV than are men, though men, too, report being hit, slapped, yelled at, and beaten (Gelles and Straus 1988).

Men who batter come from all race/ethnic groups and social classes. Though men of different race/ethnic groups may engage in different forms of violence, overall white men are *as likely to batter* as are men of any race/ethnic minority group. Though men of the lower classes are more likely to serve time in jail or attend court-ordered intervention programs (Harvey 2002; Hattery, Williams, and Smith 2004), affluent men are as likely to be verbally and physically abusive to their partners, though many have devised mechanisms that keep them out of the public's eye and/or the criminal justice system. Weitzman (1998, 2001) notes in upper income families the abuse is mostly psychological and the control mostly financial.

The "risk" factors for becoming violent are (1) growing up with a parent who is abusive to the child, and (2) growing up in a household where the mother's intimate partner abuses her. The latter triples the likelihood that one will engage in IPV in adulthood.

This last point underscores the biggest tragedy of IPV—its tendency to be repeated in subsequent generations. This is precisely why we need to take seriously those proposals to alter, curb, prevent, and interrupt all forms of IPV, especially in those households where children are "in sight or sound" of the violence.[4]

Intimate partner violence (IPV) takes a toll on all of society; the bruises and breaks are not simply born by the victims. In raw economic terms, the costs of IPV borne by the institution of health care alone are estimated at $5 million (CDC 2006) to $10 million (Finlayson et al. 1999) per year (see table 3.1). It is virtually impossible to estimate the labor force losses associated with attrition that results from many battered women being fired or quitting due to the violence they are living with, lost wages, and lost productivity due to excessive sick days. Finally, the costs associated with social services that are provided to battered women and their children are even more elusive. These include the costs of running shelters and providing various forms of social welfare—many battered women rely on Temporary Aid to Needy Families (TANF) and food stamps (Brush 2000; Brush, Raphael, and Tolman 2003)—and the costs associated with interventions for the abuser, the victim, and the children living in the household. Finally, the costs to the criminal justice system include sending police officers out to domestic disputes, prosecution and detention of abusers—especially in states like North Carolina that require mandatory arrest—intervention programs, and, finally, incarceration. These costs are borne by all American taxpayers. (See table 3.1.)

Last, I note that IPV remains an understudied problem that is underresourced in terms of care for the victims, which often include not just the woman herself but her children as well. In a paper by Tiefenthaler et al. (2005), the authors summarize the need for more funding for IPV victims at the local, county, and state level. Their research recommends government intervention, and while important, this approach is too fragmented; what I call for in my research is not only increased funding—which is easy to recommend but harder to get—but a more nuanced approach to child rearing, teaching boys and young men that it is not OK to maim, hit, or verbally abuse their sisters, classmates, mothers, girlfriends, partners, and wives.

A CULTURE RIPE FOR INTIMATE PARTNER VIOLENCE

In this book I have done several things: (1) sketched an accurate picture of IPV as it exists in twenty-first-century America, (2) paid attention to differences in IPV as they relate to race/ethnicity and social class, (3) explored experiences with IPV from the perspectives of both battered women and men who batter—many times by talking to members of the same couple, and (4) explored both micro- and macro-level causes and outcomes of IPV.

As a sociologist, I have argued that IPV is epidemic in our culture and that its roots lie in specific norms that structure our behavior. In chapter 4 I outlined norms around masculinity that contribute to a context in which men turn to physical, emotional, and sexual violence as a way to deal with threats to their masculinity and the overall loss of control they feel in their day-to-day interactions with the women in their lives.

I also examined the ways in which hegemonic femininity structures women's expectations and choices around marriage and partnership. In particular I outlined the ways in which this set of norms actually encourages women to be dependent, submissive, and inferior in their intimate partnerships. Finally, I noted the ways in which hegemonic femininity, along with wage discrimination, leads to compulsory heterosexuality, or more specifically "compulsory partnering," which leaves women vulnerable to violence in their intimate relationships. I also noted the ways in which race and class work to shape women's emotional and economic dependency on men, and this was examined in depth in chapter 4.

From the very beginning of this book I argued that one of the advantages to my research is that I have talked with and interviewed both men and women in the batterer/battered relationship. Interviewing both men and women allowed me to explore these connections between hegemonic masculinity and hegemonic femininity and the context that fosters IPV. Though hegemonic masculinity and hegemonic femininity are not necessarily codependent or flip sides of the same coin, they are, nonetheless, related, and they work to reinforce a cultural and social landscape that results in male dominance and sometimes leads to intimate partner violence.

Another important aspect to the culture of IPV in the contemporary United States is the construction of romantic love. Building on the work of Angela Browne (1987), in chapter 6 I examined the ways in which hegemonic constructions of romantic love often mask the early warning signs of IPV. As created and perpetuated by the media—movies, TV, romance novels, and even on the all-sport ESPN network, watched mainly by men, where these same images are portrayed via commercials—certain patterns common in the early stages of relationships are romanticized such that women grow to expect and even desire certain qualities and behaviors such as private dates, surprise visits, and even jealousy. When these qualities or behaviors are defined as "romantic" and are normalized, women in the early stages of abusive and controlling relationships often do not notice when private dates turn into isolation or surprise visits become stalking; they simply do not see the violence coming.

Finally, it is important to understand the relationship between the economy and IPV. In a practical sense, a variety of structural economic forces leave women dependent on and often vulnerable to their romantic partners. First, on all measures of economic well-being women come out behind. Women are less likely to work full-time, they are less likely to have health benefits with their jobs, and they are more likely to work in low-wage industries and occupations. In the final analysis, when all else is held constant, women working in the twenty-first-century U.S. economy remain subjected to gender discrimination in wages—be that in a factory or as a CEO. In 2005 women still earned less than 75 percent of the male dollar. The result: women are more likely to live in poverty. This is exacerbated by the fact that women are also more likely to be raising children alone than are men. Fully 20 percent of white women and 40 percent of African American women who are raising children on their own live below the poverty line. Thus, many women "choose" to stay with abusive partners or move in with men they barely know in order to escape or avoid homelessness and to provide shelter, food, and clothes for their children.

In chapter 3 I examined the stories of many battered women who did just this, including women who moved out of a battered women's shelter or a homeless shelter and moved in with men they had known anywhere from a few hours to a few days. Certainly choices like this, created by structured inequality, leave women vulnerable to IPV. And, actual experiences with IPV leave women economically vulnerable, as the violence often impacts their ability to go to work; as a direct result battered women often report exhausting their sick days, taking unpaid leaves, and even being fired as a result of the IPV.

Moving to a more macro-level discussion, it is important to see the ways in which IPV is situated within the context of capitalist patriarchy, as explored by bell hooks. In focusing on the particular experiences of African American women at the hands of African American men, Professor hooks makes this exceptionally pointed remark:

> White patriarchy is just as misogynist as black patriarchy and offer death as the price all women must pay if they get out of their place. (2004, 61)

That is, from birth to the grave, women are socialized to succumb to "their man" even when doing so is not in their best interest.

In order to further disentangle the relationship between race and IPV, in chapter 5 I analyzed data from the NVAW survey that allowed me to compare rates of IPV in interracial and intraracial couples. Whereas all national level research has demonstrated that African American and white men batter at the same rate, these data revealed some surprising findings; namely that African American men are more likely to batter in interracial relationships with white women than they are in intraracial relationships. In contrast, white men's rates of battering follow the reverse pattern: white men are more likely to batter same-race partners than they are to batter in interracial relationships, namely in their relationships with African American women. This analysis furthers our understanding of the ways in which race, and in particular the racial composition of the couple, shapes IPV.

NEGATIVE CONSEQUENCES ASSOCIATED WITH IPV

Throughout this book I have documented the negative outcomes associated with IPV. These range from (1) physical injury, (2) emotional hurt and pain, (3) billions of dollars in health care costs, (4) untold losses in economic productivity, (5) the costs of services for battered women and their children, and finally (6) the costs associated with the criminal justice system: responding to domestic calls, detaining batterers, and adjudicating the cases.

But the biggest negative consequences associated with IPV are not the economic costs borne by a variety of institutions, but rather the costs to families in the contemporary United States. I began this chapter by noting that most individuals who end up in violent relationships never intended for their relationships to go this way. As I noted in chapter 2, many of the women I interviewed, and in fact *all* of the African American women I interviewed, experienced sexual abuse and/or had premature "consensual" sexual relationships—I refer to this as pre-mature sex engagement—that left them impaired in their abilities to deal with abusive romantic partners. Many of the women and men I interviewed witnessed violence in the families in which they grew up. Many of the men, and this was especially true for African Americans, witnessed severe violence, even gun murders of a parent, in their homes. Many men vowed that they would never treat their romantic partners and their children this way. Yet, they did.

> But I still look at it like this. I think as far, you know, young men we come up and we gonna see our mothers and our fathers together, you know we come up and we get that thing going on, you know, like my moms was married to my real dad *I did see him slam her head on the car, I was in the car,* I did see that one, so you know, I think I think these young men when we see that when we children and as we grow up we like I'd never do that when I get married. I get married I never do that, I ain't gonna say this I ain't gonna do that to my wife, but when we grow up you know what I'm sayin', not knowin', you know what I'm sayin', in our mind, that's what we really been taught to do, that how we been taught to deal with things, you know, moms say something she smack in the mouth or somethin' like that, that kind a stick with guys you know, well guys say I ain't gonna do this, *I ain't gonna do that, but when they get in the situation that do exactly that,* you know.—Manny, twenty-something African American man, North Carolina

Will articulates the same point:

> So you know, with my boys now, all the anger and stuff that I done been through, you know, anger management class, I see it coming out in my boys. One of them . . . and now he, he a little wiry guy and wants to play football. He's rough. He had the nerves the other day, he said, Dad, I know what I want to do. I said, what? He said, I want to box. First thing that came to my mind was, oh no. It's because my dad used to get into it, used to always fight with my mother. *And he was little and he see me and his mom get into it when he was little.* He says [about his brother] I'm going to knock him out. So, right now, I'm kind of worried, he comes and tell me he wants to box. I don't think so. You know, now he got his twin brother. They go in, the other morning,

brushing their teeth, he turn around, keep messing with me, he keep messing with me. So, I just turned around and boom, popped him in the stomach [his son talking]. Then, yesterday, the day before yesterday, he had had a bad day at school and his I just kept bugging him. And he wanted to be off by himself. Sometimes that's what I'll do. If I'm peed off about something, say, leave me alone. Just leave me alone. Don't say nothing to me. Let me go off by myself, let me cool off my way. That's how he is and I just kept bugging him and bugging him and bugging him. Next thing I know, he says, if you don't leave me alone I'm going to kick you. You know, and I got kind of upset about it. Well, he won't let me. . . . I said, look, he's telling you he don't want you to bother him. Leave him alone. And he got a little upset.—Will, fifty-something African American man, Minnesota

The primary negative outcome of IPV is that it ruins individual lives and it ruins American families. Boys who grow up *witnessing* violence in their homes have triple the risk for becoming physically violent with their own romantic partners than boys who do not (Ehrensaft, Cohen, et al. 2003). Boys who grow up in families in which their fathers beat their mothers learn an important lesson: that women have no value and that women's self-interests are not linked with their own. This is similar to the findings of Scully's interviews with convicted rapists (1990).

Living with IPV can be stressful at its minimum and lethal at its most severe. For women, living with IPV can mean having to learn to apply makeup to cover cuts and bruises, learning to scream into a pillow so that the children will not hear, it can mean choosing homelessness or living in a shelter in a new city or state or region of the country in order to stay alive. For men who are abusive, the outcomes of violence include living with someone who is afraid of you, often being separated from your children, and in some cases, it may include being arrested, charged with a crime, and some sort of "punishment" ranging from attending an intervention program to incarceration.

So often scholars of IPV, and we as a culture, focus on the toll that IPV takes on its victims. But men who perpetrate this kind of violence lose as well. They lose the chance to have a loving, intimate relationship with another person. They often lose the chance to raise their children or have any sort of relationship with them. They lose the chance to fulfill that part of the American Dream that includes making and raising a family. And, they must live with the pain that they have hurt someone they claim to love and the guilt that they have created a toxic environment for their children. By exposing their children to violence they are contributing to the intergenerational nature of this poisonous phenomenon. Men, too, are hurt by the violence they perpetrate. Therefore it is in their self-interest to reduce the prevalence of this social ill.

THE INTERGENERATIONAL TRANSMISSION OF VIOLENCE

As noted throughout the book, some truth lies in the notion of the intergenerational transmission of violence. Though most men who grow up in violent households do not become violent, nevertheless, those who do are at a significantly greater risk for becoming violent. Will goes so far as to argue that it is hereditary. Though Will's adherence to this belief may in part be a mechanism to excuse his behavior, it is also clear that he understands something about the intergenerational transmission of violence in his own family history.

> So I got, I see, it is heredity. *It is heredity and a lot of people say it's not, but it is. You know, and basically, I don't think* . . . . Its heredity, but I think some people take it a different way by heredity, you know, how they pick it up. One way I think the main way, that I see it as, from seeing it. From you seeing it. Its not in your blood. Its actually from seeing it.—Will, fifty-something African American men, Minnesota

I would suggest that we need to further explore the mechanism for this intergenerational transmission. Unlike many aspects of socialization and social learning, I do not believe it is as simple as boys learning by watching their fathers. Rather, I learned a great deal about a possible mechanism for transmission when I asked the men I interviewed what advice they would give their sons. Their responses fell primarily into two categories: (1) don't get hooked up with a bad woman, and (2) don't get played.

Analyzing the advice these men gave or planned to give their sons, I would argue that what gets passed on in the intergenerational transmission are beliefs about men and women; beliefs about gender. Men intend to teach their sons how to be masculine. They may not teach them explicitly that they should hit their romantic partners, but they teach them how to be the man of the house, how to be in control, how to require certain behavior from their romantic partners. Furthermore, they teach their sons lessons about women. For example, they teach their sons about appropriate roles for women, about behaviors that are common in women, and about the ways in which women will try to manipulate and control them. In essence, they need not teach their sons to hit women, as partner violence, especially verbal abuse, will be a logical outgrowth of their general lessons about (1) the way women are, (2) what it means to be a man, and (3) the roles of men and women in relationship. If boys learn that they are the ones in charge, that women are out to manipulate them, and that real men keep their women in line, then it is quite likely that these boys will grow up to be perpetrators of IPV, even if they are bound and determined not to become batterers like their fathers.

As far as my son goes, I'm gonna teach him to stand up for himself, not to let anybody run over him. Just to *really be cautious about who he deals with*, um to really really get to know the person, not just having sex with them and stuff like that, to really get to know someone before you get involved with them, 'cause there's so many diseases, it's uh, you have some . . . out there and so he just really needs to be aware of what that person likes and dislikes and see if it matches up with some of the stuff he likes and dislikes before he gets involved with her and makes a mistake.—Ward, thirty-something African American man, North Carolina

THE LOGIC OF POWER

One advantage of face-to-face interviews—as opposed to surveys or telephone interviews—with both members of couples living with IPV is the chance to assess size and power, especially economic power. I found in interviews with many couples that IPV is a gendered phenomenon that sometimes defies what I will call "the logic of power." In fact, in many of the couples I interviewed the abuse was primarily perpetrated by the man (though some women had begun fighting back) despite the fact that the men were physically smaller and had less economic power than their female partners. Let me explain this important finding a bit further.

I return to a discussion of Chris and Wanda whom I interviewed in rural Minnesota. They are both African American, and both were born and raised in the urban Midwest (Wanda in Chicago and Chris in Toledo). They have been in an intimate relationship for the past five years or so. Wanda, a former Chicago high school basketball star, is tall, perhaps 6 feet, 2 inches, though because she desperately needs a hip replacement and cannot stand up straight it is difficult to make an accurate assessment of her true height. Wanda has worked hard her whole life as a certified nursing assistant (CNA) and is raising five children. She also reported that she endured a great deal of physical abuse from her father. The manner in which she briefly explained this abuse and then quickly, while crying, moved on to another subject makes me believe that she was subjected to incest by her father as well. Though she is quite young, only 37 or 38, the degeneration of her hip means that she spends most of her day on the couch, and she must rely on a motorized scooter in order to have any mobility at all. As a result of her disability she is reliant on social security (SSI) in order to provide for her family. Though Wanda may seem an obvious target for IPV—she has limited mobility, she is reliant/dependent on welfare to meet her economic needs—in fact, her partner Chris is in worse shape.

Chris, a man in his early sixties, was once a powerful man. He was a boxer and continues to train young men vying for the Golden Gloves. Though strong, Chris is small in stature, standing maybe 5 feet, 2 inches tall, a full foot shorter than Wanda, and when he boxed professionally he boxed as a "featherweight." More significant, however, is the fact that Chris has been fighting glaucoma for years. At the time I interviewed him in jail he had lost one eye completely (it was actually removed) and he has almost no sight in his remaining eye. He is aware that he will soon be completely blind. As a result of his disability, Chris is unable to work, and according to both him and Wanda he is not providing any income to the household. As Wanda remarked, "[I] paid the rent, the light bill, the gas bill, the phone bill and all of the groceries." (See chapter 3.)

Detracting further from Chris's "power" in the household, he is currently incarcerated and has been in jail on and off for the last year. As a result, he is entirely dependent on Wanda. The day that I interviewed him in jail, Chris was hoping Wanda would bail him out before the weekend. In the case of Chris and Wanda, and many other couples I interviewed, the "logic of power" simply does not hold. The women in these relationships are physically bigger, and perhaps more important, they provide the only source of income for their families. Yet, it is the men in these relationships who engage in the majority of the physical abuse.

This is precisely where feminism helps us to decode the data: the men in these relationships do *not* meet the culturally defined, hegemonic constructions of masculinity—they are physically smaller than their partners, they are not meeting the requirements of the role of "breadwinner," nor in many cases are they meeting the requirements of masculinity in the bedroom. In the case of Chris and Wanda she even remarked that not only was Chris not contributing to the household financially, but that he was not "doing her" in ways she wanted. Hence, she had figured out how to satisfy her sexual needs—by purchasing sex toys at the local "adult" store—and remarked that she can even "suck her own tit." Men's emotional and physical violence then can be understood as an attempt to *equalize the power* in the relationship. They may be smaller and have less access to economic resources, but they can assert their masculinity by degrading their female partners verbally and by beating them down physically. In addition, living in a capitalist patriarchy means that even if an individual man has little power outside the home, institutions will nevertheless recognize him as a member of the ruling or dominant class, and this creates access to power. Again, this is mitigated by both race and social class, but as black feminist scholars such as bell hooks (2004), Shirley Hill (2005), and Patricia Hill-Collins (2004) point out, privileges vested in patriarchy do indeed accrue even to African American men.

Outcomes? Even convicted batterers rarely serve any significant time in jail or prison (Harvey 2002; Hattery, Williams, and Smith 2004). In a culture such as ours that continues to treat IPV as a "family problem," men are rarely held accountable for battering, emotional abuse, and sexual abuse of their female partners, even when they live at the powerless margins of the poor and disenfranchised.

RISK FACTORS FOR INTIMATE PARTNER VIOLENCE

I concur with scholars who have noted the "risk factors" for IPV:

- Age (couples that partner at a younger age are at greater risk for IPV)
- Social class (lower class couples are at increased risk for IPV)
- Number of children (couples with more children are at greater risk for IPV)
- Chemical dependency (individuals addicted to drugs and or alcohol are at greater risk for perpetrating and being the victim of IPV)

Early on in the interviews I conducted, I began to learn about the ways in which IPV was interwoven with a variety of other issues that these families were dealing with, including drug abuse, unemployment, HIV/AIDS, and incarceration (for a detailed discussion of this see Hattery and Smith 2007a). Here I briefly summarize the relationship between IPV and other social problems.

Drug Abuse and IPV

Many previous scholars have noted the relationship between drug abuse and IPV (see especially the work of Jeremy Travis, especially Travis 1997). Yet, as with the intergenerational transmission of violence theory, the relationship may be more complex than has otherwise been argued. Certainly drug and alcohol use are related to aggressive behavior and violence, and a long literature substantiates this (see, for example, Pihl and Peterson 1995, 2, 141–49). However, when I interviewed men and women about their experiences with violence, I learned that the relationship between drugs and IPV is a bit more complex. In the case of drug addiction, the violence commonly erupted over disagreements about the money needed to support a drug/alcohol habit. Several of the men and many of the women I interviewed noted that physical violence often erupted out of arguments that ensued when the drug addict (typically the man) came down from a high and needed more money to get another fix. When no money was available or when his female partner refused to "ante up," the man would beat her. Two of the clearest examples come from Stella and Will, and Akim and Betty.

Akim uses crack cocaine regularly, but he indicates that he is not an addict because, in his words, he has (1) never failed a drug test, and (2) he only uses on the weekend. On a typical Friday, Akim gets paid. He cashes his check, keeps enough to get "a rock"—a nickname for crack cocaine—and then gives the rest of his pay to his wife Betty, telling her explicitly that he knows they need the money to pay bills so she is not to let him have any of it. He then goes off and gets high. When he comes down and desires another "fix" he asks Betty for some money. When she refuses, complying with his sober order, he beats her. This pattern, according to Akim and confirmed by Betty, repeats itself virtually every weekend.

Stella is also involved with a crack addict. Will has been using crack cocaine for thirty years, since he was 17. In the last few years he has done many stints in jail or prison, and for the last decade or so has been unable to hold a job. Stella endures severe beatings: Will has beaten her head against the concrete wall in their apartment and hit her in the face so hard that her teeth punctured both her bottom and top lips. When Will is in need of another fix and Stella cannot or will not give him money, he beats her. Because Will has been unemployed for the last decade his habit is entirely dependent on Stella's financial support. Stella notes that violence around Will's crack addiction occurs, on average, every other day.

Why is this nuance important? It is important because for violent couples like Betty and Akim and Stella and Will, there is very little one can do to interrupt the violence in these relationships without first addressing the drug addiction. Both of these men have been crackheads for three decades, and effective strategies for unseating this addiction must be developed before any attempts can be made to permanently stop the violence. Finally, strategies for preventing IPV in the first place must include discussions of alcohol and drug abuse and its disastrous affects on relationships and family life.

Sexually Transmitted Diseases, HIV/AIDS

One of the issues that health care providers have identified with regard to IPV is the risk of exposure to a variety of STDs, including HIV/AIDS, that many battered women face (see Gilbert 2001). Battered women are at increased risk for STDs for a variety of reasons, including the fact that they are often raped and sexually assaulted by their partners, their partners often have multiple sex partners, their partners may be drug addicts, and, especially in the African American community, their partners are likely to have spent time in jail or prison, which increases their risk for STDs and HIV/AIDS in particular.

Most of the women I interviewed noted that they had had sex with their intimate partners when they did not want to and some admitted that they had been raped by their partners. Several of the women I interviewed specifically talked about getting a sexually transmitted disease from their partners. Stella noted that her partner Will was cheating on her while she was pregnant and gave her several sexually transmitted diseases. Sally noted that she figured out what was wrong with her when she discovered crabs—pubic lice—in her partner's underwear while she was doing the laundry.

> I loved him and that's the only . . . I don't know, that was the only love I had in my life. You know what I'm saying, it's like, I went to the clinic. He gave me crabs and gonorrhea. You know, and I ain't even know he had this stuff. He's not telling me this, you know what I'm saying. I'm washing his clothes out in the washing machine, in the tub, swirling. He got blood in his boxers cause the crabs had ate him up so bad, you know.—Sally, twenty-something African American woman, North Carolina

The particular issues of HIV/AIDS, however, came up with one of the men that I interviewed. An African American man of 21, Demitrius's partner Mary talked about the fact that, in her opinion, Demitrius beats her in part because he is unable to work, and this results in feelings of inadequacy on his part and fights about money that often become violent. When I asked Mary why a young man of 21 was unable to work, she said, "well, you'll see him [she knew I was interviewing him later that day], and I'll let him tell you about it."

Demitrius is a small man, maybe 5 feet, 5 inches tall and certainly weighing less than 120 pounds. His color was not good. He had circles under his eyes and did not look healthy. When I asked Demetrius why he was not working, he said that he had "sickle cell." When I asked him to talk about that, he was intentionally vague. I asked him about treatment for his sickle cell at the local hospital, a world-renowned medical facility in Minnesota, and he remarked that he did not go to the doctor because he does not like doctors or hospitals.

After completing my interview with Demetrius, I read several well-researched *New York Times* editorials that dealt with HIV/AIDS in the African American community. Among other things, the author noted that it is common for African American men to hide an HIV/AIDS diagnosis behind one of sickle cell.[5]

A few months later, when I interviewed Ronny in the same hospital that Demetrius was afraid to go to, I arrived and found a sign on his door that visitors were to see the nurse before entering his room. I was instructed by the nurse to gown up before seeing him, and I was instructed not to touch him. On the way out of his room I was reminded by Ronny, the nurse, and a posted placard to wash my hands carefully so as not to transmit any infection. Ronny was HIV positive. Quite ill, this 27-year-old, like Demetrius, was a shell of a man, having had several toes amputated due to untreated diabetes as well as having eight gunshot wounds from "gang-banging" and no front teeth. And, at 27 years old, he had just undergone quadruple bypass surgery.

Understanding that couples dealing with IPV may also be dealing with a positive HIV/AIDS diagnosis is important for many reasons, the most important of which is the risk that the woman faces simply by being with her abusive partner. He may be exposing her to HIV/AIDS through rape, unprotected consensual sex, and because he engages in physical violence, he may expose her to HIV/AIDS every time he hits her or cuts her and they are both bleeding. In addition to the risk of exposure, an HIV/AIDS diagnosis puts tremendous strain on the individuals as well as on the couple that may involve jealousy (how was the disease acquired), the draining nature of caretaking (most often of the man by the woman), and untold financial burdens associated with the resultant unemployment and the cost of drug regimens. Thus, it is important that scholars and practitioners be aware of the possible coexistence of IPV and HIV/AIDS[6] when designing prevention and intervention programs. Battered women may need to be alerted to their possible risk; they may require health and sex education counseling, and they may need to set up plans for protecting themselves from possible exposure to HIV/AIDS as they negotiate their violent relationships.

Incarceration

In the United States, a greater percentage of Americans are incarcerated than are citizens in any other nation in the world and more than at any time in history. As many as 1 percent of our population is incarcerated at any one time, with the rate disproportionately high among African American men, of whom 25 to 33 percent are incarcerated at some time in their lives, most between the ages of 18 and 35 (Smith and Hattery 2007).

Many of the men I interviewed had spent time in jail or prison and almost all (90 percent) of the African American men I interviewed reported that they had been incarcerated. Though I interviewed men in states that have mandatory arrest laws for domestic violence—Minnesota and North Carolina—and though most of the men I interviewed were arrested and spent anywhere from a few hours[7] to three days in jail on a domestic violence charge, I did not consider mandatory arrest as "jail time" when I analyzed the data. Instead, the men I interviewed who reported that they had been incarcerated had been in county jails and/or state prisons from several months to more than a decade for their crimes, including drug charges, drug trafficking, breaking and entering, and even strong-arm robbery, felony assault, and homicide.

Though one might conclude that the connection between incarceration and IPV is that men abuse their female partners when they call the police and have them arrested and then refuse to bail them out, and this is certainly true, the issue that I illuminate here is more complex. Clearly incarceration affects family life in many ways: it is stressful for the family; it is expensive, as one pays court costs, fines, attorneys' fees, and travel expenses as many offenders are incarcerated hundreds of miles from where their families live; and it creates a period of separation for the couple (for a lengthy discussion see Hattery and Smith 2007a).

The most serious consequence associated with incarceration is that in all cases the men emerge with criminal records, and in many of the cases I learned about, their records include at least one felony. As noted in chapter 3, a felony leaves the man disenfranchised and often unable to find gainful employment. Recall that Pager's (2003) analysis demonstrates clearly the severe employment penalty African American men with a felony pay in the labor market. Thus, the primary way in which IPV and incarceration are intertwined is in the fact that men who emerge from jail or prison with a felony find it nearly impossible to obtain gainful employment, and as noted in chapter 4, this leaves them unable to fulfill the role of breadwinner.[8] Two significant results occur: (1) the family has less income, and (2) the inability to provide economically is a blow to the men's masculinity. Both of these are "triggers" for IPV.

Additionally, what I do not find in the literature on incarceration, although it is critical to understanding IPV, is a discussion of jealously and infidelity. Many, if not all, of the men I interviewed who were incarcerated and most of the women I interviewed whose partners were incarcerated reported infidelity. As noted in chapter 6, Hank said that he had women on the side while his partner was incarcerated and that this was not "cheating" because she knew about it. This interpretation was repeated over and over. Chris, who was very jealous of men hanging around his girlfriend Wanda, noted that while he was in jail he could do nothing about it, and he was not worried as long as she did not fall in love with anyone else. In fact, he reinforced this point by stating: "I sleep through the night here, [in jail] I don't have any worries."

The relationship between incarceration and IPV is critical to our understanding of IPV, but it is especially potent in the African American community in which 25 to 33 percent of men spend some time incarcerated. It is likely, therefore, that African American men who batter are also ex-cons, a situation that results in underemployment and unemployment for these men.

Both scholars and practitioners need to be cognizant of this as they seek prevention and intervention strategies that pay attention to the incarceration history of the batterer. I would argue that helping these men find gainful employment will increase the probability of success of both IPV prevention and intervention programs, whereas ignoring this reality will likely result in failing at the prevention and interruption of IPV.

Again, I say that a model that locates IPV within the context of other social ills—specifically poverty, drug addiction, HIV/AIDS, and incarceration—is not only more effective than models that treat IPV as an independent problem, but the connections only emerge when life-history interviews are collected. Collecting survey data in order to estimate the prevalence of IPV in the United States certainly has value, but this method of data collection and social inquiry will remain limited in that it does not allow for respondents to contextualize their experiences within their more complex lives (for a lengthy discussion of the strengths of qualitative methods, especially for these types of research questions, see Lamont and Small 2008).

The Relationship between Risks and "Triggers": An Illustration

One way of thinking about risks for perpetrating IPV (unemployment, incarceration, alcohol and drug abuse, age, number of children, social class) as opposed to "triggers" for IPV (failures at breadwinning and failures in one's sex life) is to use the analogy of a gun. The risks for IPV are like bullets that get loaded into the chamber of a gun. The "triggers" are the incidents (like being nagged by one's partner, jealousy) that men say lead to them erupting in violence—or pulling the trigger on the gun. The "triggers" that African American men in this study report do not differ from the "triggers" that white men report. Furthermore, these "triggers" are consistent with the threats to masculinity identified by Kimmel (2005), Messner (2002), and others. How then can we explain the greater use of force by African American men compared to their white counterparts—a fact that is well documented by national level surveys of IPV and is documented in table 5.1. I argue that the primary way in which race shapes IPV is by shaping the way in which the chamber of the gun is loaded.

African American men face many barriers to successful breadwinning and successful sex lives, as I noted above. These include a substantially higher risk for incarceration, a significantly higher rate of unemployment, wage discrimination, and so forth. If one imagines each of these experiences—incarceration, bouts of unemployment, earning sub-standard wages, etc.—as bullets that are loaded in the chamber of the gun, then we can see that for many African American men, the "guns" they hold are loaded with more bullets than those held by their white counterparts. Thus, when African American men "pull the trigger" they erupt into more severe violence than their white counterparts. This interpretation reveals the distinct way in which *race shapes IPV*: rather than the often held belief that African American men are more likely to engage in IPV—a fact that is not borne out by the data—I argue that African American men's violence is more severe—even though not more common—because of their exposure to structured inequality that, among other things, impacts their likelihood of getting a job and making a living that allows them to support their families.

RACE, CLASS, AND GENDER: AN INTERSECTIONAL APPROACH

One risk factor for becoming a battered woman is her status as a second-class citizen in other systems of domination such as the class system or the system of racial domination. Many of the battered women I interviewed had grown up on the economic margins.[9] They had little human or social capital, very few had been to college, many of them never completed high school or a GED, and some had not even entered high school, dropping out in the seventh or eighth grade. (In the interviews conducted in Minnesota often the men were similarly lacking in educational credentials.) These women were already second-class citizens when it came to social class. They had no access to economic resources let alone any power or control in the economic system. They were, as described by Ehrenreich (2002), wage slaves. They were exploited by an economic system in which the only work they could get was undervalued and grossly underpaid. They were, in a sense, easy targets for gender exploitation (IPV) because they were already exploited and oppressed by other systems of domination, in this case, capitalism.

Economic power does not exempt one from IPV. As I have noted throughout this book, affluent women report rates of IPV that are nearly as high as those reported by low income and poor women (see table 3.2). However, given that few, if any, studies of the reactions of affluent women to IPV exist,[10] I can only speculate, based on the limited number of middle-class women in my sample (and from the research of others), that middle-class and affluent women are less likely to experience the harshest forms of violence, and more important, they have more economic resources to leave an abusive relationship if they choose to. As I discussed in chapter 3, one of the main problems facing the majority of women I interviewed was the lack of access to financial resources. They simply could not feed their children and keep a roof over their heads working a minimum-wage job, if they worked at all (Ehrenreich 2002).

Thus, they stayed with their abusive partners, or they returned to them after a stint out on their own. They returned hungry and homeless, preferring a roof over their heads and food in their children's bellies over their own physical and emotional safety. Or, perhaps more disturbing, they ricocheted from one abusive partner to the next, moving in with men they barely knew because of the offer of some economic stability.

The interviews I conducted with African American men and women illuminated the ways in which a system of racial domination similarly increases the vulnerability of women of color to IPV and the increased likelihood that men of color will engage in physical violence. Just as capitalism creates a second-class category of poor and working-class Americans (Acker 2006), the system of racial domination creates a system of second-class citizens based on race. African American men and women live in an America in which the doors of opportunity for education, housing, jobs, and public office are simply not open, or they are open so slightly that it is much more difficult to get in (see Hattery and Smith 2007a). As a result, African American women are more likely to be poor. And, poor women are more economically vulnerable and thus more vulnerable to chronic, severe IPV. In a word, *race and social class and gender shape IPV.*[11]

PRESCRIPTIONS FOR PREVENTING AND INTERRUPTING IPV

The "simple" solution to eradicating IPV would be to teach boys and young men not to batter their partners, not to seek to control them, and not to seek to possess them through sex (Woolley 2007). It is clear from the previous research on IPV as well as my own interviews that this approach, though pleasing, is neither effective nor practical. I will close this book by making recommendations for preventing and interrupting IPV, though I will focus on prevention.

I have not worked with nearly the number of batterers as have social workers and counselors in this specialized field. However, the research of others, as well as my own evaluation research,[12] demonstrates a very high recidivism rate among perpetrators of IPV and that intervention programs are only minimally effective (Hattery, Williams, and Smith 2004). Furthermore, after conducting in-depth interviews with some forty batterers, I have come to the conclusion that intervention work is mostly ineffective. I certainly would endorse others to continue to modify and develop intervention programs; however, I will focus here on prevention.¹³ Finally, I will offer two approaches to prevention and intervention: individual solutions and institutional or societal level proposals.

Economic Reform/Disrupting Capitalism

One of the constant themes throughout this book has been the issue of economics, finances, and money. As I noted in chapter 4, hegemonic masculinity proscribes that men take on the role of "breadwinner." And many, if not most, women expect their male partners to contribute significantly to the economy of the household (Bianchi, Robinson, and Milkie 2007). When men are unable to meet the economic needs of the family, they often report being nagged by their female partners, and they often feel their masculinity threatened. Many, if not most, couples admitted that they fought over money and that sometimes these arguments turned violent.

> So Justin had lost his job—and I get very cranky when that happens—and—it's happened too many times since we've been together, I guess. I've had the same job for this many years and he's, he's changed jobs so many times and—Well, some of it's—a lot of his work is seasonal so then he gets laid off and unemployment just doesn't cut it. So, then, he'd have to find a new one and the new one and then he'd get like a—I'd complain so much, he'd get, like, a telemarketing job. No. Six-fifty an hour—we can't pay bills on that—you gotta look— So he'd just get like these stupid like little jobs in between the bigger couple year jobs, or whatever . . . and so I just couldn't really take it that much any more.—Kylie, twenty-something white woman, Minnesota

Certainly I would agree that most men (and women) should be contributing economically to their households unless they are incapable of doing so (as some of the men I interviewed were) or unless they are "stay-at-home" dads, a relatively rare "occupation." Certainly some of the men I interviewed needed to take more economic responsibility for their families. However, I argue that in order to make serious headway on the problem of IPV as it is associated with economics, we need to demand serious economic reform. The truth of the matter is that even in the best case scenario, where a hardworking man is working full time, all year round, he will have to make at least nine dollars an hour in order to keep his family above the federally established poverty line. And, as most poverty experts note, living above the poverty line does not mean that you are "making ends meet" (Edin and Lein 1997). I suspect that over time we would see a decline in IPV if we returned to an economy that offered a living wage to all employees, not just those with special skills and advanced education (Ehrenreich 2002).

The situation worsens for men who have a criminal record. As noted throughout this book, men with a criminal record, especially a felony record, find it virtually impossible to obtain employment, even minimum-wage employment (for a lengthy discussion see Hattery and Smith 2007a). For men in the African American community this is a serious problem given that 25 to 33 percent of African American men are incarcerated at one time or another. Thus, until two key issues, (1) the disproportionately high rate of incarceration of African American men[14] and (2) the employment discrimination faced by men with criminal records, are addressed, IPV will continue to be an epidemic in the African American community. Furthermore, until all African American men, including *those who have never been incarcerated*, no longer face employment and wage discrimination, they will continue to find it difficult if not impossible to provide economically for their families, and we will continue to see fights about "breadwinning" erupt into violence in these relationships.

Economic reform that provides a living wage to men is not the only key to disrupting IPV. As discussed at length in chapter 3, women are vulnerable to IPV because of the economic oppression they suffer. As long as women continue to earn only a portion of men's wages—currently women earn seventy-one cents on the male dollar—they will be dependent on men in order to provide economic stability for their families. The outcome of the gendered wage gap is, according to Rich (1980, 1995), compulsory heterosexuality, or as I argued in chapter 4, "compulsory partnering." Battered women stay in abusive relationships because they cannot leave *and* feed their children. Battered women who do leave often jump quickly into relationships with men they barely know out of sheer economic need. They need someone to help pay the rent and fill the refrigerator. And the men with whom they jump into relationships often become abusive as well. Thus, economic reform that provides a livable wage to all workers and addresses the gendered wage gap is critical to making women less economically vulnerable to their male partners and thus reducing IPV.

Table 7.1. Mean Hourly Wages for Selected Occupations in North Carolina and Minnesota

	North Carolina	Minnesota
McDonald's/KF	$ 6.69	$ 7.35
Laborer	$10.13	$17.33
Retail clerk (Wal-Mart)	$ 8.98	$ 7.84
Nurse (CNA)	$15.47	$15.60
Teacher	$19.26	$20.81

Source: North Carolina Occupational Employment and Wages, http://eslmi23.esc.state.nc.us/oeswage/.

Gender Equality/Dismantling Patriarchy

Throughout this book and specifically in this chapter I have argued that IPV is a "logical" byproduct of patriarchy. Inside a system of male domination, in which men are defined as superior and women inferior, in which men have social, political, and economic power and women have little to none (Zweigenhaft and Domhoff 2006), the hegemonic model of gender relations is one of domination, power, and control. Acker (2006) describes this as a gender inequality regime. In a system designed around oppression and inequality, it is not surprising—in fact one would *expect*—that the dominant group uses a variety of means to control the subordinate group. Clearly not all men are batterers, but as Andrea Dworkin (1987) argued, all heterosexual relationships contain the elements necessary for IPV. What is remarkable, frankly, is that some men *choose not to* exercise the power and control they have under patriarchy.

Patriarchy is, at its most fundamental level, a system of privilege. Part of the privilege is, as noted, the power to choose when and how to exercise power. Another and equally important aspect of the privilege is the ability to render women and women's "interests" invisible. Scully's study of convicted rapists provides insight into this part of privilege:

> Since patriarchal societies produce men whose frame of reference excludes women's perspectives, men are able to ignore sexual violence, especially since their culture provides them with such a convenient array of justifications. . . . *Indeed, it appears that . . . a man rapes because his value system provides no compelling reason for him not to do so.* (Scully 1990, 116, emphasis mine)

I could easily replace "sexual violence" with "intimate partner violence," and it would accurately reflect what men who batter report. The structural rendering of the "victim" or "oppressed" as invisible allows the oppressor to feel justified in his or her[15] behavior. Men batter because they can get away with it and because they do not see the interests of their partners as inextricably tied to their own.

In examining the relationships of these men and women living with violence, several patterns emerged. As I discussed at length in chapter 4, many men identify a similar trigger to their violence: their inability to meet the demands as a breadwinner. One of the traps of any system of domination, and patriarchy is no exception, is that it defines very rigid roles for both men and women. Women are relegated to the status of second-class citizen with little power and few choices. But men are also relegated to a narrow set of available roles: the primary role being that of economic provider. This rigid role assignment is strictly enforced. How do we know? Despite the fact that men—as well as women—are eligible for the provisions of the Family and Medical Leave Act (FMLA), allowing them time off from work when they have a new baby—or adopt a child or have a sick family member that needs to be cared for—fewer than 10 percent of men take advantage of this. Some report they are not given "permission" by employers to take advantage of this provision to which they are legally entitled (Hattery 2001b). And, the ranks of the stay-at-home father, though growing, are relatively small, at about 8 percent (nationally). As I noted in other research, when men do stay at home, they incur a great deal of negative feedback for this decision (Hattery 2001b).

Another distinct pattern that emerges in these couples is that men's use of violence and attempts to control their female partners are often triggered by events and actions that signal that their female partners are simply behaving as if they do not live under patriarchy. In short, women are verbally berated, beaten, and abused when they are *acting as if they are free*.[16]

Women are abused and beaten when they take too long on an errand or return home later than expected. They are abused and beaten when they have lunch with a coworker their partner does not like—which he may define as any man besides himself. They are abused and beaten when they decide they are not going to clean up after their male partners, especially if this involves cleaning up or preparing food for their partners' male friends as they watch sport events, like football or boxing. They are abused and beaten when they decide to change the dinner menu or the time the meal is served. And, mostly, women are abused and beaten when they talk to or express any interest in a man other than their male partner. Even though the expression may simply be of the friendship or collegial variety. When women exercise agency, engage in their own decision making, or attempt to wield power, they are verbally berated, beaten, and sexually assaulted. In other words, IPV is a form not only of "rule" enforcement (or discipline) but of "role" enforcement. This pattern of violence can only be explained as part of a larger system that is designed to keep women in their "rightful" place, as second-class citizens on this earth to serve the needs of their male partners.

Harsh? I suppose. But accurate, I believe, as this is borne out by my own data and the research of other scholars.

I am reminded that it is no less harsh than the treatment battered women receive every day. Stella was hit so hard in the mouth that her teeth ripped through both her bottom and top lips. Lara was beaten in the head with a ball-peen hammer—a hammer that has one round and one flat end and is *normally* used in working metal. Candy had her pelvis broken on the stick shift of her car, and her partner bit her in the face. How does one avoid becoming a battered woman? Be careful how you choose your mate. The greatest risk factor for becoming a battered woman is simply being a woman.

In addition, I add here at least two other significant risk factors that emerged in my study. First, I argued in chapter 2 that being a victim of early childhood and adolescent sexual abuse (or premature sex engagement) puts one at risk for becoming a victim of IPV. Why? As a sociologist I would argue that the connection is not very complex: when a woman has been a victim of one kind of gendered violence (rape, sexual abuse) that is used to maintain a system of male power and privilege, her second-class citizenship status is potently reinforced. And when she later encounters men, including her male partner(s), who treat her as a second-class citizen, as someone to be controlled, she "accepts" this behavior as "normal," as simply part of the way that men and women interact. The normalcy aspect of IPV was very apparent in all of my interviews regardless of race or ethnicity. In contrast, women who have not had early experiences that reinforced their second-class citizenship status were more shocked if and when their male partner(s) attempted to control and abuse them, and they were more likely to react by leaving the situation after just one or at most two episodes (recall the experiences of Josie).

THE FINAL WORD: RELATIONSHIPS AS PARTNERSHIPS

Understanding IPV requires understanding systems of domination and the ways that they are interconnected. IPV is a logical outcome of patriarchy, but it is reinforced by other systems of domination such as class exploitation and racial domination. Fighting the epidemic of IPV means dismantling patriarchy so as to empower women, but it also means that roles for men must be expanded as well. Men who are boxed into evaluating themselves within a narrow framework of masculinity will almost always fail. Few such men can succeed as breadwinners. This avenue is almost entirely restricted to white men who were born with some class privilege. Poor men and minority men are likely to fall short. Thus, revising our constructions of masculinity (as well as femininity) will offer men more opportunities for success and a richer life experience. What does this mean? Practically, it can mean associating masculinity with being a "good dad" and being a supportive partner as being a "real man." It means transforming heterosexual relationships into partnerships. Referring to the discussion in chapter 4, this would mean defining both men and women in relation to their intimate relationships and in relation to the labor market. As long as men continue to be defined in relation to the labor market and women in relation to their relationships (Tom's wife) heterosexual relationships cannot be transformed into true partnerships.

Destroying the notion that men must be breadwinners and women must be restricted to the role of "support" (taking care of the home and the children, being supportive of her man) and replacing it with a notion that men and women in heterosexual relationships are in partnerships would have many positive outcomes. It would offer both men and women a chance for fuller lives, the chance to explore their talents and their preferences for everything from jobs to household labor to child care. The notion of partnership suggests equality and interdependence. Interdependency suggests that each partner's self-interest is best served by supporting rather than harming or sabotaging the other. If men and women identified their self-interests as interconnected, the result would be healthier, happier, more fulfilling relationships, and violence would become a rare event.

Dismantling patriarchy, however, means more than simply creating new constructions of masculinity and femininity and new norms around gender relations in heterosexual relationships. For true equality to arise and for a serious reduction in IPV, women must be given access to real social, political, and economic power. Women must be paid a fair wage, women must have the opportunity for political leadership, and women must have the access to social leadership as well.

What sets this book apart from others on the issue is that I have argued throughout that though IPV is *primarily* a result of gender oppression—patriarchy—yet every aspect of IPV is shaped by the forces of capitalism and racial domination as well. The system of racial domination shapes the "bullets" that are loaded into the "gun" that is triggered in men who become violent. The exploitation and dual-labor market features of capitalism shape women's economic dependency on men and contribute to the compulsory nature of heterosexual partnering. Thus, disrupting IPV will require more than dismantling patriarchy and creating gender equality, it will also require the simultaneous dismantling of racial domination[17] and reformation of the economy.

In order for men and women to live healthy, productive lives in relationships with each other, both men *and* women need to be freed from the severe economic exploitation that currently exists in the capitalist political economy of the United States. The rich continue to get rich by stealing the labor of the poor. Every time a worker is paid less than he or she is worth, the net gain goes to the business owner. Only when men and women are paid a fair and living wage for their work, only when all are offered opportunities for economic advancement based on fair principles, not the exploitation of others, will men and women be able to live in healthy relationships with each other, relationships that are free of violence.

Finally, minority men must not be treated as second-class citizens in economic, political, or social life—and especially in the criminal justice system—if they are to develop a healthy masculine self. Similarly, the battering of minority women cannot be justified by invoking a system that devalues them and their bodies. True equality for men and women is tied to equality for *all* men and *all* women, regardless of race or ethnicity (see Davis 1983).

NOTES

1. In my next book I will explore the issues related to children in the household per my relationship with the program (the Domestic Violence Response Team) in Olmsted County, Minnesota.

2. This "one incident" is a very conservative estimate in that IPV, like rape, is severely underreported.

3. Although I limit my work here to women in the United States, it is important to note that with expanded news coverage on the Middle East, Iraq, etc., we have rich accounts from journalists around the globe of IPV in a variety of ethnic/religious groups. See Kristof (2004).

4. The program that I partnered with in Olmsted County, Minnesota, is designed precisely around this goal: to keep the children safe. Furthermore, the professionals in this program recognize that *witnessing* violence constitutes the maltreatment of a child. Thus, their focus is on reducing the likelihood that children will witness IPV, and when they do, these children and their families are referred to child protective services.

5. See especially Clemetson (2004). As with William, Louise's infection is mostly unacknowledged in her family. When a male relative died recently of AIDS, she said, his illness was generally referred to within the family as sickle cell anemia.

6. This is especially important when dealing with African American men and women as they are currently the population with the highest percentage of new HIV/AIDS cases.

7. Mandatory arrest requires a seventy-two-hour lockup; however, if a man can bail out, then he is free to leave as soon as he is arraigned and bail is set. For affluent men this may be a matter of a few hours.

8. On the day that *USA Today* reported on the "scars" men carry with them when exiting prison, I had exonerated felon Darryl Hunt in to talk with my Social Inequality class. Hunt had been convicted and sentenced to death for the rape and murder of a white female in Winston-Salem, North Carolina. After spending eighteen years in prison, DNA evidence cleared him of these crimes. In his talk to my class very early on he made it clear that no one was willing to hire him and even noted that employers asked him about the eighteen years missing from his resume (see Armour 2004).

9. Sociology as a discipline has always looked at the underrepresented in society. For an example, see Wilson and Taub (2007).

10. For the best study of affluent IPV see Weitzman (2001).

11. In our book (Hattery and Smith 2007a), we devote an entire chapter (chapter 5) to a discussion of IPV in the African American community. I refer the interested reader to this chapter for a more in-depth discussion of the ways in which race shapes

IPV. It is also here that we offer specific solutions designed to address the unique circumstances facing African Americans living with IPV.

12. Along with Professor Earl Smith and Melissa Williams, I conducted a program evaluation for a social services agency in North Carolina. Our results demonstrated that (1) recidivism is high overall and (2) participation in the intervention program is no more successful than not.

13. Prevention is also critical because, as noted previously, boys who observe IPV are at greatest risk for perpetrating violence themselves, one thousand times more likely than boys who do not observe IPV.

14. Recently, the Drug Sentencing Reform and Cocaine Kingpin Trafficking Act (S. 171), sponsored by Senator Joe Biden, was enacted. The new law changes the crack cocaine laws and reduces the mandatory minimum sentences. http://biden.senate.gov/

15. This argument can be applied to other systems of domination such as racial superiority or capitalism.

16. See Auerbach (2004) for a good explanation of the interlocking web of violence, HIV/AIDS, and IPV.

17. This issue is explored in much greater length in Hattery and Smith (2007a).

Appendix

An Overview of Sampling, Instruments, and Strategies

CONSTRUCTING THE SAMPLE

Interviews were conducted in two states: North Carolina and Minnesota. Because the research focused on intimate partner violence all the subjects were selected *because* they were known to have experienced at least one incident of IPV that had come to the attention of either the criminal justice system or social services.

For a variety of reasons we felt it was important to collect data in more than one part of the United States. The South has such a particular (and peculiar) social, political economy and thus collecting data in the Midwest allowed for a "comparison" sample. The Midwest is less racially diverse, for example. The African American population in Minnesota is very small (in the particular county where interviews were conducted African Americans make up only 2.5 percent of the residents). Furthermore, most of the African Americans in this county migrated there in the last generation. Because we chose the Midwest specifically to create variation in the sample, we did not want to interview African Americans in the Midwest who had been reared in the South where, among other things, the racial politics are decidedly less progressive. Thus, we restricted our sample in Minnesota to African Americans who had *not ever* lived in the South. In this way we would ensure a midwestern sample that had not lived, for example, under the vestiges of Jim Crow–style segregation. They would not have grown up in the heat of the school desegregation battles of the early 1970s, nor would they have attended racially segregated schools or witnessed the KKK presence we still see today.

The Midwest provides variation in many other ways as well. States in the upper Midwest, namely Minnesota, Wisconsin, and to a lesser degree Michigan, have a history of progressive politics on issues such as race, social class, and gender. For example, states like Minnesota were at the forefront of progressive laws regarding violence against women (rape and battering). Some of these differences in state law influence family form. For example, in Minnesota, families experiencing an incident of violence may continue to live together as long as their safety is monitored by a social worker, whereas in North Carolina the parents must physically separate. This shaped our sample such that most of the women we interviewed in the Minnesota sample were still living with their partners, whereas none of the women we interviewed in North Carolina were.[1]

In terms of class politics, it is important to note that the most important political party in these upper midwestern states is the Democratic Farm Labor party, a party with strong ties to rural labor organizing and labor organizing among miners in the Iron Range.[2] In contrast, the South has historically been the most resistant to labor organizing. As a result, both class relations and attitudes toward class politics are more progressive in the Midwest than in the South, thus creating differences in the workplace that may affect employment, the availability of health insurance, and so forth.

The Midwest provides an interesting contrast site in many other ways as well. First, the midwestern states and Minnesota in particular have been at the forefront of domestic violence legislation and intervention. The county we partnered with, Olmsted County, has been awarded several pilot grants from the Department of Justice to create innovative intervention and prevention approaches.[3] Second, states like Minnesota were at the forefront of progressive laws regarding violence against women (rape and battering). For example, in Minnesota domestic violence is defined in a genderless manner that makes room for including women who batter men and same-sex battering. In North Carolina, however, domestic violence is defined in a gendered way: the only conceivable pattern is men beating women. Thus the charge, "assault on a female," retains the vestiges of patriarchy.

North Carolina Sample

Men   All of the sixteen men interviewed in North Carolina were participants in the TimeOut Program, a batterers' intervention program administered by Family Services, Inc. Forsyth County, North Carolina. All of the men who were recruited for interview had been court-ordered to this program as a result of being charged in the criminal justice system with "assault on a female," which is the North Carolina charge applied to any physical battering behavior that a man commits against a woman. All of the men interviewed were offered the opportunity to participate in Time-Out (a twenty-six-week program) rather than serve time in jail. Fourteen of the men interviewed were African American, and two were white. All of the interviews were conducted by the author and colleague and all were taped and professionally transcribed.

Women The women were recruited at a local battered women's shelter in the same midsize city in North Carolina. All of the women were living in the shelter at the time of the interview, and all of the interviews were conducted in the shelter by the author and colleague. All of the interviews were taped and professionally transcribed. Of the twenty-four women interviewed in the shelter, fourteen were African American and nine were white. Many had children living with them in the shelter.

Although the study design had originally called for interviewing partners, in the North Carolina sample we were able to conduct interviews with only two couples: one white and one African American, only those with partners are denoted.

NC WOMEN

C (AA)	Amy (W)
Cheri (AA)	Betty (AA) (Akim's partner)
Candy (AA)	Charlotte (W) (Perry's partner)
Connie (AA)	Debby (W)
Evie (AA)	Dawn (W)
Jessica (AA)	Johnetta (AA)
Rose (AA)	Josie (W)
Sally (AA)	Lucy (W)
Sheri (AA)	Rose (AA)
Crystal (W)	Princess (AA)
Vicki (W)	Susy (W)

NC MEN

Cass (AA)	Warren (AA)
Eddie (AA)	Darren (W)
Fred (AA)	Akim (AA) (Betty's partner)
Gus (AA)	Daryl (AA)
Jason (AA)	Lowell (W)
Jerry (AA)	Tim (AA)
Manny (AA)	Taurus (AA)
Richard (AA)	Perry (W) (Charlotte's partner)
Ward (AA)	

Minnesota Sample

We partnered with the Domestic Violence Unit which is administered within Child Protective Services (CPS). All of the men and women we interviewed were involved with social services, not the court system. Minnesota law requires an officer responding to a domestic violence incident that involves children "within sight or sound" to refer the family to CPS. Among other things, this allowed us to generate a sample that included couples. We conducted twenty interviews in Minnesota with ten men and ten women. We conducted interviews with six intact couples (we interviewed both members of the couple, though for confidentiality and safety reasons the interviews were conducted separately). The remaining interviews were conducted with one member of the couple, the other member either refusing to be interviewed or being unavailable for interview (several of the partners had moved out of state or were in prison in other counties). Nine of the ten women we interviewed in Minnesota were African American and one was white; the same is true for the men: 90 percent were African American.[4] In any case, most of the battered women we interviewed in the Minnesota sample are still living with their batterers, whereas none of the battered women we interviewed in North Carolina were.

Minnesota Women
Andi (AA) no partner
Candi (AA) no partner
Kylie (AA) Jon (AA)
Lara (AA) no partner
Mary (AA) Demitrius (AA)
Stella (W) Will (AA)
Tammy (AA) Ronnie (AA)
Tanya (AA) no partner
Veta (AA) Wells (AA)
Wanda (AA) Chris (AA)

Minnesota Men
Chris (AA) Wanda (AA)
Ellis (AA) no partner
Ethan (AA) no partner
Hank (AA) no partner
Jon (W) Kylie (AA)
Ronnie (AA) Tammy (AA)
Wells (AA) Veta (AA)
Will (AA) Stella (AA)
Demetrius (AA) Mary (AA)

The Interview

Interviews were designed to follow a semistructured set of questions. The men and women we interviewed were asked to begin by talking about the families in which they grew up, what the relationships were like between their parents, among their siblings, with grandparents, and so on. Then the men and women were asked to talk about their experiences with dating and marriage or cohabitation. The focus was on both their "healthy" or violence-free relationships as well as the relationships that involved IPV. Thus the interviews were essentially mini life histories, each taking between an hour and a half and two hours.

ANALYSIS OF SECONDARY DATA

In order to explore the prevalence of intimate partner violence in interracial couples, we performed secondary analyses of data contained in the National Violence Against Women (NVAW) Survey conducted by Patricia Tjaden and Nancy Thoennes. The data are available for analysis through the Interuniversity Consortium for Political and Social Research (ICPSR) distributed through the University of Michigan. Interviews were conducted with more than sixteen thousand men and women. The sample is nationally representative. Interviews were conducted in 1995 and 1996.

> Respondents to the NVAW Survey were queried about (1) their general fear of violence and the ways in which they managed their fears, (2) emotional abuse they had experienced by marital and cohabiting partners, (3) physical assault they had experienced as children by adult caretakers, (4) physical assault they had experienced as adults by any type of perpetrator, (5) forcible rape or stalking they had experienced by any type of perpetrator, and (6) incidents of threatened violence they had experienced by any type of perpetrator. Respondents disclosing victimization were asked detailed questions about the characteristics and consequences of victimization as they experienced it, including injuries sustained and use of medical services. Incidents were recorded that had occurred at any time during the respondent's lifetime and also those that occurred within the 12 months prior to the interview. (Tjaden and Thoennes 1999)

Sampling Restrictions

The same data were used to examine race and class differences in IPV as reported in chapters 2 (race) and 4 (social class). Whereas the data presented in chapters 2 and 4 were based on analyses of the entire sample, for the analyses presented in chapter 5 I applied specific restrictions to the data, and it is important to detail these.

African American–white relationships are the most contentious of all interracial relationships in the United States. Thus, I decided to restrict the sample analyzed for chapter 5 accordingly. Second, in order to disentangle the independent effects of the race of the perpetrator and the race of the victim, I also included African American and white *intraracial* couples, thus allowing for race/gender comparisons. The racial composition of the couples included in the sample is shown in table A.1.

Table A.1.   Racial Composition of the Couples (total number of couples = 803)

	Race of Male Partner		
	African American	*White*	*Total*
Race of Female Partner			
African American	308	11	319
White	43	441	484
Totals	351	452	803

NOTES

1. All of these sorts of variation in the sample will be addressed when appropriate. We would argue, however, that rather than making the sample less consistent, these variations contribute to a sample that better represents the experiences of women in the United States who are living with IPV. Thus, we think the sample is one of the strengths of the study.

2. Minnesota senator Paul Wellstone was a member of the Democratic Farm Labor Party and organized farmers throughout southern Minnesota and miners in the northern Iron Range region.

3. For example, Minnesota was among the first states to experiment with mandatory arrest laws.

4. We note that the two white individuals were not in the same couple. Both were in interracial relationships.

References

Acker, Joan. 2006. *Class Questions, Feminist Answers*. New York: Routledge.

Adams, D. 1988. Treatment Models of Men Who Batter: A Profeminist Analysis. In *Feminist Perspectives on Wife Abuse*, ed. Kersti Yllo and Michele Bograd, Newbury Park, CA: Sage.

Alan Guttmacher Institute. 2006. *U.S. Teenage Pregnancy Statistics Overall Trends, Trends by Race and Ethnicity and State-by-State Information*. http://www.guttmacher.org/sections/index.php?page=stats.

Andersen, M. L. 2001. Restructuring for Whom? Race, Class, Gender, and the Ideology of Invisibility. *Sociological Forum* 16:181–201.

Armour, Stephanie. 2004. "Wrongly Convicted Walk Away with Scars." *USA Today*, October 13.

Auerbach, Judith. 2004. "The Overlooked Victims of AIDS." *Washington Post*, October 14.

Benedict, Jeff, and Don Yaeger. 1998. *Pros and Cons: The Criminals Who Play in the NFL*. New York: Warner.

Bianchi, Suzanne, John P. Robinson, and Melissa A. Milkie. 2007. *Changing Rhythms of American Family Life*. New York: Russell Sage Foundation.

Bombardieri, Marcella. 2005. Summer's Remarks on Women Draws Fire. *Boston Globe*, January 17, 2005, A1.

Bonilla-Silva, Eduardo, and Tyrone A. Forman. 2000. I Am Not a Racist But. *Discourse and Society* 11:50–85.

Brandt, J. 2006. Why She Left. The Psychological, Relational, and Contextual Variables That Contribute to a Woman's Decision to Leave an Abusive Relationship. Unpublished PhD dissertation, City University of New York. DAI-B 66/08, February 2006, p. 4473.

Browne, A. 1987. *When Battered Women Kill*. New York: Free Press.

Browne, A., and D. Finkelhor. 1986. Impact of Child Sexual Abuse: A Review of the Research. *Psychological Bulletin* 99:66–77.

Brownmiller, Susan. 1975. *Against Our Will: Men, Women, and Rape*. New York: Bantam.

Brush, Lisa D. 2000. Battering, Traumatic Stress, and Welfare-to-Work Transition. *Violence against Women* 6 (10):1039–65.

———. 2001. Poverty, Battering, Race, and Welfare Reform: Black-White Differences in Women's Welfare-to-Work Transitions. *Journal of Poverty* 5:67–89.

———. 2006. When Domestic Violence Spills Over to Work. Presentation at the annual meeting of the Society for the Study of Social Problems, Montreal, Quebec.

Brush, Lisa D., Jody Raphael, and Richard Tolman. 2003. Effects of Work on Hitting and Hurting. *Violence against Women* 9 (10):1213–30.

Bureau of Justice Statistics. 1995. *Special Report: Violence against Women: Estimates from the Redesigned Survey* (NCJ-154348), August 1995, p. 3.

———. 2003. *Crime Data Brief: Intimate Partner Violence, 1993–2001*. Washington, DC: U.S. Department of Justice.

Burton, Linda. 1990. Teenage Childbearing as an Alternative Life-Course Strategy in Multi-generational Black Families. *Human Nature* 1 (2):58–81.

Campbell, Doris Williams, Phyllis W. Sharps, Faye Gary, Jacquelyn C. Campbell, and Loretta M. Lopez. 2002. Intimate Partner Violence in African American Women. *Journal of On-line Nursing* 7 (1):1–21.

Centers for Disease Control and Prevention. 2004. *Diagnoses of HIV* 53:1106–10.

———. 2006. Understanding Intimate Partner Violence Fact Sheet.

Childs, Erica Chito. 2005. Looking behind the Stereotypes of the Angry Black Woman: An Exploration of Black Women's Responses to Interracial Relationships. *Gender and Society* 19:544–61.

Clemetson, Lynette. 2004. "Links between Prison and AIDS Affecting Blacks Inside and Out." *New York Times*, August 6.

Collins, Randall. 1992. Love and Property. In *Sociological Insight: An Introduction to Non-obvious Sociology*. 2nd ed. London: Oxford University Press.

Compton, Vicki, and Ellen Zelda Kessner. 2003. *Saving Beauty from the Beast: How to Protect Your Daughter from an Unhealthy Relationship*. Boston: Little Brown.

Conley, Dalton. 1999. *Being Black, Living in the Red: Race, Wealth, and Social Policy in America*. Berkeley: University of California Press.

Connell, R. W. 1990. An Iron Man: The Body and Some Contradictions of Hegemonic Masculinity. In *Sport, Men, and the Gender Order: Critical Feminist Perspectives*, ed. M. Messner and D. Sabo, 83–95. Champaign, IL: Human Kinetics.

———. 1995. *Masculinities*. Berkeley, CA: University of California Press.

———. 2008. Keynote Remarks. Conference on Masculinity. Wake Forest University, April 2–4.

Coontz, Stephanie. 1992. *The Way We Never Were: American Families and the Nostalgia Trap*. New York: Basic Books.

———. 1997. *The Way We Really Are: Coming to Terms with America's Changing Families*. New York: Basic Books.

Crenshaw, K. 1991. Mapping the Margins: Intersectionality, Identity Politics, and Violence against Women of Color. *Stanford Law Review* 43 (6):1241–99.

Datzman, Jeanine, and Carol Brooks. 2000. In My Mind, We Are All Humans: Notes on the Public Management of Black-White Interracial Romantic Relationships. *Marriage and Family Review* 30:5–16.

Davis, Angela. 1983. *Women, Race, and Class*. New York: Vintage.

Dobash, R. E., and R. Dobash. 1979. *Violence against Wives: A Case against Patriarchy*. New York: Free Press.

Drake, St. Clair, and Horace R. Cayton. 1945. *Black Metropolis: A Study of Negro Life in a Northern City*. Chicago: University of Chicago Press.

DuBois, William Edward Burghardt. 1951. Preface in *A Documentary History of the Negro People in the United States*, ed. Herbert Aptheker. New York: Citadel.

Duneier, Mitchell. 1992. *Slim's Table: Race, Respectability and Masculinity*. Chicago: University of Chicago Press.

Dunham, Charlotte. 2005. Good Girls Don't Get Paid. Paper presented at the annual meeting of the American Library Association, Chicago.

Durkheim, Emile. 1982. *The Rules of the Sociological Method*. Ed. Steven Lukes. Trans. W. D. Halls. New York: Free Press.

Durose, Matthew R., Caroline Wolf Harlow, Patrick A. Langan, Mark Motivans, Ramona R. Rantala, and Erica L. Smith. 2005. *Family Violence Statistics Including Statistics on Strangers and Acquaintances*. Report NCJ 207846. Washington, DC: Bureau of Justice Statistics.

Dworkin, Andrea. 1987. *Intercourse*. New York: Free Press.

Dye, J. L. 2005. *Fertility of American Women: June 2004*, no. P20-555. Washington, DC: U.S. Census Bureau.

Edin, Kathryn, and Laura Lein. 1997. *Making Ends Meet: How Single Mothers Survive Welfare and Low Wage Work*. New York: Russell Sage Foundation.

Eggebeen, David J., and Alan J. Hawkins. 1990. "Economic Need and Wives' Employment." *Journal of Family Issues* 11:48-66.

Ehrenreich, Barbara. 2002. *Nickle and Dimed: On NOT Getting By in America*. New York: Holt.

Ehrensaft, Miriam K., Patricia Cohen, Jocelyn Brown, Elizabeth Smailes, Henian Chen, and Jeffrey G. Johnson. 2003. Intergenerational Transmission of Partner Violence: A 20-Year Prospective Study. *Journal of Consulting and Clinical Psychology* 71 (4):741–53.

Engels, Friedrich. 1884. *The Origin of the Family, Private Property, and the State*. Introduction by Eleanor Leacock. New York: International Publishers.

England, Paula. 2005. Gender Inequality in Labor Markets: The Role of Motherhood and Segregation. *Social Politics* 12:264–88.

Epstein, Cynthia Fuchs. 2007. Great Divides: The Cultural, Cognitive, and Social Bases of the Global Subordination of Women. *American Sociological Review* 72:1–22.

ESPN. October 26, 2007. http://sports.espn.go.com/ncw/news/story?id=3081048.

Esqueda, C. 2005. The Influence of Gender Role Stereotypes, the Woman's Race, and Level of Provocation and Resistance on Domestic Violence Culpability Attributions. *Sex Roles: A Journal of Research*.

Felson, Richard. 2006. Is Violence against Women about Women or about Violence? *Contexts* 5 (2):21–25.

Fields, M. 1977–1978. Wife-Beating: Facts and Figures. *Victimology International Journal* 2:653–57.

Finkelhor, D., and K. Yllo. 1982. Forced Sex in Marriage: A Preliminary Research Report. *Crime and Delinquency* 28 (3):459–78.

Finlayson, T. J., L. E. Saltzman, D. J. Sheridan, and W. K. Taylor. 1999. Estimating Hospital Charges Associated with Intimate Violence. *Violence against Women* 5 (3):313–35.

Fisher, B. S., F. T. Cullen, and M. G. Turner. 2000. *The Sexual Victimization of College Women*. NCJ 182369. Washington, DC: Bureau of Justice Statistics.

Franklin, Clyde. 1984. *The Changing Definition of Masculinity*. New York: Plenum.

Friedman, Thomas. 2006. *The World Is Flat: A Brief History of the 21st Century*. New York: Farrar, Straus and Giroux.

Gaarder, E., and J. Belknap. 2002. Tenuous Borders: Girls Transferred to Adult Court. *Criminology* 40 (3):481–517.

Garey, Anita I. 1999. *Weaving Work and Motherhood*. Philadelphia: Temple University Press.

Geffner, R., ed. 1997. *Violence and Sexual Abuse at Home*. Binghamton, NY: Haworth.

Gelles, R. J. 1974. *The Violent Home*. Beverly Hills, CA: Sage.

———. 1997. *Intimate Violence in Families*. 3rd ed. Thousand Oaks, CA: Sage.

Gelles, R. J., and M. A. Straus. 1988. *Intimate Violence*. New York: Simon and Schuster.

Gilbert, Louisa. 2001. "Intimate Violence and STDs among Women in an ED." Paper presented at the 129th annual meeting of the American Public Health Association, Atlanta, Georgia, October 21–25.

Glassner, Barry. 2000. *The Culture of Fear: Why Americans Are Afraid of the Wrong Things*. New York: Basic Books.

Gondolf, Edward. 1997. Patterns of Reassault in Batterer Programs. *Violence and Victims* 12:373–87.

———. 1999. A Comparison of Reassault Rates in Four Batterer Programs: Do Court Referral, Program Length and Services Matter? *Journal of Interpersonal Violence* 14:41–61.

Goodkind, S., I. Ng, and R. C. Sarri. 2006. The Impact of Sexual Abuse in the Lives of Young Women Involved or at Risk of Involvement with the Juvenile Justice System. *Violence against Women* 12 (5):456–77.

Goodrum, S., D. Umberson, and K. L. Anderson. 2001. The Batterer's View of the Self and Others in Domestic Violence. *Sociological Inquiry* 71 (2):221–31.

Graetz, Naomi. 1998. *Silence Is Deadly: Judaism Confronts Wifebeating*. Lanham, MD: Jason Aronson.

Griffin, Susan. 1979. *Rape: The Politics of Consciousness*. New York: Harper & Row.

Griffing, S., D. F. Ragin, S. M. Morrison, R. E. Sage, L. Madry, and B. J. Primm. 2005. Reasons for Returning to Abusive Relationships: Effects of Prior Victimization. *Journal of Family Violence* 20:341–48.

Gutman, Herbert. 1976. *The Black Family in Slavery and Freedom, 1750–1925*. New York: Vintage.

Haj-Yahia, Muhammad. 2000. The Incidence of Wife Abuse and Battering and Some Sociodemographic Correlates as Revealed by Two National Surveys in Palestinian Society. *Journal of Family Violence* 15 (4):347–74.

Halsell, Grace. 1969. *Soul Sister*. New York: World.

Hampton, R. L., and R. J. Gelles. 1991. A Profile of Violence toward Black Children. In *Black Family Violence: Current Research and Theory*, ed. R. L. Hampton. Lexington, MA: Lexington Books.

Hampton, R. L., R. J. Gelles, and J. Harrop. 1991. Is Violence in Black Families Increasing? A Comparison of 1975 and 1985 National Survey Rates. In *Black Family Violence: Current Research and Theory*, ed. R. L. Hampton. Lexington, MA: Lexington Books.

Hampton, R. L., W. Oliver, and L. Magarian. 2003. Domestic Violence in the African American Community: An Analysis of Social and Structural Factors. *Violence against Women* 9 (5):533–57.

Hanson, R. K. 1990. The Psychological Impact of Sexual Assault on Women and Children: A Review. *Annals of Sex Research* 3:187–232.

Hanson, R. K., O. Cadsky, A. Harris, and C. Lalonde. 1997. Correlates of Battering among 997 Men: Family History, Adjustment, and Attitudinal Difference. *Violence and Victims* 12:191–208.

Harper, C. W. 1985. Black Aristocrats: Domestic Servants on the Antebellum Plantation. *Phylon* 46:123–35.

Harvey, L. K. 2002. *Domestic Violence in Winston-Salem/Forsyth County: A Study of Domestic Court Cases in 2001*. Winston-Salem, NC: Center for Community Safety, Winston-Salem State University.

Hattery, Angela J. 2001a. Tag-Team Parenting: Costs and Benefits of Utilizing Non-overlapping Shift Work Patterns in Families with Young Children. *Families in Society* 82 (4):419–27.

———. 2001b. *Women, Work, and Family: Balancing and Weaving*. Thousand Oaks, CA: Sage.

Hattery, Angela J., and Emily W. Kane. 1995. Men's and Women's Perceptions of Non-consensual Sexual Intercourse. *Sex Roles* 33:785–802.

Hattery, Angela J., and Earl Smith. 2003. Intimate Partner Violence in the African American Community: A Race-Class-Gender Approach. Presented at the fourth annual conference of Trapped by Poverty, Trapped by Violence, Austin, Texas.

———. 2005. Dirty Little Secret: Intimate Partner Violence in the African American Community. Presented at the annual midwinter meeting of Sociologists for Women in Society, Miami, Florida.

———. 2007a. *African American Families*. Thousand Oaks, CA: Sage.

———. 2007b. Duke Lacrosse: An Exploration of Race, Class, Power, and Privilege. In *Learning Culture through Sports*, vol. 2, ed. Sandra Spickard Prettyman and Brian Lampman. New York: Rowman & Littlefield.

——. 2008. Cultural Contradictions in the Southern Mode of Segregation: Black Tits, White Only Water Fountains, Bad Blood, and the Transmission of Semen. *Mississippi Quarterly*.

Hattery, Angela J., Melissa Williams, and Earl Smith. 2004. *The Efficacy of the Time Out Intervention Program in Forsyth County*. Report.

Hays, Sharon. 1996. *The Cultural Contradictions of Motherhood*. New Haven, CT: Yale University Press.

Hill, Shirley. 2005. *Black Intimacies: A Gender Perspective on Families and Relationships*. Lanham, MD: Altamira.

Hill-Collins, Patricia. 1994. Shifting the Center: Race, Class, and Feminist Theorizing about Motherhood. In *Mothering: Ideology, Experience, and Agency*, ed. E. Glenn, G. Chang, and L. Forcey. New York: Routledge, pp. 45–66.

——. 2004. *Black Sexual Politics: African Americans, Gender, and the New Racism*. New York: Routledge.

Hirschel, J. D., I. W. Hutchison III, and C. W. Dean. 1992. The Failure of Arrest to Deter Spouse Abuse. *Journal of Research in Crime and Delinquency* 29:7–34.

Hochschild, Arlie Russell. 1989. *The Second Shift*. New York: Penguin.

Holtzworth-Munroe, A., and G. L. Stuart. 1994. Typologies of Male Batterers: Three Sub-types and the Differences among Them. *Psychological Bulletin* 116:476–97.

hooks, bell. 2000. *Feminist Theory: From Margin to Center*. Cambridge, MA: South End.

——. 2004. *We Real Cool: Black Men and Masculinity*. New York: Routledge.

Isaacs, Dan. 2002. "Nigeria in Crisis over Sharia Law," *BBC News*. March 26. http://news.bbc.co.uk/1/hi/world/.

Johnson, J., and V. F. Sacco. 1995. Researching Violence against Women: Statistics Canada's National Survey. *Canadian Journal of Criminology* 37:281–304.

Johnson, Michael P., and Kathleen J. Ferraro. 2000. Research on Domestic Violence in the 1990s: Making Distinctions. *Journal of Marriage and the Family* 62:948–63.

Johnston, James H. 1970. *Race Relations in Virginia and Miscegenation in the South, 1776–1860*. Amherst: University of Massachusetts Press.

Kalmijn, Matthijs. 1993. Trends in Black/White Intermarriage. *Social Forces* 72 (1): 119–46.

Kane, Emily. 2006. No Way My Boys Are Going to Be Like That: Parents' Responses to Children's Gender Nonconformity. *Gender and Society* 20:149–76.

Kaufman, Joan, and Edward Zigler. 1987. Do Abused Children Become Abusive Parents? *Journal of Orthopsychiatry* 57:186–92.

Kaufman, Michael. 1992. The Construction of Masculinity and the Triad of Men's Violence. In *Men's Lives*, ed. Michael Kimmel and Michael Messner. New York: Macmillan.

Kelly, Henry A. 1994. Rule of Thumb and the Folklaw of the Husband's Stick. *Journal of Legal Education* 44 (3):341–65.

Kendall-Tackett, K., L. Williams, and D. Finkelhor. 1993. Impact of Sexual Abuse on Children: A Review and Synthesis of Recent Empirical Studies. *Psychological Bulletin* 113:164–80.

Kimmel, Michael. 1995. *Manhood in America*. New York: Free Press.

———. 2005. *Manhood in America*. 2nd ed. New York: Oxford University Press.

King, D. 1988. Multiple Jeopardy, Multiple Consciousness: The Context of a Black Feminist Ideology. *Signs* 14 (1):42–72.

Kingsnorth, Rodney F., Randall C. MacIntosh, Terceira Berdahl, Carrie Blades, and Steve Rossi. 2001. Domestic Violence: The Role of Interracial/Ethnic Dyads in Criminal Court Processing. *Journal of Contemporary Criminal Justice* 17:123–41.

Kirkwood, Catherine. 1993. *Leaving Abusive Partners: From the Scars of Survival to the Wisdom for Change*. Newbury Park, CA: Sage.

Korstad, R. 2003. *Civil Rights Unionism: Tobacco Workers and the Struggle for Democracy in the Mid-Twentieth Century South*. Chapel Hill: University of North Carolina Press.

Koss, M. P. 1985. The Hidden Rape Victim: Personality, Attitudinal, and Situational Characteristics. *Psychology of Women Quarterly* 9:193–212.

Koss, M. P., L. A. Goodman, A. Browne, L. F. Fitzgerald, G. P. Keita, and N. F. Russo.1994. *No Safe Haven: Male Violence against Women at Home, at Work, and in the Community*. Washington, DC: American Psychological Association.

Kristof, Nicholas D. 2004. Sentenced to Be Raped. *New York Times*, September 29.

Lamont, Michèle, and Mario Luis Small. 2008. How Culture Matters for the Understanding of Poverty: Enriching Our Undertanding. In *The Colors of Poverty: Why Racial and Ethnic Disparities Persist*, ed. Ann Lin and David Harris. Russell Sage Foundation.

Lanier, S. 2000. *Jefferson's Children: The Story of One American Family*. New York: Random House.

Lawless, E. J. 2001. *Women Escaping Violence: Empowerment through Narrative*. Columbia: University of Missouri Press.

Leone, Janel M., Michael P. Johnson, Catherine L. Cohan, and Susan E. Lloyd. 2004. Consequences of Male Partner Violence for Low-Income Minority Women. *Journal of Marriage and Family* 66 (2):472–90.

Levine, Linda. n.d. The Male-Female Wage Gap: A Fact Sheet. *CRS Report for Congress*. www.ncseonline.org/nle/crsreports/economics/econ-65.cfm?&CFID= 3106828&CFTOKEN=69609068 (accessed October 20, 2007).

Lindsey, Sue. 2007. Too Few Warnings at Virginia Tech? *Time-CNN*. www.time .com/time/nation/article/0,8599,1610857,00.html (accessed May 14, 2007).

Luker, Kristin. 1985. *Abortion and the Politics of Motherhood*. Berkeley: University of California Press.

MacKinnon, Catharine. 1989. *Toward a Feminist Theory of the State*. Cambridge, MA: Harvard University Press.

Majors, Richard, and Janet Bilson. 1992. *Cool Pose: The Dilemmas of African American Manhood in America*. New York: Lexington.

Marx, Karl. 1869. *The Eighteenth Brumaire of Louis Bonaparte*. New York: International Publishers.

Mason, James O. 1993. The Dimensions of an Epidemic of Violence. *Public Health Reports* 108:1–3.

Massey, D. S. 2005. Racial Discrimination in Housing: A Moving Target. *Social Problems* 52 (2):148–51.

Massey, D. S., and N. A. Denton. 1993. *American Apartheid: Segregation and the Making of the Underclass*. Cambridge, MA: Harvard University Press.

Mauer, Marc. 2001. *Race to Incarcerate*. New York: New Press.

———. 2002. Race, Poverty and Felon Disenfranchisement. *Poverty and Race Research Council* 11 (4):1–2.

Mauer, Marc, and Meda Chesney-Lind. 2002. *Invisible Punishment*. New York: New Press.

Maume, David J. 1999. Glass Ceilings and Glass Escalators: Occupational Segregation and Race and Sex Differences in Managerial Promotions. *Work and Occupations* 26 (4):483–509.

Mauss, Marcel. 2000. *The Gift: The Form and Reason for Exchange in Archaic Societies*. New York: Norton. (First published in English in 1954. Trans. Ian Cunnison. Glencoe, IL: Free Press.)

Maynard, Rebecca A. 1997. *Kids Having Kids: Economic Costs and Social Consequences of Teen Pregnancy*. Washington, DC: Urban Institute Press.

Merton, Robert K., and Elinor Barber. 2004. *The Travels and Adventures of Serendipity*. Princeton, NJ: Princeton University Press

Messner, Michael. 2002. *Taking the Field: Women, Men, and Sports*. Minneapolis: University of Minnesota Press.

Monto, M. A., and N. Hotaling. 2001. Predictors of Rape Myth Acceptance among Male Clients of Female Street Prostitutes. *Violence against Women* 7:275–93.

Murdock, George Peter. 1954, 1983. *The Outline of World Cultures*. New Haven, CT: Human Relations Area Files.

National Center for Injury Prevention and Control. 2003. *Costs of Intimate Partner Violence against Women in the United States*. Atlanta, GA: Centers for Disease Control and Prevention.

Newman, Katherine S., Cybelle Fox, Wendy Roth, Jal Mehta, and David Harding. 2005. *Rampage: The Social Roots of School Shootings*. New York: Basic Books.

Newsweek. Doubts about Dole. February 5, 1996.

Odem, M. E. 1995. *Delinquent Daughters: Protecting and Policing Adolescent Female Sexuality in the United States, 1885–1920*. Chapel Hill: University of North Carolina Press.

Padavic, Irene, and Barbara F. Reskin. 2002. *Women and Men at Work*. Thousand Oaks, CA: Pine Forge.

Pagelow, M. D. 1981. *Woman-Battering: Victims and Their Experiences*. Thousand Oaks, CA: Sage.

Pager, Devah. 2003. The Mark of a Criminal Record. *American Journal of Sociology* 108:937–75.

Parsons, Talcott, and Robert Bales. 1955. *Family, Socialization, and the Interaction Process*. Glencoe, IL: Free Press.

Pate, A. M., and E. E. Hamilton. 1992. Formal and Informal Deterrents to Domestic Violence: The Dade County Spouse Assault Experiment. *American Sociological Review* 57:691–97.

Patterson, Orlando. 1999. *Rituals of Blood: Consequences of Slavery in Two American Centuries*. New York: Civitas.

Pihl, R. O., and J. Peterson. 1995. "Drugs and Aggression: Correlations, Crime and Human Manipulative Studies and Some Proposed Mechanisms." *Journal of Psychiatry and Neuroscience*, March 20.

Pipher, M. B. 1994. *Reviving Ophelia: Saving the Selves of Adolescent Girls.* New York: Putnam.

Pirog-Good, Maureen A., and Jan E. Stets. 1989. Violence in Dating Relationships: Emerging Social Issues. New York: Praeger.

Potter, Hillary. 2004. *Intimate Partner Violence against African American Women: The Effects of Social Structure and Black Culture on Patterns of Abuse.* PhD dissertation, University of Colorado, Boulder. (Publication Number: AAT 3153870.)

Qian, Zhenchao. 2005. Breaking the Last Taboo: Interracial Marriage in America. *Contexts* 4:33–37.

Quinney, Richard. 1970. *The Problem of Crime.* New York: Harper & Row.

——. 1980. *Class, State, and Crime.* London: Longman.

Raphael, J. 2004. *Listening to Olivia: Violence, Poverty and Prostitution.* Boston: Northeastern University Press.

Regoeczi, Wendy. 2001. Exploring Racial Variations in the Spousal Sex Ratio of Killing. *Violence and Victims* 16:591–606.

Rennison, Callie Marie. 2003. *Intimate Partner Violence, 1993–2001.* Washington, DC: U.S. Department of Justice, Bureau of Justice Statistics.

Renzetti, Claire M. 1989. Sexuality in Intimate Relationships Building a Second Closet: Third Party Responses to Victims of Lesbian Partner Abuse. *Family Relations* 38 (2):157–63.

——. 1992. *Violent Betrayal: Partner Abuse in Lesbian Relationships.* Newbury Park, CA: Sage.

——. 2001. One Strike and You're Out: Implications of a Federal Crime Control Policy for Battered Women. *Violence against Women* 7 (6):685–98.

Reskin, Barbara, and Irene Padavic. 1994. *Women and Men at Work.* Thousand Oaks, CA: Pine Forge.

Rich, Adrienne. 1980. Compulsory Heterosexuality and Lesbian Existence. *Signs* 5:631–60.

——. 1995. *Of Woman Born: Motherhood as Experience and Institution.* New York: Norton.

Richardson, Diane. 1996. *Theorising Heterosexuality: Telling It Straight.* Buckingham, UK: Open University Press, 1996.

Richie, B. 1985. Battered Black Women: A Challenge for the Black Community. *Black Scholar* 16 (2):40–44.

Rind, B., P. Tromovitch, and R. Bauserman. 1998. A Meta-Analytic Examination of Assumed Properties of Child Sexual Abuse Using College Samples. *Psychological Bulletin* 124:22–53.

Romero, Mary. 1992. *Maid in the U.S.A.* New York: Routledge.

Sanday, P. R. 1981. The Socio-Cultural Context of Rape: A Cross-Cultural Study. *Journal of Social Issues* 37 (4):5–27.

——. 1990/2007. *Fraternity Gang Rape.* New York: New York University Press.

Satcher, David. 2001. *Youth Violence: A Report from the Surgeon General.* www .surgeongeneral.gov/library/youthviolence/report.html.

Scully, Diana. 1990. *Understanding Sexual Violence: A Study of Convicted Rapists.* Boston: Unwin Hyman.

Segura, Denise A. 1994. Working at Motherhood: Chicana and Mexican Immigrant Mothers and Employment. In *Mothering: Ideology, Experience, and Agency*, ed. Evelyn Nakano Glenn and Grace Chang. New York: Routledge.

Shapiro, T. 2003. *The Hidden Cost of Being African American: How Wealth Perpetuates Inequality.* New York: Oxford University Press.

Sherman, L. W., J. D. Schmidt, D. A. Smith, and D. Rogan. 1992. Crime, Punishment, and Stake in Conformity: Legal and Informal Control of Domestic Violence. *American Sociological Review* 57:680–91.

Shir, J. S. 1999. Battered Women's Perceptions and Expectations of Their Current and Ideal Marital Relationship. *Journal of Family Violence* 14:71–82.

Simmons, Tavia, and Martin O'Connell. 2003. *Married-Couple and Unmarried-Partner Households: 2000 Census 2000 Special Reports.* Washington, DC: US Bureau of the Census.

Smith, Earl. 2007. *Race, Sport and the American Dream.* Durham, NC: Carolina Academic Press.

——. 2008. African American Men and Intimate Partner Violence. *Journal of African American Studies* 12:156–79.

Smith, Earl, and Angela Hattery. 2007. If We Build It They Will Come: Human Rights Violations and the Prison Industrial Complex. *Societies without Borders.*

Smith, M. D. 1987. The Incidence and Prevalence of Women Abuse in Toronto. *Violence and Victims* 2:173–87.

Smith, V. 1998. *Not Just Race, Not Just Gender: Black Feminist Readings.* London: Routledge.

Staples, B. 2004. Fighting the AIDS Epidemic by Issuing Condoms in the Prisons. *New York Times*, September 7.

Steinbugler, Amy C. 2005. Visibility as Privilege and Danger: Heterosexual and Same-Sex Interracial Intimacy in the 21st Century. *Sexualities* 8:425–43.

Straus, Murray A. 1991. Response to Alternate Viewpoints: New Theory and Old Canards about Family Violence Research. *Social Problems* 38 (2):180–97.

Straus, Murray A., and Richard J. Gelles. 1995. *Physical Violence in American Families.* New Jersey: Transaction.

Strauss, Anselm, and Juliet Corbin. 1990. *Basics of Qualitative Research: Grounded Theory Procedures and Techniques.* Newbury Park, CA: Sage.

Sturza, M. L., and R. Campbell. 2005. An Exploratory Study of Rape Survivors' Prescription Drug Use as a Means of Coping with Sexual Assault. *Psychology of Women Quarterly* 29:353–63.

Summers, Lawrence. 2005. Remarks at National Bureau of Economic Research Conference on Diversifying the Science and Engineering Workforce. Office of the President, Harvard University. Cambridge, Massachusetts. January 14.

Sweet, N., and R. Tewksbury. 2000. What's a Nice Girl Like You Doing in a Place Like This? Pathways to a Career in Stripping. *Sociological Spectrum* 20:325–43.

Taylor Institute. 1997. *Trapped by Poverty, Trapped by Abuse: New Evidence Documenting the Relationship between Violence and Welfare.*

Therborn, Göran. 1980. *The Ideology of Power and the Power of Ideology.* London: Verso.

Thomas, Dorothy, and W. I. Thomas. 1923. *The Unadjusted Girl.* Boston: Little, Brown.

Tiefenthaler, Jill, Amy Farmer, and Amandine Sambira. 2005. The Availability of Services for Victims of Domestic Violence in the US: Equity and Efficiency Considerations. *Journal of Marriage and the Family* 67 (3):565–79.

Tjaden, Patricia, and Nancy Thoennes. 2000. *Full Report of the Prevalence, Incidence, and Consequences of Violence against Women: Findings from the National Violence against Women Survey.* NCJ 183781, Washington, DC: U.S. Department of Justice, National Institute of Justice.

Travis, Jeremy. 1997. *Drugs, Alcohol, and Domestic Violence in Memphis.* National Institute of Justice Series: NIJ Research Preview. U.S. Department of Justice.

Tursi, F. 1994. *Winston-Salem: A History.* Winston-Salem, NC: John F. Blair.

USA Today. 2003. Study: Partners Blamed for One-Fifth of Violence against Women. February 24. www.ojp.usdoj.gov/bjs/homicide/gender.htm.

U.S. Bureau of the Census. 1972. *U.S. Census of Population: 1970.* Vol. 1. Washington, DC: Government Printing Office.

———. 1999. *Race of Wife by Race of Husband: 1999.* Washington, DC: Government Printing Office.

U.S. Commission on Civil Rights. 1982. *Under the Rule of Thumb: Battered Women and the Administration of Justice.*

Walker, L. 1979. *The Battered Woman.* New York: Harper.

———. 1984. *The Battered Woman Syndrome.* New York: Springer.

Warshaw, R. 1988. *I Never Called It Rape: The MS. Report on Recognizing, Fighting, and Surviving Date and Acquaintance Rape.* New York: Harper & Row.

Weber, Max. 1903–1917. *The Methodology of the Social Sciences.* Translated and edited by Edward A. Shils and Henry A. Finch, 1997. New York: Free Press.

Weitzman, Susan. 1998. *Upscale Violence: The Lived Experience of Domestic Abuse among Upper Socioeconomic Status Women.* Unpublished DSW dissertation, Loyola University, Chicago.

———. 2001. *Not to People Like Us: Hidden Abuse in Upscale Marriages.* New York: Basic Books.

Wesley, J. K. 2006. Considering the Context of Women's Violence: Gender, Lived Experiences, and Cumulative Victimization. *Feminist Criminology* 1 (4):303–28.

Wesley, J. K., and J. D. Wright. 2005. The Pertinence of Partners Examining Intersections between Women's Homelessness and Their Adult Relationships. *American Behavioral Scientist* 48 (8):1082–1101.

West, Candace, and Don H. Zimmerman. 1987. Doing Gender. *Gender and Society* 1:125–51.

Western, B. 2006. *Punishment and Inequality in America.* New York: Russell Sage.

Widom, C. S., and M. G. Maxfield. 2001. *An Update on the "Cycle of Violence."* Washington, DC: National Institutes of Justice.

Wilson, Julius, and Richard P. Taub. 2007. *There Goes the Neighborhood: Racial, Ethnic, and Class Tensions in Four Chicago Neighborhoods and Their Meaning for America.* New York: Random House/Vintage.

Wilson, William J. 1987. *The Truly Disadvantaged: The Inner City, the Underclass, and Public Policy.* Chicago: University of Chicago Press.

Wolf, N. 1992. *The Beauty Myth: How Images of Beauty Are Used against Women.* New York: Anchor.

Woolley, Morgan Lee. 2007. Marital Rape: A Unique Blend of Domestic Violence and Non-marital Rape Issues. *Hastings Women's Law Journal* 18:269.

Zambito, Thomas. 2007. Isaiah Explains Double Standard on Slurs in Garden Trial. *New York Daily News*, September 18. www.nydailynews.com/sports/basketball/knicks/2007/09/18/2007-09-18_isiah_explains_double_standard_on_slurs_.html.

Zimbardo, Phillip. 2007. *The Lucifer Effect: Understanding How Good People Become Evil.* New York: Random House.

Zinn, Maxine Baca, and B. Thornton Dill. 2005. Theorizing Differences from Multicultural Feminism. In *Gender Through the Prism of Difference*, ed. M. B. Zinn, P. Hondagneu-Sotelo, and M. A. Messner. London: Oxford University Press.

Zweigenhaft, Richard, and G. William Domhoff. 2006. *Diversity in the Power Elite.* New York: Rowman & Littlefield.

Index

abuse, child, 12, 25–27, 42–43, 48–49, 146

abuse, emotional, 63, 65, 105, 129–30, 164, 185

abuse and intimate partner violence, 34, 38, 53, 56, 62, 105, 107, 130, 151, 154–56, 162, 176; pathway to intimate partner violence, 26–27, 34, 43

abusive partners, 15, 32, 53, 62–63, 65–68, 109, 135, 143, 145, 149, 155–57, 167, 171, 193

abusive relationships, 14, 35–36, 54, 68, 106, 108–9, 145, 148, 152, 170, 173, 187, 190

Acker, Joan, 3, 5, 18, 57, 76, 111, 151, 171, 174

Adams, David, 16

Adams, John, 135

affluence and intimate partner violence, 6, 17–18, 20–21, 35, 53–54, 82, 99, 109, 155, 170, 176

African American Community, 19, 20, 41, 46, 95, 165–66

African American men, 8, 16–20, 46–47, 62, 68, 76–77, 117; breadwinning and, 74, 95; employment and, 67, 173; HIV/AIDS and, 69, 70, 166;

incarceration and, 67, 69, 71–73, 143, 167–68, 173; intimate partner violence and, 16, 46, 63, 72, 121–24, 126–27, 143, 158, 168, 170; masculinity and, 81–83, 95, 125–26; myths of violence and, 121–22, 127, 170; patriarchy and, 125, 163; triggers to violence and, 169–70

African Americans, 5, 8, 9, 16–20, 22; children and sexual abuse, 29, 30, 41–42; discrimination and, 68–69, 76, 109, 171; drug use and, 70; education and, 117; employment and, 29, 31, 67; families, 59, 62, 67, 70, 72, 74, 138; HIV/AIDS and, 70; illegitimate economy and, 31–32; incarceration and, 73; marriage and, 95, 109, 116–17; unemployment and, 29, 69, 95

African American/white interracial relationships, 47, 116–18, 122, 124–27, 185

African American women, 19, 20, 29, 30, 37, 41–43, 46–48, 59, 108, 117; employment and, 59, 66–67, 95, 97, 108–9; femininity and, 109; HIV/AIDS and, 70; intimate partner violence, and, 19, 20, 42, 47, 72, 108–9, 119–20, 122–26, 158; poverty

About the Author

Angela J. Hattery is professor of sociology and women's and gender studies at Wake Forest University. She completed her BA at Carleton College and her MS and PhD at the University of Wisconsin, Madison, before joining the faculty of Wake Forest in 1998. She will spend the 2008–2009 academic year at Colgate University as the A. Lindsay O'Connor Professor of American Institutions, Department of Sociology. Her research focuses on social stratification, gender, family, and race. She is the author of numerous articles, book chapters, and books, including *Globalization and America: Race, Human Rights, and Inequality* (Rowman & Littlefield 2008), *African American Families* (2007), *Women, Work, and Family: Balancing and Weaving* (2001), and her forthcoming book *Interracial Intimacies Across the Color Line*.